Japan's 'Lost Decade'

Understanding the 'lost decade' of the 1990s is central to explaining Japan today. Following a period of record high growth, the chronic downturn after 1990 raised fundamental questions about the course of the world's third largest economy. This crisis also presented Japan with the opportunity for transformative change. Changes have followed, some of them less than might be expected, and some of them far more sweeping than is generally realized.

This volume presents a wide range of international perspectives on post-bubble Japan, exploring the effects of the long downturn of the eyes of the Japanese business community.

to what degree has Japan's traumatic corporate crisis prompted institutional and economic changes, corporate governance, business strategy, and the long-term recovery of the economy?

This book was originally published as a special issue of Business Review.

W. Miles Fletcher III is Professor in History at the University of North Carolina-Chapel Hill, USA. His research interests include business, political and intellectual history during the post-war period. He has written on trade policy, and the development of the cotton textile industry in modern Japan.

Peter W. von Staden is Senior Lecturer in International Business at Bristol Business School, part of the University of the West of England, UK. His research focuses on governance and business relations in modern Japan. His previous work has examined the role of business in political decision-making in the late twentieth century.

Japan's 'Lost Decade'

Causes, Legacies and Issues of
Transformative Change

Edited by
W. Miles Fletcher III and Peter W. von Staden

Routledge
Taylor & Francis Group

LONDON AND NEW YORK

First published 2013
by Routledge
2 Park Square, Milton Park, Abingdon, Oxfordshire OX14 4RN

Simultaneously published in the USA and Canada
by Routledge
711 Third Avenue, New York, NY 10017

First issued in paperback 2014

Routledge is an imprint of the Taylor and Francis Group, an informa business

British Library Cataloguing in Publication Data
A catalogue record for this book is available from the British Library

ISBN 978-0-415-78320-0 (hbk)

ISBN 978-1-138-84479-7 (pbk)

Typeset in Times New Roman
by Taylor & Francis Books

Publisher's Note
The publisher would like to make readers aware that the chapters in this book may be referred to as articles as they are identical to the articles published in the special issue. The publisher accepts responsibility for any inconsistencies that may have arisen in the course of preparing this volume for print.

Contents

CONTENTS

Citation Information

The chapters in this book were originally published in *Asia Pacific Business Review*, volume 18, issue 2 (April 2012). When citing this material, please use the original page numbering for each article, as follows:

Chapter 1
Introduction: Japan at an inflection point
Mark Metzler
Asia Pacific Business Review, volume 18, issue 2 (April 2012) pp. 135-147

Chapter 2
Dreams of economic transformation and the reality of economic crisis in Japan: Keidanren in the era of the 'bubble' and the onset of the 'lost decade,' from the mid-1980s to the mid-1990s
W. Miles Fletcher III
Asia Pacific Business Review, volume 18, issue 2 (April 2012) pp. 149-165

Chapter 3
From developmental state to the 'New Japan': the strategic inflection point in Japanese business
Ulrike Schaede
Asia Pacific Business Review, volume 18, issue 2 (April 2012) pp. 167-185

Chapter 4
Fettered by the past in the march forward: ideology as an explanation for today's malaise in Japan
Peter von Staden
Asia Pacific Business Review, volume 18, issue 2 (April 2012) pp. 187-202

Chapter 5
Family and non-family business resilience in an economic downturn
Bruno Amann and Jacques Jaussaud
Asia Pacific Business Review, volume 18, issue 2 (April 2012) pp. 203-223

Chapter 6
Characteristics of R&D expenditures in Japan's pharmaceutical industry
Sophie Nivoix and Pascal Nguyen

Notes on Contributors

Bruno Amann is Professor in Management Sciences at the University Paul Sabatier of Toulouse, France. He is the Director of the "Management and Cognition" Research Team of that University. He has published a number of contributions in leading academic journals on Family business, Corprorate governance, and on International Management. His most recent publications have been released in the *Asia Pacific Business Review* (2011), the *Journal of Transition Economies* (2010), *Ebisu* (2010), the *Journal of Family Business Strategy* (2010) and *Family Business Review* (2008).

Naoki Ando earned his PhD at Seoul National University, Korea. He is an Associate Professor in the Faculty of Business Administration, Hosei University, Japan. His research interests lie in management of MNCs, strategic alliance, expatriate policy, and strategy in emerging economies.

W. Miles Fletcher III is Professor of History at the University of North Carolina-Chapel Hill, USA. His previous work has examined Japanese political and intellectual history during the pre-war period, the history of Japanese trade policy, and the development of the cotton textile industry in modern Japan.

Jun Ishikawa is Professor of Organizational Behaviour and Human Resource Management at Rikkyo University, Japan. He received his Ph.D. from Keio University, Japan. His research interests include leadership, R&D management, and strategic human resource management.

Jacques Jaussaud is Professor in Management Sciences at the University of Pau, France, and is the Director of the CREG Management Research team of that University. He is currently driving a three year research program with Yokohama National University, Japan, financed by the Agency for National Research (ANR, France) and the Japan Society for the Promotion of Science (JSPS, Japan). This research investigates organisation and control in Japanese and French multinational firms in Asia. He has published in several academic journals, including *Asian Business and Management* (2004, 2007), *Ebisu* (1996, 2003, 2010), *Journal of International Management* (2006) and *Asia Pacific Business Review* (2011).

Mark Metzler is Associate Professor of History and Asian Studies at the University of Texas at Austin, USA. He has also worked professionally in the computer and software industries. His research program focuses on deflation and its effects in long-run historical perspective, in Japan and around the world. He has recently completed a study of capital creation illustrated by Japan's experience, entitled *Capital as*

Will and Imagination: Schumpeter's Guide to the Postwar Japanese Miracle, to be published in 2013. He is now writing a global history of the 'Great Depression' of 1873 – 1896.

Pascal Nguyen is Senior Lecturer in the School of Finance and Economics at the University of Technology, Sydney, Australia. His research is related to risk management and corporate governance. He has published in the *Geneva Risk and Insurance Review,* the *Journal of Risk and Insurance,* and the *Journal of Economic Dynamics and Control,* and is also the author of *Investissements: Evaluation du Risque et Gestion d'Actifs* (2000).

Sophie Nivoix is Associate Professor of Finance in the Faculty of Law and Social Sciences at the University of Poitiers, France. Her main research interests are stock market valuation, risk and return, with a particular focus on Japanese firms. She is the author of book chapters in *The Economic Relations between Asia and Europe: Organization, Control, Trade and Investment* (2007), *Evolving Corporate Structures and Cultures in Asia: The Impact of Globalization* (2008), and *Les Paradoxes de la Globalisation des Marchés* (2009) and is also the editor of *Les Territoires dans la Mondialisation* (2010).

Ulrike Schaede is Professor of Japanese Business at the School of International Relations and Pacific Studies (IR/PS), at the University of California, San Diego, USA. Her research interests include Japanese corporate strategy and management, financial markets, regulation and antitrust. She has written many books and papers about Japan's political economy and its companies, most recently *Choose and Focus: Japanese Business Strategies for the 21st Century* (2008) which argues that Japan's business organization has undergone a strategic inflection point so fundamental that our existing knowledge is no longer adequate for a full understanding of Japan.

Peter W. von Staden is Senior Lecturer of International Business at Bristol Business School, part of the University of the West of England, UK. His research focuses on government and business relations in modern Japan. His previous work has examined the role of business in political decision-making in the early twentieth century.

Introduction: Japan at an inflection point

Mark Metzler

Department of History, B7000, University of Texas at Austin, Austin, TX 78712, USA

Japan, inadvertently, has become the outstanding forerunner in a new set of global developments that can be described under the three headings of *deflation*, *downsizing*, and *demography*. New 'lessons from Japan' are to be discovered here, and these are not only admonitory ones. Far from it, for recent Japanese practice exemplifies the new 'choose and focus' strategies that can make an era of general, quantitative business slowdown into one of remarkable sectoral and qualitative development. The implications touch upon wide domains of activity, particularly strategic planning and finance. This introduction surveys some relevant and under-appreciated features of this recent history, in order to understand and project a few main lines of present and near-future developments in connection with the contributions that make up this special issue.

Introduction

In twenty years retrospect, the significance of Japan's great bubble and its deflationary aftermath seems only to grow. Its multiple implications, mostly not perceived at the time, appear in increasingly many social and economic dimensions. Two deserve special notice here. First, deflation is back in Japan, and it now seems that it never really went away. Not only that: historically speaking, this is the longest-lasting deflationary trend period in a very long time. Depending how one views it, Japan's deflation has nearly equalled or surpassed in duration the deflation that affected the Western countries in the so-called 'Great Depression' of 1873–1896. In the stream of Japan's own history, even more strikingly, this is the longest deflationary trend period since the days of the Tokugawa shogunate (Metzler 1994, Iwasaki 1996).

Second, great bubbles are now, manifestly, a global enterprise. We have only begun to perceive their wider effects. In this domain of experience, Japan got there first, and the lessons learned by Japanese businesses under deflation are worth some judicious attention from the rest of the world.

This special issue brings together a collection of studies that consider developments in the world of Japanese enterprise today and in the recent-historical sweep of the years since the deflation of the great bubble. This introduction provides a framework and contextualization for thinking about these developments, surveying, by reference to the contributions to this issue, some basic aspects of the new situation in Japan and the nature of some of the business responses that have come out of it.

The 'three Ds', post-bubble *deflation*, corporate *downsizing*, and shrinking-population *demography*, have come together over the past two decades in a mutually reinforcing way.

These considerations are all conditioned by the great slowdown of economic growth. They raise broad and deep questions, for Japan faces a great turning point in reconceptualizing growth. And not only Japan. These questions touch on the conduct and finance of business, revealing some unforeseen liabilities and some unexpected sources of advantage in the new environment.

The age of deflation

The appearance of deflation in Japan has been epoch-making, as Japan in the 1990s underwent the first extended period of price deflation, anywhere in the world, since the Great Depression of the 1930s. Very short-term deflations occurred in early post-war Japan, in 1949–1950 and in 1953. Since then, the word had been applied rather to deflation *policies*, whose effects stopped short of bringing actual price deflation. Thus, by 1990, price deflation was no longer in the lived experience of any but the oldest of the current generation of policy-makers and entrepreneurs; people did not really remember what it was.

Deflation is frequently mistakenly treated, for example in the Japanese government's 2007 Economic and Fiscal White Paper, as a phenomenon that began with the Asian economic crisis of 1997–1998. Yet general deflation in consumer prices first appeared two years before that, in 1995. Consumer-price deflation was then interrupted by the fleeting economic recovery of 1996, and thereafter persisted as a trend from 1998 to the present, notwithstanding a slight and fleeting pick-up of prices between 2006–2008. Overall, consumer prices in 2010 stand at the same level that they stood 18 years before, in 1992.

If one looks instead at the GDP deflator, which incorporates wholesale prices, deflation began earlier, in 1994, and continued from then until the present. Where the consumer price index has been practically flat, the GDP deflator has fallen 14% over the period.

If one looks at asset prices, the deflation began still earlier. The deflation of share prices ran from 1990–2003. Share prices recovered from then until 2007, and fell back sharply again after mid 2007. The deflation of urban land prices ran from 1991 to the present. As of the end of 2010, both share prices and land prices remain, respectively, some 75% and 60% below their peaks of 1990–1991. Commercial land prices in the largest urban areas, after a temporarily strong recovery in 2006–2008, are now 85% off of their bubble-era peak (Statistics Bureau 2011).

The course of wholesale prices may be even more significant and has been much less heralded. Here, deflation began *before the bubble*, in late 1982, and became substantial in 1985, with the great appreciation of the yen and the international collapse of prices for petroleum and other commodities. The domestic bubble (that is, the great run-up of asset prices) at the end of the 1980s temporarily masked this underlying deflationary movement, which by this measure has, as of writing this, persisted as a tendency for 28 years.

The macro-level environment

More care is also needed in describing the period since the bubble, which continues to be frequently and inaccurately described as if it were one undifferentiated period of stagnation. The 'lost decade' of the 1990s, as introduced by W. Miles Fletcher's (2012) contribution to this issue, was itself contoured by three successive recessions, beginning respectively in 1991, 1997, and 2000. Each recession culminated in an acute financial crisis, followed by an interval of recovery.

These downs and ups of the business cycle were connected to swings in policy, seen conspicuously in two dimensions. First, there was a stop-go cycle of fiscal retrenchment versus Keynesian stimulus. Second, a series of drives for 'neoliberal' regulatory reform along Anglo-US lines cycled with renewed efforts to maintain more protective 'Japan, Inc.' style arrangements (Metzler 2008). One could diagram this policy space in two dimensions as follows:[1]

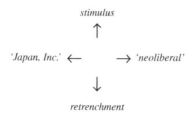

In practice, policy combinations in the 1990s tended to cycle between the 'northwest' (stimulus/Japan, Inc.) quadrant and the 'southeast' (retrenchment/neoliberal) quadrant of this policy space.

Through each of the three stages of recession, deflation tended to intensify. The core bad-debt crisis in the banking sector grew worse, culminating in severe banking crises in 1997–1998 and again around 2003. Out of the latter crisis emerged the mega-banks, the products of repeated mergers. The banks were supported to a critical extent by massive infusions of central bank and governmental funding. At this point, policy also shifted into the 'northeast' quadrant, that is, combining neoliberal structural reform and massive credit creation, which was now directed above all to the rescue and consolidation of the banks themselves.

Even before this final round of banking crisis, there began the long-slow recovery that continued until 2006, the longest economic expansion in the whole post-war record (if also the most modestly paced one). The nature of this recovery is analysed from multiple dimensions by Ulrike Schaede (2008, 2012), whose book is one of the most important contributions to the study of Japanese business to appear in many years. Indeed, Schaede describes a new world of Japanese business. With the collapse of the Western economic bubble in 2007–2008 came renewed recession and deflation in Japan – but this time without a financial crisis. Indeed, though the magnitude of the shock was extreme, Japanese enterprise seemed relatively accustomed to the new situation.

The response of the business world

The 'business world' – *zaikai* – has a particular meaning in Japanese, referring to the politically organized peak business organizations, of which the Federation of Economic Organizations (Keidanren) forms the umbrella group. Bank consolidation is a classic response to depression, seen in many times and places. This financial consolidation happened within the larger context of the reorganization of the old *keiretsu* business groups. Consolidation also happened at the level of the *zaikai* itself, with the amalgamation of Keidanren with the Japan Federation of Employers' Associations (Nikkeiren) into Nippon Keidanren in 2002.

Throughout the long slowdown, Keidanren pushed for regulatory easing, which they said would liberate the energy, flexibility, and creativity of the private sector. Miles Fletcher (2012), in this issue, explicates this movement, continuing his ongoing longitudinal study of peak business organizations in Japan, which extends back to the country's primary industrialization phase in the late nineteenth century (Fletcher 1989, 1996, 1998, 2000, 2005). Prior work by two other contributors to this issue, Peter von

Staden (2008) and Ulrike Schaede (2000), also contributes to this study of *zaikai* organization over the very long run. Fletcher's timely extension of this work focuses on a question that seems likely to grow in importance, as Keidanren displays the ambition to articulate big strategic visions in the way that the Ministry of Economy, Trade and Industry (METI) and other government agencies are accustomed to doing. However, in this case, we also see a pattern of inflexibility and adherence to outmoded world-models similar to that diagnosed by Malcolm Warner (2011) and in this issue by Peter von Staden (2012), a perspective that blinded business leaders to the new situation and ended up contributing to the systemic impasse.

A schema in two dimensions of the national policy space was offered above. One can also consider Keidanren's own internal policy field, which shifted in response to its environmental circumstances. This is a question of the internal balance of forces within the Keidanren and of the main competing standpoints vying for representation. Here as in the larger political world, there has been a tension between a stimulus-oriented policy and a retrenchment-oriented policy. For example, Keidanren representatives called for stimulus in 1991 and 1992, as did officials of the ruling Liberal Democratic Party (LDP). They then returned to calling for retrenchment in 1996, as, simultaneously, did LDP officials.

One sees here also the contradictions between stated goals, appearing most plainly when Keidanren representatives call, on one hand, for restraining labour costs and increasing the consumption tax – both tending to suppress domestic demand – while calling on the other hand for 'expanding the domestic market'. How does one have it both ways? In Japan, the conventional way out is by means of massive industrial investment, which has historically constituted an extraordinarily large share of total domestic demand. But with investment demand maxed out as a result of bubble-era over-investment and low growth, and with mountains of private debt looming on all sides, where was new demand to come from? In practice, it has come from the other source on which Japanese business had grown to rely, overseas demand. In the early twenty-first century, the new demand was above all from China.

Has Keidanren been a force for innovation or a source of inertia? Certainly Keidanren representatives sounded radical, even Marxist in talking about the way that old practices (meaning in practice the regulatory system) were 'shackles' on the forces of production. Peter von Staden (2012), in this issue, also considers some systemic ideological 'fetters of the past', in an ambitious and theoretical account that starts with mind itself and finds its empirical grounding in a discussion of the system of business-government deliberation councils (*shingikai*). Like Fletcher's work, this account draws on Japanese language documentation to present a new account of events. These deliberation councils play a little noticed but pivotal role at the centre of the Japanese policy system. First, they provide inputs to the policymaking process. On the output side, they serve as channels of communication, coordination, implementation, and corrective feedback. This work also builds on a longer longitudinal study (von Staden 2008), and provides a remarkable window into core debates over social values, which are at the heart of the process that Schaede (2012) describes as a strategic inflection point.

Downsizing and upgrading

Here we come to the age of 'choose and focus' – a great shift of emphasis from prioritizing of revenues and market share during the high-growth era to a new, low-growth era priority given to profit and reconsolidation around core competencies. This can also be described as a shift from a more extensive to a more intensive mode of operation.

As Ulrike Schaede (2012) explains in her contribution to this issue, synthesized from an extraordinary range of source material and interviews, Japan has come to the end of the long post-war era and entered a new institutional era, emerging out of the so-called 'lost decade' interval. Even in the early 1990s, historians were unsure whether Japan's seemingly endless 'postwar present' could properly be treated as history (Gordon 1993). There were practical reasons for this doubt. The transformation after World War II was manifestly historic and epoch-making. But then, after the mid to late 1950s, despite enormous quantitative growth and upgrading of the Japanese economy, the basic institutional framework – and the framework of economic regulation particularly – were truly and remarkably stable. Indeed things were stable to the point of being boring, presenting little of the drama people seek in history. But that era is well past; we now speak of our own age as the post-bubble era. In the process, a system that had come to seem 'slow and unwilling to reform' in fact underwent a great wave of reform, beginning in 1998, with the great financial crisis of that year. The reform drive intensified in the early 2000s and resulted by 2006 in a comprehensive reformation of the business and legal/regulatory framework, as Schaede details. This has been accompanied by a great shift in the system of regulation from a 'parental' style of informal, actor-based bureaucratic regulation to a more rule-based, transaction-focused type of regulation.

This reformation is of the very type described in various theoretical traditions as a transformation of the 'regime of regulation', or of the 'social structure of accumulation', or of technological and organizational paradigms (Kotz *et al.* 1994, Jessop and Sum 2006, Freeman and Louçã 2001). The differences between these various analytical schools and their political valences seem less interesting than the fact that they are all more or less apt to the current transformation, and their commonalities deserve discussion. All of them also draw more or less directly on the ideas of Joseph Schumpeter (1939). In all of these views, one sees a picture of multi-decadal periods of predictable growth within an established framework, alternating with periods of extended crisis and technological revolution, the latter bound up with organizational innovation at the level of the firm and with national- and international-level changes of basic regulatory regimes. The high-growth era exemplified the first type of situation; the period since then exemplifies the second.

At one level, 'choose and focus' is a typical recession-era dynamic. Historically, the processes of downsizing, consolidation, and aggregation can be seen to accompany any severe or extended recession. This tendency is especially noticeable during long-extended deflation periods – though the last of those to happen in Japan was the deflation of 1920–1932, which came in the aftermath of the great boom and bubble of the late 1910s (Metzler 2006). In Schumpeterian fashion, that deflationary period was also one of tremendous technological revolutionization and upgrading. As summarized by Freeman and Louçã, a similar wave of technological and organizational revolutions happened in the 1980s and 1990s, associated above all with the new information and communication technologies. On a shorter timescale and to a lesser degree, shakeout and consolidation happens during regular business-cycle downswings – though an important implication of Schaede's argument is that this consolidation/liquidation dynamic *was substantially forestalled* during the recessions of Japan's long post-war boom. This forestalling was accomplished by means of a panoply of state and business-group mutual insurance policies, including such institutions as recession cartels, keiretsu linkages, price fixing by industrial groups, and so on. This forestalling itself is now widely perceived to be one cause of the serious and extended nature of the consolidation and liquidation process that followed the deflation of the 1989 bubble. This liquidation process is the destructive side of Schumpeter-style 'creative destruction', a result more or less explicitly aimed at in many financially oriented neoliberal reform plans.

Thus, after five or six years of more or less contained crisis, the trouble became very acute in 1997–1998. Social distress deepened simultaneously, seen in a highly visible increase in homelessness and, as Schaede explains, in a striking ramping up of the suicide rate in 1998, which was closely connected to the wave of bankruptcies. All of this opened a 'window of opportunity' for reform. But did Japanese authorities jump through the right window?

Internalizing 'global standards': Japan's strategic genuflection?

'Global standards' has been a slogan of the age in Japan and a core conception in the reform process, which has taken a mainly neoliberal direction. Fletcher's (2012) and von Staden's (2102) contributions give a view of this internal Japanese discussion from the basic standpoints of values and ideology, while Schaede (2012) analyses the results of the process. Under the high-speed growth system, the rule of the containing international economic environment and the rules of the 'embedded' domestic environment were substantially different. Now the rules of the containing environment have been, to a substantial degree, adopted into the internal (domestic) environment. This is a result toward which US 'foreign pressure' (*gaiatsu*) has long been directed, but the Japanese system has ample reserves of organizational resistance, and in the end this result has come about as the result of Japanese initiatives.

We see also in this connection big shifts in ownership structures, simultaneous with the strengthening of shareholder rights and the weakening of employee rights. First, the big banks divested substantially especially after 1998. Yet shareholding by the trust banks simultaneously, increased by nearly the same amount. Simultaneously against the expectations raised by the liberal individualist model, *individual* shareholding actually fell slightly. Most dramatic of all was the great increase in foreign shareholding, rising from only about 4% of the total at the end of the Japanese bubble to a peak at 28% in 2006. The year 2006 is also when the US bubble was reaching its peak.

Thus, not only did Japanese companies begin to be governed by a more US-style model; increasingly many of them also had actual US and other foreign owners. As described in a surge of popular business and economics books on the subject in the late 1990s and early 2000s, this shift was widely taken as an expression of Japan's historic 'money defeat' (*manē haisen*; Kikkawa 1998). This language put the neoliberal reforms of the era on a par with what happened in 1945.

There is both less and more to this than meets the eye. Less, because much of the money invested through US funds was actually Japanese money. In this, Japanese institutional investors can be compared to Chinese investors who round-tripped their money out of China in order to be able to invest it in China under the rules applied to foreign investors. And there was more than meets the eye, because this meant that investors acting in this way were utilising US rules to create a beachhead into the Japanese system. US investment was also funded, as we know now, by an unsustainable kind of credit creation. And in another twist, one of the great wellsprings of US bubble-era credit creation was the carry trade in Japanese yen – in other words, Japanese credit, for Japan, in this period, never ceased being the world's super-creditor. This fact has been overlooked in discussions that compared weak and ailing post-bubble Japan with seemingly robust Britain and America – as the banks of the latter countries inflated their own immense credit bubbles.

In connection with this discussion of internationalization of ownership, we can also consider movement in the other direction, namely Japanese outward foreign direct investment, which has also continued to be very considerable. Naoki Ando (2012), in his contribution to this issue, addresses an aspect of this question. He treats ownership structure (percentage of ownership of a subsidiary company's shares) as a dependent variable and argues that, other things being equal, Japanese firms hold smaller stakes in subsidiaries based in countries that are institutionally more distant from Japan, as measured by the World Bank's 'Governance Indicators' index. He emphasizes the importance of learning and partnering in reducing environmental uncertainty.

In any case, it now looks like what happened in Japan from 1998 into the early 2000s was one of the last of the big neoliberal reforms of the Neoliberal era in world history. The Neoliberal era, indeed, now appears as a definite historical era, which can tentatively be dated as 1979–2008. Japan's reform was also in many ways (though with some big exceptions) one of the most modest and judicious of these reforms. Altogether, as Schaede's research delineates in detail, this was a comprehensive and remarkably systematic reform of the business legal and regulatory framework.

This question of a shift in regulatory regime also ends in a new political question, raised by the current phase of government by the Democratic Party of Japan (DPJ). At a minimum, the DPJ government has radically disrupted the pattern of one-party government that began in 1955. Clearly the Hatoyama and Kan cabinets do not represent a neoliberal viewpoint – yet neither do they reflect the old Liberal Democratic Party (LDP) type of corporatist Japan, Inc. vision. What will emerge out of this may be too early to say, but it does seem that both the old 'Japanese'-style vision and the 'Anglo-American'-style critique of it are used up. The first was discredited by the great Japanese bubble that peaked in 1989 and the second by the great Anglo-American bubble that peaked in 2007.

The demographic slowdown

If the course of deflation displays something beyond just another business cycle, so too do the basic demographic indicators tell the story of an epochal shift. Birthrates are falling and populations are ageing all over the already-industrialized world. Demographically, Japan is thus at the leading edge of a movement affecting much of Europe and prospectively East Asia as well (Goodman and Harper 2007). However, in Japan, this prospective future is already here in a way that has not yet happened elsewhere, as the national population actually began to decline in 2005 (Smil 2007). Is societal ageing and population decline compatible with extensive economic growth of the twentieth century type? If so, how and to what sustainable extent? These are questions the twentieth century did not have to ask.

What we confront here is the assumption that growth is a given necessity. Indeed, one can hear it said that because the society is ageing so fast, the economy will have to grow even faster! This growth assumption is pervasive and often unconscious. A nation of 60 year olds will not behave in the same way as a nation of 20 year olds, but it remains to be seen how such a nation will be different. Individual companies in individual sectors will continue to enjoy strong quantitative growth, but one cannot take that as a norm in an age of static or shrinking/ageing populations and stable or falling prices.

Up to a certain point, most people agree that growth is good; but past a certain point of sufficiency, the accumulation of possessions in a limited living space will appear more and more as an obsessive and damaging neurosis. What will be appropriate at a certain stage of 'maturity' is rather intellectual, cultural, and spiritual development. If this were only a question of moral desirability, one could debate it endlessly. But more than that, a return to the old type of growth seems unlikely to be possible. The demand of such an age is qualitative growth, something that we are only beginning to perceive, much less conceptualize fully. Minimally, growth will need to be reoriented and redefined. In some ways, many of them doubtless still invisible to us, this is already happening.

Implications of a deflationary environment at the level of the firm

There has been enormous attention to deflation inside Japan but little notice of the question outside of Japan. It has been assumed outside of the country that Japan's problems were Japan's; they have not been approached in the spirit of learning about generalizable problems of deflation. There is, moreover, a natural desire to learn from success and little interest in learning from what has appeared to be failure. In fact, surviving and even thriving under conditions of deflation reflects anything but failure, and much wider attention is called for among foreign researchers.

Peter von Staden (2012) addresses the question of institutional evolution in a hopeful way, with the suggestion that we humans move by stages from the domain of necessity – of genetically and historically given conditions – to the domain of free, conscious intentionality. Here we are talking about the deliberate design and reformation of social institutions, in an environment that is itself undergoing significant transformation.

Practical lessons for firms operating in a deflationary environment are offered in two distinct dimensions by Sophie Nivoix and Pascal Nguyen (2012) and by Bruno Amann and Jacques Jaussaud (2012). Both contributions connect to questions of finance, particularly to the hazards of debt. Here it bears repeating the obvious, that in an inflationary environment of the kind usual in the latter twentieth century, a given debt becomes over time lighter and easier to repay, whereas under deflation, debts grow heavier over time. Even zero interest is a positive number under deflation. The systemic behaviour of debts and their serviceability is rife with threshold effects, and under highly leveraged conditions, failures can rapidly cascade through a system. Managerial intuitions and common sense formed out of the matrix of the most inflationary century in history may be acutely maladapted to an age of deflation. Indeed, in respect to credit and debt, 'nineteenth century'-style business intuitions might form a better guide.

Qualitative development and differentiation in a low-growth environment

Japan is an exceptionally research and development-intensive country, as Nivoix and Nguyen (2012) point out. The Japanese state is also coordinating some big new recent initiatives in national-level innovation systems (Jackson and Debroux 2008, Ibata-Arens 2008). Skepticism concerning such initiatives is understandable and no doubt justified to an extent, but these initiatives might also be brought into the inflection-point framework offered by Schaede (2012), suggesting that more is at work here than just more of the same.

There is less skepticism concerning the effectiveness of research and development (R&D) efforts at the firm level. Nivoix and Nguyen (2012) study the question here by examining an exceptionally R&D-intensive industry. As they indicate, R&D-intensive firms tend to do better in downturns, because their highly differentiated products cannot easily be substituted by cheaper alternatives. The point is critical when facing an environment of general deflationary price pressure.

There is another critical lesson here, that debt leverage appeared as a clearly negative factor for R&D. High levels of debt tend to hold back R&D. Leveraged buy-outs that saddle a company with new debt are also noted as an inhibiting factor for R&D spending: this debt-leveraged version of aggregation would appear to weaken a company's ability to withstand the pressures of recession, deflation and an ongoing low-growth environment. In this domain, the type of capital is therefore critical. As in other connections, this is not necessarily a matter of debt versus equity so much as a matter of stable or patient (or own) capital, versus capital that demands quick returns at high levels. Like other industries, the pharmaceutical industry has been greatly consolidated since 1990, though it still remains relatively fragmented. Larger firms also tend to devote more resources to R&D.

Japanese ways of research and development may also be a significant aspect of Japanese difference, as suggested by Ishikawa's (2012) study of R&D team performance, also in this issue. There is a point here directly relevant to new ownership structures that include a large Western, particularly US ownership share, because the implication of Ishikawa's study is that efforts at Western-style team leadership may actually inhibit innovation within the Japanese context. Ishikawa points to the need for more specific study of such questions in specifically Asian contexts. This conclusion also challenges a teleology implicitly held in mind by many Western (especially US) practitioners and analysts, to the effect that the direction of future development in Japan must be toward individualism or toward charismatic 'one-man' leadership styles. One repeatedly sees Western observers applying the same set of expectations to the Japanese political system, where these expectations of 'convergence' are regularly and predictably disappointed. The implication of this external view of Japan is that more collective and social modes of operation are developmentally residual or backward. In fact, it seems more the case that times of economic constraint and reconsolidation have the effect of reconsolidating rather than loosening solidary social structures.

There is also a methodological point to note here. Within the ever-changing *conjunctural* (or business-cyclic) environment of a firm, the appearance of deflation is a critical development. By and large, however, scholars have not taken deflation explicitly into account. Because of this, straight comparisons between the way firms operate in a deflationary environment (Japan) and in an inflationary environment (for example, the pharmaceutical industry in the United States) may be telling us more about conjunctural 'phase' differences than they do about national differences. One must be careful not to jump to conclusions about the essence of either system when comparing such dissimilar price-phase environments. But this too may be a domain where it is now other countries that are 'catching up' to Japan rather than vice versa.

Beyond 'grow or die': acting like a family

Bruno Amann and Jacques Jaussaud (2012) indicate that family firms display more resilience in a downturn. A number of organizational and 'moral' reasons (or in von Staden's terms, ideological factors [von Staden 2012]) are suggested by the literature on family business, including the ideas of stewardship, parsimony, familiness, and socio-emotional wealth. This is a set of vocabulary that would sound quite alien in reference to many other types of company environments. Are we seeing here also a residual survival of an older form of business practice? Or again, in a new low-growth, potentially shrinking-population environment, are there lessons for emergent best practice for business enterprises in general?

Finance is again particularly indicated, with family firms tending to have a sounder financial structure. It appears that a critical difference is that family firms carry lower overall debt levels and maintain substantially larger cash balances. Deflation and recession put a premium on this kind of conservative, long-term orientation, which gives priority to organizational continuity rather than to investors' short-term profit demands or creditors' debt-service demands. These latter tend to place a firm in a 'grow or die' situation.

The key feature may thus be the lack of bank pressure (as exists in the Japanese system) or investor pressures (as in US/UK-style systems) for a certain level of return. For a wholly-owned, unindebted enterprise, low growth or no growth is manageable. Family farms and other family businesses have operated on this kind of relatively steady-state basis for centuries. The leveraged, financially driven grow-or-die dynamics of the modern age (so positively evaluated by Schumpeter) indeed produced extraordinary industrial growth in the first century and a half of modern industrialism (Schumpeter 1934 [1926], Mark Metzler forthcoming). However, in an age of demographic stasis or decline, there is a radical mismatch between grow-or-die financing and the new environmental circumstances.

There are also fresh research implications here. Alfred Chandler and many who have followed him had a very high evaluation of the US-style corporate form and a rather negative evaluation of partnerships and family enterprise. Do these familistic and personalistic forms now need much fuller description and theorization in their own right, particularly in Asian contexts?[2] Might such study offer lessons for business enterprise in general? It is also notable that Amann and Jaussaud (2012) are studying here the least 'family-like' of family businesses – large listed companies – in order to filter out other factors and allow easy comparison between family and non-family firms. Descriptive empirical research into more family-like small and medium enterprises may be even more revealing. The implication for non-family businesses may well be that in a deflationary environment, it can be advantageous to learn to operate in more family-like ways.

Altogether, the suggestions must remain modest at this point, pending a broad and focused programme of research into the conduct of business under deflation. Nonetheless, one may venture, based on contributions to this special issue, a few lessons for deflationary times:

- choose and focus;
- minimize debt;
- research, develop and differentiate;
- act like a family.

Conclusion

Contemporary business studies often lack a larger historical or developmental framework. In 'mid-regime' times of long-lasting institutional stability – for example, in Japan from the late 1950s into the 1980s – such an absence can be overlooked, as things operate within a more or less well known and determined social framework. In times of rapid institutional change and regime transformation, the absence of a wider vision becomes a critical lack. A longer-run intellectual time horizon not only helps one to identify and understand the transformations around oneself. Such an understanding may also save organizations from running into cul-de-sacs, chasing after formerly available possibilities that are just at the point of disappearing even while new opportunities open up in unlooked-to directions. A wider temporal awareness also engages imaginative and innovative vision to the tasks of the future. Joseph Schumpeter's intensively historical *and* future-oriented vision of the nature of innovation continues to serve as a wellspring of ideas in considering these questions. Moments of systemic transformations and shifts in regulatory regimes are, by definition, points when entire sets of rules and behaviours change in a short interval. To grasp such changes requires an essentially historical approach. In a similar spirit, Kathryn Ibata-Arens, Julian Dierkes and Dirk Zorn (2006) highlight a trend to reincorporate history into contemporary business scholarship. They emphasize the importance of history for grasping local and contingent factors. Even more broadly than that, to work with a wider mental time horizon enables a grasp of basic dynamic forces, trends, and turning points that are not otherwise visible.

Increasingly, Japan's present transformation appears to be significant on a time scale far greater than that of an ordinary business-cyclic downturn. After a century-long programme to 'catch up and overtake' the more technologically advanced Western countries, Japanese industry more or less achieved that goal in the 1980s. Practically simultaneously, this time without any planned volition, Japan emerged as a forerunner in a new set of post-growth developments. In historical retrospect, this may constitute the beginning of a second age of industrial capitalism. My own conclusion thus differs from that of Peter von Staden (2012) who argues that 'Japan needs to unite itself behind a new vision'. Is a new unified vision likely or even possible in the new environment? The history of a hegemonic *national* vision is, in effect, Japan's story ever since the Meiji Restoration in 1868: the creation of a modern national identity was bound up with the creation of a national goal of catching up with the advanced Western countries. But now we indeed seem to be at a turning point – not just the end of the 'postwar' era but also of the *post-Meiji* era. The market model of distributed decision-making itself suggests that it is time to let a thousand visions bloom.

One institutional legacy of the twentieth century is a bank-centred system built for highly leveraged high-speed growth. Now, with different underlying fundamentals, above all in the demographic domain, these 'legacy' institutions generate speculative bubbles rather than industrial growth. If Japan cannot and will not get back to the high-growth rates of the past, it is doubly clear that leveraged financial structures premised upon high-growth rates themselves now constitute the burden of the past. Indeed, debt itself is such a burden – a storing up of past claims on future production – and itself represents a kind of inertial force.

Here we may step out to the level of the whole global economy and the current Western-world financial mess, which itself is another massive debt crisis centred on the largest banks. Again we see the bailout of the great banks, mostly accomplished in a quiet, semi-public way by the central banks, something that was no more 'left to the market' in the US or UK than it was in Japan's ostensibly market-oriented reform. Far from being the end of the socializing of business risk, this was, in sheer magnitude, the greatest single socialization of 'risk' (debt) ever. This is now a repeated story, as the US and other central banks have broken Japan's previous record. The similarity of these bubble phenomena points to something systematic: a mismatch between the highly leveraged capital-creation process developed out of an age of rapid industrial growth, and the realities of a new era.

All of this suggests that we need to think more deeply about what economic activity is for, as a moral and as a practical question. What *is* economic growth? Are the established metrics of growth the most relevant ones? Which metrics are most relevant in circumstances of industrial and demographic 'maturity'? What would qualitative economic growth look like? What does capitalism as a whole system and what do enterprises individually look like in an environment of zero or negative population growth? For example, what does sustained low growth or even no growth mean for leveraged ownership structures that demand growth? In this connection, might 'traditional' family ownership structures be a great societal resource and fund of lessons for the future? Historically speaking, the understanding of economic growth as a basic ground of economic existence is itself a rather new idea. The history of some older forms of social organization may provide lessons that did not seem relevant amid the extensive industrial growth phase of the nineteenth and twentieth centuries.

Notes

1. For the idea of policy space, see Metzler (2010).
2. Thanks to Professor Kohei Wakimura for this suggestion.

References

Amann, B. and Jaussaud, J., 2012. Family and non-family business resilience in an economic downturn. *Asia Pacific business review*, 18 (2), 201–221.

Ando, N., 2012. The ownership structure of foreign subsidiaries and the effect of institutional distance: a case study of Japanese firms. *Asia Pacific business review*, 18 (2), 257–272.

Fletcher, W.M., 1989. *The Japanese business community and national trade policy, 1920–1942*. Chapel Hill: University of North Carolina Press.

Fletcher, W.M., 1996. The Japan spinners association: creating industrial policy in Meiji Japan. *Journal of Japanese studies*, 22 (1) 49–75.

Fletcher, W.M., 1998. Co-operation and competition in the rise of the Japanese cotton spinning industry, 1890–1926. *Asia Pacific business review*, 5 (1) 45–70.

Fletcher, W.M., 2000. Economic power and political influence: the Japan spinners association, 1900–1930. *Asia Pacific business review*, 7 (2), 39–62.

Fletcher, W.M., 2005. The impact of the great depression: the Japan spinners association, 1927–1936. *In*: Morris Low, ed. *Building a modern Japan*. New York: Palgrave MacMillan, 207–232.

Fletcher, W.M., 2012. Dreams of economic transformation and the reality of economic crisis: Keidanran in the era of the 'bubble' and the 'lost decade' from the mid-1980s to the mid-1990s. *Asia Pacific business review*, 18 (2), 149–165.

Freeman, C. and Louçã, F., 2001. *As time goes by: from the industrial revolutions to the information revolution*. Oxford: Oxford University Press.

Goodman, R. and Harper, S., eds, 2007. *Ageing in Asia: Asia's position in the new global demography*. London: Routledge.

Gordon, A., 1993. *Postwar Japan as history*. Berkeley: University of California Press.

Ibata-Arens, K., 2008. Comparing national innovation systems in Japan and the United States: push, pull, drag and jump factors in the development of new technology. *Asia Pacific business review*, 14 (3), 315–338.

Ibata-Arens, K., Dierkes, J. and Zorn, D., 2006. Theoretical introduction to the special issue on the embedded enterprise. *Enterprise and society*, 7 (1), 1–18.

Ishikawa, J., 2012. Leadership and performance in Japanese R&D teams. *Asia Pacific business review*, 18 (2), 239–256.

Iwasaki, M., 1996. Bukka to keiki hendō [Prices and economic conjuncture]. *In*: S. Nishikawa, K. Odaka and O. Saitō eds. *Nihon keizai no 200 nen*. Tokyo: Nihon Hyōronsha, 55–75.

Jackson, K. and Debroux, P., 2008. Innovation in Japan: an introduction. *Asia Pacific business review*, 14 (3), 285–291.

Jessop, B. and Sum, N.-L., 2006. *Beyond the regulation approach: putting capitalist economies in their place*. Cheltenham: Edward Elgar.

Kikkawa, M., 1998. *Manē haisen* [Money defeat]. Tokyo: Bungei Shunju.

Kotz, D., Terrence McDonough, T. and Reich, M., eds, 1994. *Social structures of accumulation: the political economy of growth and crisis*. Cambridge: Cambridge University Press.

Metzler, M., 1994. Capitalist boom, feudal bust: long waves in economics and politics in pre-industrial Japan. *Review* (Fernand Braudel Center), 17 (1), 57–119.

Metzler, M., 2006. *Lever of empire: the international gold standard and the crisis of liberalism in prewar Japan*. Berkeley: University of California Press.

Metzler, M., 2008. Toward a financial history of Japan's long stagnation, 1991–2003. *Journal of Asian studies*, 67 (2), 653–674.

Metzler, M., 2010. Policy space, polarities, and regimes. *In*: B. Gramlich-Oka and G. Smits eds. *Economic thought in early modern Japan*. Leiden: Brill, 217–250.

Metzler, M., Forthcoming. *Capital as will and imagination: Schumpeterian Finance and the invention of high-speed growth*. Ithaca: Cornell University Press.

Murphy, R.T., 1997. *The weight of the yen*. New York: W.W. Norton.

Nivoix, S. and Nguyen, P., 2012. Characteristics of R&D expenditures in Japan's pharmaceutical industry. *Asia Pacific business review*, 18 (2), 223–238.

Schaede, U., 2000. *Cooperative capitalism: self-regulation, trade associations and the antimonopoly law in Japan*. Oxford University Press.

Schaede, U., 2008. *Choose and focus: Japanese business strategies for the 21st century*. Ithaca, NY: Cornell University Press.

Schaede, U., 2012. The strategic inflection point in Japanese business. *Asia Pacific business review*, 18 (2), 167–184.

Schumpeter, J.A., 1934 [1926]. *The theory of economic development: an inquiry into profits, capital, credit, interest, and the business cycle*. Cambridge, MA: Harvard University Press.

Schumpeter, J.A., 1939. *Business cycles, a theoretical, historical, and statistical analysis of the capitalist process*. 2 vols. New York: McGraw-Hill.

Smil, V., 2007. The unprecedented shift in Japan's population: numbers, age, and prospects. *Japan Focus*, 19 April. Available from: www.japanfocus.org/-Vaclav-Smil/2411.

Statistics Bureau, 2011. *Japan statistical yearbook 2011*, Ministry of Internal Affairs and Communications, Japan. Available from: www.stat.go.jp/english/data/nenkan/index.htm [Accessed 23 March 2011].

von Staden, P., 2008. *Business–government relations in prewar Japan*. Oxon: Routledge.

von Staden, P., 2012. Fettered by the past in the march forward: ideology as an explanation for the malaise in today's Japan. *Asia Pacific business review*, 18 (2), 185–200.

Warner, M., 2011. Whither Japan? Economy, management and society. *Asia Pacific business review*, 17 (1).

Dreams of economic transformation and the reality of economic crisis in Japan: Keidanren in the era of the 'bubble' and the onset of the 'lost decade,' from the mid-1980s to the mid-1990s

W. Miles Fletcher III

Department of History, C.B. 3195, Hamilton Hall, University of North Carolina, Chapel Hill, NC 27599-3195, USA

This study examines the dynamics of the development of Japan's notorious 'lost decade' from 1990–2003. This economic downturn marked the end of four decades of strong economic growth and is still affecting the Japanese economy today. While previous studies have focused on government policies to explain the nation's slow response to this crisis, the attitudes of the Japanese business community merit more attention. For example, the leaders of Keidanren, the powerful representative of big business in Japan, defined a set of economic challenges facing Japan in the late 1980s and neoliberal solutions that blinded them to the significance of the economic bubble that developed at that time and its subsequent collapse. Since then, Keidanren's prescriptions for reviving the Japanese economy have remained essentially the same.

Introduction

The economic stagnation that Japan experienced between 1990–2003, what the Japanese have dubbed as the lost decade, marked the end of four decades of impressive economic growth. After nearly 15 years of rapid growth starting in the late 1950s, the economy had weathered the oil crisis of 1973–1974 to resume a more moderate but still steady pace of expansion. The nation's economic prowess prompted scholars to search for the reasons for this success (Vogel 1979, Johnson 1982). Now, studies often focus instead on the causes and effects of the economic crisis that gripped Japan during the 1990s, commonly known as the lost decade (Katz 1998, Grimes 2001, Lincoln 2001, Amyx 2004, Beason and Patterson 2004, Rosenbluth and Thies 2010).

Although economic growth picked up for several years after 2003, the global financial crisis of 2008 pushed Japan back into the economic doldrums. Hence, examining the causes of the lost decade assumes even more importance, as Japan is still feeling its direct effects. Investigating and delineating the causes of the 'lost decade' can help in figuring out how to avoid similar crises in the future and perhaps even to find a way out of the current lingering morass. One impression that emerges is the need for an accurate understanding of recent economic developments and a questioning of whether proposals formed initially under a much different set of circumstances decades ago should continue to influence national economic policies.

This study finds that a determination that evolved in the late 1980s to carry through a specific program of economic reforms shaped the slow response of the business community, as represented by Keidanren (The Federation of Economic Organizations), to the onset of the nation's economic crisis in the early 1990s. This commitment inhibited rapid and bold intervention by the government to stimulate the economy. On the other hand, this reform agenda encouraged the types of major legal changes and shifts in management practices that Ulrike Schaede's contribution to this volume argues have now occurred in Japan (Schaede 2012). Today, Keidanren (now Nippon Keidanren) is still advocating the same basic policies that it did 25 years ago.

The contours of what happened during the lost decade are well known (see Warner 2011). The trouble started after 1985 with financial speculation that fueled a rise in the prices of stocks and then in the price of real estate. The Nikkei average on the Tokyo stock exchange tripled from 13,000 yen in 1986 to 39,000 yen by the end of 1989. The price of land quintupled between 1985–1991 (Itō 2007, p. 124). By 1989, concern about these trends led officials at the Bank of Japan to begin a rapid increase in its discount rate. It rose from 2.5% to 3.25% in May 1989, to 3.75% in October, and to 4.25% in December 1989. By August 1990, the discount rate reached 6%. Meanwhile, starting in 1990, the Bank of Japan sharply reduced the growth in the supply of money (Grimes 2001, pp. 141–142, Flath 2005, p. 132). Although Japanese officials were trying to engineer a soft landing by gradually deflating the speculative bubble, it burst with surprising speed. By October 1990, the Nikkei had fallen to nearly 20,000 yen. The price of real estate began its descent in 1991 (Flath 2005, pp. 141, 145). Underscoring the continuing effects of the collapse of the markets, the stock market in 2003 remained mired at the level of 7,000 yen, while by 2005 land prices had given up all of their gains of the late 1980s (Itō 2007, p. 140). Non-performing loans piled up at banks. Economic growth virtually ground to a halt, as it averaged only 1% per year from 1990–2003.

Review of the literature

As one might expect, analysts are still trying to discern the causes of this economic collapse. As Kikkawa Takeo points out, Japanese scholars have often seemed at a loss to explain in a systematic way how characteristics of corporate governance and management that drove economic success for decades suddenly failed after 1990 (Kikkawa 2005, pp. 22–28). Among Western scholars, one approach to explaining this course of events has centered on arguing that despite Japan's impressive record of economic growth during the previous four decades, major sectors of the economy had become inefficient (Katz 1998, Beason and Patterson 2004, Rosenbluth and Thies 2010) as a result of government protectionism. This argument, however, poses several problems. First, it entails disavowing the credit that previous studies had often allotted to officials in the Ministry of International Trade and Industry (MITI) and the Ministry of Finance (MOF) for helping to guide the nation's success and, instead, charging the opposite, that these officials, far from being economic wizards, had ended up coddling unproductive industries. One could also ask: if the government's policies were so counter-productive, what actions in the private sector could account for the Japanese 'miracle' from the 1950s through to the 1980s, especially in the face of governmental policies now deemed to be detrimental to economic growth? Could, as one study asserts, mere increases in 'standard factors of production,' such as labor and capital, have sufficed to drive Japan's economic growth under such trying circumstances (Beason and Patterson 2004, pp. 86 87)?

Other analyses have focused on the specific ways in which the economic collapse unfolded after 1989. These studies have assumed that systemic problems did not make the 'lost decade' inevitable and that a more effective response early on might have mitigated the crisis. Why, many have asked, did the Japanese respond so slowly? Noting that Japan experienced an 'extraordinary delay' of eight years in responding to the banks' problem of bad debt, one scholar describes the 'mismanagement of banking sector woes' as 'enigmatic,' especially in light of the previously impressive reputation of the Ministry of Finance (Amyx 2004, pp. 1–2, 6). The Bank of Japan eventually slashed its discount rate to nearly 0%, but it took five years to reach that point. The Ministry of Finance matched that slow pace by also taking five years to issue its first estimate of the total amount of bad loans held by Japanese banks. According to one observer, before 1998 only the budgets of 1994 and 1995 were 'truly stimulatory' (Metzler 2008, p. 657). To explain the slow reaction to the developing financial crisis, studies have focused on examining the policies and actions of the Bank of Japan and the Ministry of Finance (Grimes 2001, Amyx 2004).

The aim of this contribution is to examine the attitudes and actions of Keidanren, as the economic crisis developed during the early 1990s. Carrying on the legacy of the Japan Economic League (Nihon Keizai Renmeikai) in the interwar period, Keidanren during the post-1945 era has been considered the most powerful representative of big business in Japan. It encompassed a membership of hundreds of large firms and industrial associations. During several decades prior to 1990, the Japanese business community had astutely sized up changing economic circumstances and had adjusted accordingly. The first oil crisis of 1973–1974, when the Arab oil embargo and a resulting spike in oil prices brought both a recession and high inflation, had provided the most recent example. Japanese firms had responded by becoming much more energy efficient (Kikkawa 2005, p. 17). Why then, in this instance, did the Japanese business community miss the boat, so to speak?

Propositions

The perspective of the Japanese business community during the crisis has not received adequate attention. Presumably, if Japanese business leaders had been clamoring in the late 1980s for measures to prevent a speculative bubble or in the early 1990s to respond promptly and forcefully to its collapse, those opinions would have had some impact on government officials. The question then arises as to why business leaders did not make these demands.

One could conjecture the following: (1) that Japanese executives had incentives not to confront publically Japan's economic crisis, because they did not wish to advertize their mismanagement. For example, banks initially may not have wanted to draw attention to their rapidly increasing stockpile of non-performing loans and resultant weak financial condition (Amyx 2004, chap. 7). Firms in some other sectors, however, might well have not felt the same constraints. (2) One could also conjecture that what one might call the 'mind-set' of a broad segment of the Japanese business community, represented by Keidanren, in the late 1980s and early 1990s represented a major obstacle.

The leaders of Keidanren had developed by the late 1980s such a firm definition of the economic challenges facing Japan and of the necessary solutions that this perspective blinded them to the crisis that was building underneath their feet and, once it erupted, to the need for the quick action that it demanded. This stance became manifest in the *Keidanren shūhō [Keidanren Weekly Reports]*,[1] as well as special reports issued by the federation and public statements by its leaders.

17

Evidence and analysis: envisioning an historic shift in the Japanese economy

To understand the attitudes of Keidanren toward developments in the Japanese economy in the early 1990s, one first has to examine the specific circumstances of the mid-1980s and the federation's response to them. A decade before, the nation's impressive record of nearly double-digit annual growth rates over 15 years had ended with the first oil crisis of 1973–1974. Afterwards the economy recovered to assume a steady, strong rate of annual growth of 4–5%. Only the Islamic Revolution in Iran in 1979, which again disrupted oil supplies, caused a brief hiatus in this trajectory. Meanwhile, the continued expansion of the nation's foreign trade surplus caused severe friction with Japan's largest market, the United States. American officials placed intense pressure on the Japanese to invest in the United States, to liberalize trade by removing barriers to imports, and to allow the yen to appreciate in value.

In this atmosphere, the Economic Investigation Group (Keizai Chōsakai) of the federation issued a major report in 1985, enunciating the need for basic changes in Japan's financial and economic policies. The nation, the report argued, faced a 'turning point' (*Keidanren shūhō* 1985, p. 2). It placed a top priority on reducing overseas criticism of Japanese exports by 'devising a policy to resolve severe foreign economic friction.' Japan had to remove barriers to imports and create a strategy for orderly exports. A focus on enlarging domestic demand would aid in achieving both of these goals and stabilize the economy. Noting that the nation had recovered from the second oil crisis just two years before and that the American government was running a huge fiscal deficit, the group warned that in the near future the 'world economy could again enter a situation in which [the economy] would be shaken' (*Keidanren shūhō* 1985, pp. 2–4).

The report also posited that fiscal and administrative reforms of the government were essential to reviving the economy's vitality to meet the demands of a new era. Claiming that Japan's fiscal situation was 'the worst among advanced nations,' Keidanren pleaded for a balanced national budget. The report noted with approval that a Temporary Administrative Research Council appointed by the government had begun work in March 1981, on ways to streamline the bureaucracy. Because raising taxes to pay for national bonds would exhaust the economy, Japan had to aim to 'emerge from a dependence on deficit national bonds by 1990.' Meanwhile, the authors of the report recognized that the aging of the society would bring pressure on the government to provide more medical care and pensions (*Keidanren shūhō* 1985, pp. 5–6). The prospect of this future demand made current fiscal reform even more imperative.

In general, the Japanese had to unleash the potential dynamism of the private sector both to raise the people's quality of life and to become more economically competitive. Japan, according to the report, had a large Gross National Product (GNP) but fewer real assets than other developed nations in terms of infrastructure, such as roads, housing, sewers, and parks. Japanese may have been rich, but they did not feel well off. One solution was for the private sector to play a greater role in providing these resources (*Keidanren shūhō* 1985, pp. 6–7). Of course, to do so companies would have to create and keep more capital. Unfortunately, Japanese firms were poorly capitalized, invested too little in research, and had a comparatively low rate of profitability. Moreover, they had to prepare for a future drop in the famously high savings rate of Japanese families as the society continued to age (*Keidanren shūhō* 1985, pp. 7–9).

The authors of the report took inspiration from economic policies evolving across the Pacific in the form of deregulation and tax cuts. 'Such frailty of the strength of [Japanese] enterprises depends to a great extent on the difference in trends in the policies of Japan and other nations. Especially in America, President [Ronald] Reagan, based on a goal of creating a strong America, has positively acted to strengthen enterprises and to reform the character of the economy' (*Keidanren shūhō* 1985, p. 9). As a result, businessmen had recovered their confidence in the economy: 'In Japan, too, there is a need to take such actions as a model and to develop a new industrial policy to demonstrate the vitality of business' (*Keidanren shūhō* 1985, p. 9). Certainly, companies had to strive to expand their research operations, earn more profits by avoiding 'excessive competition,' and restrain labor costs because they had outstripped gains in productivity since the mid-1960s. The government, however, could most effectively help firms by imposing itself less on the private sector. In the past, a 'fragmentary' industrial policy had 'obstructed the autonomous activity of enterprises.' In contrast, in the future there must be a priority on spurring the 'creativity of enterprises' and 'revising the circumstances of enterprise management starting with deregulation.' The report's emphasis on the comparatively low corporate tax rate in Britain and the United States and on the increase in the Japanese rate since 1980 suggested the need for a major reform of the national tax structure (*Keidanren shūhō* 1985, pp. 9–10).

In brief, this report of May 1985, represented a lengthy and major statement by Keidanren about its perception of the economic challenges facing Japan and needed reforms. The authors viewed their proposed reforms as having historical significance in altering the fundamental principles of previous economic policy. To confront the primary challenge of blunting foreign criticism of Japan's growing trade surplus, the economy had to switch from growth led by exports to growth centered on the expansion of the domestic market. To achieve this goal and to improve the quality of life for ordinary citizens, the basic character of the government's role in the economy had to change from one of enhancing regulation of the private sector to liberating the energy of private enterprise. If the tax cuts and deregulation being implemented in the United States provided an attractive model, Keidanren differed from the Reagan Administration by insisting on ending deficit financing by the national government. To this end, 'administrative reform' had to reduce government operations and expenses.

Just a few months after this report, the so-called Plaza Accord confirmed the importance of Keidanren's stated priority of mollifying international criticism of Japan's surplus in foreign trade. In September 1985, the Group of Five–France, Japan, the United Kingdom, the United States, and West Germany–agreed in New York City to coordinate their policies to effect a depreciation of the value of the US dollar relative to other currencies, including the Japanese yen. The prospect of a sharply appreciating yen caused considerable alarm within Japanese business circles because of the obvious potential effect on the nation's trade balance. In October, Prime Minister Nakasone Yasuhiro appointed a task force headed by a former governor of the Bank of Japan, Maekawa Haruo, to formulate a strategy for dealing with this new circumstance. In April 1986, Maekawa's commission recommended various policies, including increased government spending, deregulation, and changes in tax policy in order to expand domestic demand and to reduce the current account surplus (Keizai Dantai Rengōkai 1999, p. 536, Flath 2005, p. 181).

In 1985 and 1986, efforts to reform national taxes became the focus of Keidanren's activity. Its leaders continued to complain that Japan's corporate tax rate was higher than that of other developed nations and that the income tax unfairly burdened Japan's managerial employees, popularly referred to as the archetypal '*salaryman*.' Ideally, the tax system should spread the burden of financing the government more equally among all citizens. A report in September, 1986, recommended 'a reduction of the income tax centered on the middle income class,' a 'drop in the corporate tax burden to an international balanced level,' and an 'indirect tax system in which the people would share the burden thinly and widely' (Keizai Dantai Rengōkai 1999, p. 623). In December, the governing Liberal Democratic Party (LDP) proposed a 'moderation' of the graduated nature of the income tax, a lowering of the corporate tax below 50%, and the introduction of a 5% national sales tax (Keizai Dantai Rengōkai 1999, p. 625).

The federation participated actively in the national debate that followed. In early 1987, Saitō Eishirō, the chairman of Keidanren, declared that 'there is no reason that only Japan rejects a sales tax that is common internationally.' In April, the group supported a large rally for the LDP's plan organized by the Salaryman Happy Life Club in the Hibiya Public Hall in Tokyo. After the LDP in 1988 endorsed a cut in the corporate tax rate to 37.5% and a reduction in the proposed new sales tax to 3%, Keidanren convened a conference of 2500 *salaryman* to discuss tax reform (Keizai Dantai Rengōkai 1999, pp. 627, 632–633). In October, a report of the federation's Tax System Committee noted approvingly that the current plan of the LDP 'basically follows our thinking.' A 'very large' tax cut for the middle income group represented by the '*salaryman*' would stimulate consumption and advance 'the arrival of an economy led by domestic demand.' Japan would also join other advanced nations by slashing the corporate tax to 37.5%. Pointing out that over one-half of government revenue came from the corporate tax and the income tax, the Committee argued that the corporate tax would become too onerous in an aging society if the current tax rates continued (*Keidanren shūhō* 1988b, pp. 2–4). The Diet finally passed the legislation at the end of the year. Subsequently, the cabinet maintained its incipient trend of lessening its budgetary dependence on bonds, so that from 1990–1993 the government issued no deficit bonds (Grimes 2001, p. 77).

If the representatives of large corporations in Japan focused their efforts on lessening their tax burden, they also pursued other aspects of their reform agenda, such as reducing trade friction in major markets. After 1985, the persistence of Japan's large trade surplus further inflamed American public opinion, even though American exports to Japan increased significantly. In 1988 the American Congress passed the Omnibus Trade and Competitiveness Act, and in 1989 the United States Trade Representative, Carla Hills, invoked the so-called Super 301 clause of that bill against Japanese trade barriers in three areas: supercomputers, satellites, and wood products. She also listed Japan along with Brazil and India as a nation that engaged in unfair trading practices. In that same year, Structural Impediments Initiative talks began between American and Japanese officials with the aim of liberalizing trade between the two nations (Keizai Dantai Rengōkai 1999, pp. 585–586). Facing this hostility from Japan's largest trading partner, the federation from 1986–1989 consistently advocated the goal of reducing trade friction by eliminating barriers to imports and stimulating internal demand (Keizai Dantai Rengōkai 1999, pp. 523–526, 582). Many members backed the deregulation of agricultural imports, more efficient handling of imports, and substantial reform of the Large Store Law that strictly regulated the spread of supermarkets and large retail stores in commercial areas populated by small shops (Keizai Dantai Rengōkai 1999, pp. 556–557, 589–594).

As a more general strategy, the federation firmly supported a broad movement to reduce the role and size of government through 'administrative reform.' This campaign had started in the early 1980s with the government's appointment of a Temporary Administrative Study Commission. Keidanren later proposed 'to make 1988 the year of implementing "small government"' with a ceiling on the national budget and the continued privatization of public corporations. At the end of 1988, Chairman Otsuki Bunpei explained the need to reverse previous attitudes toward government interference in the private sector by 'making the principle freedom, the exception regulation,' minimizing 'administrative guidance,' and instilling the 'principle of the self-responsibility of the people' (Keizai Dantai Rengōkai 1999, pp. 557–559). In 1990 Vice-Chairman Matsuzawa Takuji criticized a recent report of the Administrative Reform Council for not going far enough. The Council's recommendation to eliminate various types of regulations of economic activity had followed Keidanren's thinking in trying to 'reform the system that has tended toward public regulation and the protection of industry for more than 120 years since the Meiji [era from 1868–1911] and create a society that respects multiple choices by consumers.' Still, he complained that the report avoided the major issue of ending the tight control of food imports and backed away from setting an ambitious goal of eliminating 50% of all regulations (Keizai Dantai Rengōkai 1999, pp. 562–563).

Administrative reform and the ideal of small government held importance for the leaders of Keidanren for several reasons. Reducing the cost of government would leave more resources in the hands of a re-energized private sector that could both provide the means to improve the quality of life of citizens and keep the Japanese economy competitive as other nations pursued deregulation. Moreover, a more vital domestic economy would stimulate more demand for imports. Paring the thicket of regulations would also help internationalize the economy by easing the entry of both foreign investment and goods. These changes would both accord with the cutting edge of changes in economic policy elsewhere, especially in the United States, and begin an historic reversal of the direction of economic policy that had for over a century tended toward increasing regulation.

Evidence and analysis: coping with a disaster

Overall, economic trends in the late 1980s inspired confidence in the economy. Real economic growth chugged along at a real rate of 4–5% per year. The issuance of government bonds fell, the proportion of manufactured goods in Japanese imports rose, and the trade surplus declined. In 1988, the government White Paper on the economy claimed that Japan had 'overcome the high yen recession since the fall of 1985' and had switched to a pattern of 'economic growth led by domestic demand.' By June 1990, Japan had experienced 43 months of economic expansion (Keizai Dantai Rengōkai 1999, pp. 542–544). In this context, the soaring prices of stocks and of real estate may have appeared as simply irksome aberrations because other economic indicators were so strong. For example, a Keidanren report in June 1988, acknowledged the soaring price of land but viewed this development not as a threat to overall economic growth but as just a specific obstacle to solving the problem of overcrowding in some urban areas. According to the report, deregulation would lead to better planning for the use of land and increasing its supply (*Keidanren shūhō* 1988a, p. 5). Members of the Economic Policy Committee accepted without challenge a positive economic forecast of officials from the Economic Planning Agency who took comfort from the low unemployment rate and three years of stable prices (*Keidanren shūhō* 1989a, pp. 2–3).

Indeed, because the leaders of Keidanren harbored a fear of inflation, they would view the initial descent of the price of land as benign. While the federation issued a generally favorable outlook for the economy in 1990, the group's forecast included a concern about the importance of keeping prices stable. From this perspective, the pressure of the demand for labor and manufactured goods and the previous rise in the value of land were 'materials for concern' (*Keidanren shūhō* 1989b, p. 6). A major assessment of the economy in early 1991 cited land speculation as one of the major problems of the 1980s that could carry over to the new decade. In this perspective, the fall of stock prices and land prices represented a positive 'correction of asset inflation.' In fact, the authors of this report welcomed a further drop in the price of real estate to enhance the general welfare by making homes more affordable (*Keidanren shūhō* 1991, pp. 3–4).

If this assessment anticipated no immediate economic problems, it continued the drumbeat for a fundamental shift in national economic policies. On the positive side, the report took pride in the nation's recovery from the second oil crisis of 1979 and the threat posed by the rapidly appreciating yen after the Plaza Accord by switching from an export-led economy to one fueled more by domestic growth. Moreover, the 'emergence from reliance on bonds' to finance deficit spending had begun. The authors predicted a respectable real economic growth rate of 4% in the first half of the 1990s and 3.5% in the second half of the decade (*Keidanren shūhō* 1991, pp. 3, 5). Still, the times demanded change. The broadest challenge lay in moderating the strong bureaucratic leadership evident since the Meiji era and 'creating a "market economy" led by the private sector' that would be 'strong and flexible.' 'The 1990s' would be nothing less than a 'turning point in world history' because of the spread of globalization and increased competition. 'Japan's national economic society had reached an important turning point' as well. The maturing of the economy and the aging of society threatened to bring a dramatic drop in economic dynamism. Various areas of the economy, such as the distribution and retail sector, had to become more productive through the introduction of market principles. To compensate for a labor shortage of 5 million people, companies would have to encourage the elderly and women to work. Moreover, Japan should also contribute to 'global development' by becoming 'a truly open international market for capital and finance.' Touting a 'new economic democracy,' Keidanren advocated that '[a]s needs diversify Japanese must reject government interference and advance deregulation.' The government, however, would have to help in new ways. Its economic role had to become more 'maneuverable and flexible.' For example, while decreasing its regulation of the private sector, the government should increase its support of companies' research expenses to equal the contributions of the American, German, and French governments to firms in those nations (*Keidanren shūhō* 1991, pp. 3, 6–10).

In general, the federation was hardly alone in its relative optimism about the coming decade. The business community as a whole showed few signs of awareness about the financial and economic crisis that was about to unfold. For example, in April 1991, the Japan Bankers Association (Zenkoku Ginkō Kyōkai/JBA) released figures for the 12 city banks, the nation's largest banks, which revealed mixed results in performance for 1990. The city banks' deposits rose sharply but the increase in lending fell to the lowest rate since 1949 at 6.1%, in stark contrast to the double-digit pace attained since 1981 (*Yomiuri shinbun* 1991a).[2] Even though the recent increases in the Bank of Japan's discount rate had hindered lending, the chairman of the JBA, Suematsu Ken'ichi, refused to advocate a cut in that rate, because 'there is [some] doubt as to whether speculation has disappeared (in relation to land, etc.)' (*Yomiuri shinbun* 1991b). In other words, bankers still feared that speculation in land or stocks could flare up again. Two months later, the 1990 results released for all 154 members of the JBA brought further disappointment, as deposits and the value of financial assets fell for the first time since 1948 and the rise in lending for all members reached a rate of only 5.1% (*Yomiuri shinbun* 1991d). This time, Suematsu termed a cut in the discount rate 'appropriate,' but he cautioned that 'one cannot say that the bubble economy has calmed down uniformly across the entire country. The magma remains underneath. In the future, vigilance is necessary' (*Yomiuri shinbun* 1991e). Bankers, in fact, during the early 1990s seemed more concerned about competition from the government's postal savings system than with the direction of the economy. Disturbed by the postal savings system offering a slightly higher interest rate on deposits than private banks, Suematsu warned that this measure would 'invite confusion in the financial markets' and declared that 'the oppression of the management of private financial institutions is feared and cannot be approved' (*Yomiuri shinbun* 1991c).

Gradually, leaders of the business community began to realize the severity of the economic crisis that was unfolding through the steep drop in first the stock market and then the price of real estate. By December 1991, the JBA reported that banks' mid-year settling of accounts showed that total deposits had declined again and that lending had grown at the miniscule rate of 0.08%, even though firms' 'pure profit' had increased (*Yomiuri shinbun* 1991f). In September, Hiraiwa Gaishi, the chairman of Keidanren, had joined the call for lowering the Bank of Japan's discount rate and reiterated his support in December while noting that 'the freezing of the investment mind-set *[maindo]* of enterprises is severe beyond expectations' (*Yomiuri shinbun*, 1991g). The first cut in the discount rate occurred in the second half of 1991, and over the next three years it declined step-by-step to 0.5% in 1995 (Grimes 2001, p. 95). Some business leaders, however, advocated further action. Saitō Hiroshi, the chairman of the Japan Steel Federation (Nihon Tekkō Renmeikai), fumed, 'one cannot say that the cut [in the discount rate] is adequate. I want to expect from now on flexible policies from the authorities' (*Yomiuri shinbun* 1991g). After observing two months later that the 'slowdown in business conditions is accelerating,' Suematsu raised the same point by hinting at the need for an expansive fiscal policy: '... there is some unease as to whether one can revive with only financial measures the frozen mind-set of enterprises. One must have some vitality from the side of public finance' (*Yomiuri shinbun* 1992a).

The steep fall of the average stock market price by March 1992, below 20,000 yen, a drop of almost 50% since early 1990, sparked a new sense of urgency. Nagano Ken, chairman of the Japan Employers Federation (Nikkeiren) advocated 'enhancing the mentality of the management of enterprises with financial and fiscal policies.' Ishikawa Rokurō, the chairman of the Japan Chamber of Commerce, which represented small and medium-sized businesses, pleaded for the 'prompt enactment of every type of recovery policy in finance, fiscal matters, the tax system, etc.' A vice-president of the New Japan Steel Company (Shin Nihon Seitetsu) favored a commitment to more public investment in the national budget. Suematsu complained that the decline in the value of financial assets in the form of both stocks and land meant that Japanese banks might not be able to meet the standard for self-capitalization set by the Bank for International Settlements (*Yomiuri shinbun* 1992b).

Sentiment within the business community leaned toward support for two measures: a large-scale supplement to the national budget to stimulate demand and major cuts in taxes on investment and/or on income (*Yomiuri shinbun* 1992c) Even though the banking sector began to lend its backing to reducing taxes and utilizing deficit spending to stimulate the economy (*Yomiuri shinbun* 1993a), most of those leading the charge in pushing for such policies came from the manufacturing and retail sectors. In August 1992, the chairman of the Japan Electrical Machine Manufacturers Association (Nihon Denshi Kikai Kōgyōkai) complained about the cabinet not including a tax cut in its recently released comprehensive economic policy. The president of the Daiei Department Store Chain added that an 'income tax cut was necessary to revive the consumption mind-set.' Muramatsu Atsushi, the vice-president of the Nissan Automobile Company, and Nakamura Tameaki, the president of Sumitomo Metal Industries, each predicted that the cabinet's timidity would delay economic recovery by a year (*Yomiuri shinbun* 1992d). A year later, Saitō argued forcefully for a 'united mobilization of financial, fiscal, and tax system policies–a large cut in income taxes, radical fiscal measures, and financial deregulation.' Kume Yutaka, chairman of the Japan Automobile Manufacturers Association (Nihon Jidōsha Kōgyōkai) declared, 'I would like to have [the government] first reduce taxes and stimulate consumption. There is no alternative to issuing deficit bonds' (*Yomiuri shinbun* 1993b).

As pressure grew for a tax cut, the Tax System Investigation Committee appointed by the government issued an interim report that proposed a compromise of combining a reduction in the income tax with raising the consumption tax. Hiraiwa, the chairman of Keidanren, voiced support by saying that he 'could understand including together a reduction in the income tax and a raise in the consumption tax.' The burden of the income tax, he implied, far outweighed the negative effects of the consumption tax. He added that 'attention should focus on the negative effects of the land tax and the heavy corporate tax rather than the negative effects that the increase in the consumption tax would bring to business conditions . . . .' Inaba, the chairman of the Japan Chamber of Commerce, made the obvious point, however, that raising one tax would offset whatever benefits might accrue from lowering the other tax. Sekimoto Tadahiro, chairman of the Japan Electrical Manufacturers Association, exclaimed in exasperation, 'The idea of lowering the income tax and raising the consumption tax as a package is a product of people who do not realize the severity of business conditions.' He favored reducing the income tax first and deciding about the consumption tax after the economy had improved. Itakura Yoshiaki, chairman of the Japan Department Store Association, asserted that increasing the consumption tax would 'ignore the psychology (*shinri*) of consumers' (*Yomiuri shinbun* 1993c).

Meanwhile, banks began to push for the strategy of using public funds to help clear away their growing stores of non-performing loans. To be sure, this was a sensitive issue. The *Yomiuri* newspaper reported that in August 1992, when Prime Minister Miyazawa Ki'ichi had suggested using public funds to help banks, 'public opinion reacted all at once that "it is absurd to pour blood taxes into financial institutions that fanned the bubble." From the business world, too, the arrows of criticism concentrated on the high wages in banks' (*Yomiuri shinbun* 1992e). By 1994, however, the continuing financial crisis appeared to reach a new level. After the Ministry of Finance finally required banks to report the total amount of their non-performing loans at the year-end settlement of accounts in March 1993, according to new standard criteria set by the Japan Bankers Association, the subsequent mid-year accounting revealed an increase in non-performing loans of at least 7.7%. As complaints about the tightening of credit 'becoming shackles on the recovery of business conditions' escalated, banks felt more pressure to redeem bad debt to create 'assets that will generate profit.' In this context arose the idea of using public funds to help financial institutions with this task (*Yomiuri shinbun* 1994). The issue continued to percolate over the next two years.

By late autumn 1995, the Bank of Japan and the Ministry of Finance were exploring the use of public funds to replenish the capital of banks as they redeemed their own non-performing loans and those of seven subsidiary 'mortgage institutions' (*jūtaku kinyū senmon kaisha/jūsen*) that faced bankruptcy (*Yomiuri shinbun* 1995e). Meanwhile, the JBA expressed caution about using public funds by declaring that doing so would require the 'persuasion of the people and consensus' and, in any case, should be used only if deposit insurance funds did not suffice (*Yomiuri shinbun* 1995a, 1995b). By November, however, Hashimoto Toru, the chairman of the JBA, was advocating a strategy of 'partial redemption' of non-performing loans that would take several years as opposed to a quick redemption, which would require a much larger one-time infusion of public funds (*Yomiuri shinbun* 1995d).

As other business groups called for more forceful government intervention, Keidanren essentially held fast to its comprehensive prescription for the economy that it presented in 1985. This strategy included a healthy dose of fiscal conservatism. In 1992, when the Tokyo Stock Exchange cratered to 60% of its value in 1989, Hiraiwa Gaishi, as chairman of Keidanren, finally advocated more public spending to spur the economy (Keizai Dantai Rengōkai 1999, pp. 879–880). Other groups and business leaders, though, took the lead in pushing this cause more forcefully. As noted above, in 1993 Hiraiwa backed a cut in the income tax only if it was balanced by an increase in the consumption tax; many other business leaders favored an immediate tax cut despite the predicted loss of revenue. The leaders of Keidanren rarely took their eye off of what they considered their main long-term goal of promoting small government and altering the basic character of the Japanese economy by liberating the private sector from bureaucratic constraints.

Accordingly, the federation continued to devote much of its energy to pushing for structural changes, such as administrative reform and deregulation in order to invigorate the private sector, rationalize and 'slim' the government, and spur 'competition and the transparency' of the economy as a whole. The group proudly noted that in July 1994, the cabinet of Prime Minister Hosokawa Morihiro adopted 112 of the 163 proposals that the group had submitted for eliminating regulations (Keizai Dantai Rengōkai 1999, pp. 853–860). This stance generally resonated with other business groups, as they, too, could agree in principle with the goal of reducing bureaucratic interference in the economy, even if they also wanted more governmental action to stimulate the economy. The Japan Chamber of Commerce presented a particularly interesting example. The chamber bitterly opposed the efforts to eliminate or substantially reform the Large Store Law, a cause that Keidanren championed as part of administrative reform (*Yomiuri shinbun* 1990, 1995c). Even though the chamber warned that changes to the law would cause the failure of many small and medium businesses, increase unemployment, and hurt small businesses outside of the main urban centers, the group still expressed support for the policy of deregulation in general as 'a very effective means to plan to energize small and medium-sized enterprises' (*Yomiuri shinbun* 1995f).

By 1995, the leaders of the federation had yielded some ground on budgetary issues but still advocated fiscal restraint. In 1992, representatives of Keidanren had rejected a suggestion by Prime Minister Miyazawa Ki'ichi to use public funds to help banks with non-performing loans (Amyx 2004, p. 159). Only three years later, in June 1995, did the Ministry of Finance again ask for the organization's opinion on this matter. Keidanren then responded more positively in a report in early July: 'From the standpoint of depositors, [the government] had to invest public funds to solve the problem of non-performing loans.' Moreover, the report pointed out that the deepening of this problem would weaken financial institutions to the point of influencing their ability to raise capital and be competitive. Because the amount of non-performing loans had exceeded 4 billion yen, leaving this problem to the private sector to solve would only postpone a resolution and increase the ultimate cost of dealing with it. The group added that in the medium and long term, 'measures that stress regulation of the [financial] market [were] necessary' to prevent further problems in the future (Keizai Dantai Rengōkai 1999, pp. 876–877). Subsequently, the federation forcefully backed the use of public funds in order to prevent further damage to the stock market within Japan and to restore international confidence in Japan's financial markets (*Yomiuri shinbun* 1996b, 1996c). Still, the leaders of Keidanren remained cautious. In December 1995, the chairman, Toyoda Shōichirō, reacted to the expansive national budget proposed for 1996 by advising, 'Now, it's important to plan an increase in taxes with the recovery of business conditions and with a radical reform of tax finances in the medium and long term to reform the fiscal situation' (*Yomiuri shinbun* 1995g).

In keeping with Keidanren's previous stance, a major report that the group issued in October 1995, emphasized the need for basic structural reforms. Once again, the federation depicted a critical turning point. Mired in a 'deep recession,' the economy confronted 'an important crossroads of the continuance of prosperity or its decline'. 'The cause of the structural difficulties that Japan is facing today,' the report intoned, 'is the stagnation of the social system since [the] Meiji [era] of bureaucratic leadership and central authority.' The 'Japanese economic system of "catch up, surpass" has made a contribution in the achievement of goals in expanding the scale of the economy, but [this economic system] has become a set of shackles today when [firms] must demonstrate creativity in every area in a period of historical change.' The main agent of change seemed to be the United States, which in the 1980s had reduced corporate and income taxes and introduced 'thorough deregulation.' The United States also 'boast[ed] overwhelming competitive power in the information and communications field that [was] said to be the leading industry of the twenty-first century.' In general, the forces of globalization and the spread of the market economy were making the Japanese economy face 'the largest changes in its circumstances in the postwar period.' With the collapse of the Cold War, Eastern Europe, the former Soviet Union, and China were entering the world economy and ushering in an 'era of mega competition of contention by economic power' (*Keidanren hōkoku* 1995, pp. 1–3).

To respond, the Japanese had to create a more flexible and innovative economic system. Not only the government, but large companies also had to change their ways. Their policies of 'long term stable employment and seniority pay' had helped create a 'stable and safe society,' but these practices were 'becoming an obstacle in realizing a society in which the Japanese economy is active through the creation of new industries and businesses and changes in the structure of industry' (*Keidanren hōkoku* 1995, p. 5). Japanese firms faced formidable challenges to 'respond to the needs of diversified consumers, quickly develop new goods and services, and deliver them at low cost....' This effort would require the creation of new technology, the output of 'superior manufactured goods, technology, and services that are unique,' as well as efforts to make the distribution of goods more efficient (*Keidanren hōkoku* 1995, pp. 6–8).

This adjustment, according to the report, required basic structural reforms carried out by the government through changes in the tax system and deregulation. The former changes included lowering the corporate tax to the level in the United States and abolishing the taxes on dividends, securities transactions, and land. The latter changes included the 'abolition of the Large Store Law by stages' (*Keidanren hōkoku* 1995, pp. 10–11). With these suggested reforms, the report predicted, the economy would end its stagnation to grow for the next five years at a real rate of 3% per year. Without such reforms, manufacturing would lose its vitality, the trade balance would fall into deficit, unemployment would increase, and annual economic growth would lag at just 1% per year (*Keidanren hōkoku* 1995, pp. 12–13).

In January 1996, Toyoda Shōichirō unveiled Keidanren's long-term vision for the economy over the next quarter-century. To realize an 'active global nation' with an average growth rate of 3% per year, the Japanese had to reduce direct taxes, such as the income and corporate tax, and increase the consumption tax as an indirect levy. Ideally the consumption tax would rise from 3% to 5% in 1997, to 7% in 2000, and to 10–12% by 2005. Depending on the rate of increase in the consumption tax, the government would cease issuing all bonds either in 2010 or 2020 (*Yomiuri shinbun* 1996a). A few months later the federation's Tax System Committee proposed raising the consumption tax to compensate for slashing Japan's 'heavy' income and corporate taxes. In particular, the effective tax rate for the corporate tax, including regional taxes, had to drop from 50% to the 40% level that prevailed in the United States (*Yomiuri shinbun* 1996d). At the end of the year, the Public Finance System Committee recommended that the use of special public bonds end in 2002 and that by 2006 all public expenditures at the local and national level, including support for public corporations, fall below the current level of 45% of gross domestic product (GDP) (Keizai Dantai Rengōkai 1999, pp. 884–885).

Discussion

The basic attitudes of Keidanren, arguably the most powerful business group in Japan, became a major reason for the nation's slow response to the economic crisis that developed rapidly in the early 1990s. In the mid-1980s, the federation had begun to advocate what it viewed as historic changes in Japan's economic policies in lobbying for the liberation of the energy, flexibility, and creativity of the private sector. These structural reforms would entail fewer governmental controls over the economy, a substantial cut in government spending, lower taxes for corporations and their managers, higher taxes for consumers, a reduction of barriers to imports, and an emphasis on increasing domestic demand. The need to respond to severe criticism from major trading partners, especially the United States, weighed heavily on the minds of the leaders of Keidanren as did the prospect of the rapid aging of Japanese society. Taking inspiration from the neo-liberal economic policies of the Reagan administration in the United States, they became convinced that the goals of keeping Japanese industry competitive in the international marketplace and ensuring the future prosperity of the nation required structural reforms. In the late 1980s, these business leaders simply were not prepared to view speculation in stocks or real estate as a major problem. In the early 1990s they initially viewed the decline in the price of real estate as a positive development.

As the ramifications of the sharp drop in the stock market and the real estate market became increasingly evident in the early 1990s, Keidanren stuck with impressive consistency to its original prescription to solve Japan's economic ills, even while other business groups lobbied for more forceful efforts to stimulate the economy through increased government expenditures and/or tax cuts. In fact, the federation would countenance a cut in the income tax only if it were offset by raising the levy on consumption. Even when the federation agreed in 1995 to the use of public funds to help resolve the problem of non-performing loans, it did so reluctantly while urging a return to fiscal restraint within several years. Its reports neglected measures for short-term recovery to keep a focus on structural reforms to enhance the long-term vitality of the Japanese economy.

If, as Peter von Staden suggests elsewhere in this volume (von Staden 2012), Japanese officials and politicians hesitated during the 1990s and afterwards to contemplate basic changes in economic policy, Keidanren welcomed such reforms. In fact, its proud backing for 'administrative reform' provided a basis for the important legal and managerial policy changes that Ulrike Schaede's essay contends have, in fact, occurred, along with significant progress in deregulation (Schaede 2012). As one study has concluded, 'The 1990s was [the decade] for the actualization of the advancement of deregulation.' Indeed, the period from 1990–2001 saw the implementation of over 3500 items out of more than 4000 that the Administrative Reform Commission proposed for deregulation, including changes to the Large Store Law (Ogawa and Matsumura 2005, pp. 105–112). For better or worse, Keidanren consistently followed a strategy of eschewing actions to cure the economy in the short-term to push for structural reforms that its leaders thought would enhance the long-term growth of the economy.

Implications for research

Clearly, Keidanren, as a major business group, merits attention as a major participant in the formation of Japanese national economic policy during the lost decade. Tracing the positions that the group took during the period of the economic bubble and the subsequent onset of the economic crisis reveals parallels between proposals of the federation and policies of the government. One area into which research could expand would be to broaden the examination of the business community to include other groups. Another fruitful topic would center on an investigation of how members of appointed study committees within Keidanren reconciled differences among themselves to produce their proposals. The federation embraced a variety of business sectors and, as some of the preceding analysis illustrates, leaders of different sectors could disagree on recommendations for national policy. Finally, one could further probe the ways in which Keidanren sought to influence government officials. The *Keidanren Weekly Reports* (*Keidanren shūhō*) record regular interaction between members and government officials through organized discussions, and the group regularly sent proposals about various issues to government agencies and ministries. The challenge would be to track more precisely the trail of an idea as it moved from the private sector to enactment as public policy.

Conclusions

As suggested by proposition 2 previously, one simply cannot understand the dynamics of the initially slow and ineffective Japanese response to the collapse of the 'bubble' economy during the early 1990s without taking into account the views of the business community. During the onset of the lost decade, Keidanren's emphasis on deregulation and on fiscal restraint had a particularly strong impact on national policies. As noted previously, the Japanese government did not dramatically increase spending until 1994. As the economy showed signs of positive economic growth in 1996, the cabinet in 1997 duly enacted a raise in the consumption tax from 3% to 5%, just as Keidanren proposed. It is a sobering thought that shortly after this bold act of fiscal probity the Japanese economy suffered a relapse that lasted another six years. Meanwhile, Keidanren continued to push for deregulation, and the government complied.

During 2010, the policies of Keidanren remained essentially the same as they were 25 years earlier. As one might expect, the federation continued to advocate deregulation (*Yomiuri shinbun* 2010c). In addition, the group campaigned for a lowering of the corporate tax and, to maintain fiscal soundness, a rise in the consumption tax. In April 2010, the group began to advocate a gradual increase in the consumption tax to a level of 10%, a doubling of the levy, by the latter half of the 2020s in order to restore confidence in social security programs and in the government's finances (*Yomiuri shinbun* 2010a, 2010b, 2010d). Not long afterwards, members began pushing for a 5% cut in the corporate tax. As before, the justification centered on the need to help Japanese firms become more internationally competitive by reducing the comparatively high rate of the levy, which was approximately 40% (*Yomiuri shinbun* 2010e). A later statement even argued for a more dramatic drop, because in order to keep companies from moving abroad and to attract firms to Japan, the rate should fall to 30% (*Yomiuri shinbun* 2010f). These types of proposals had evolved under much different circumstances in the 1980s, and their track record does not inspire confidence for impressive results in boosting the economy and expanding employment, even if one could assume an absence of major crises. The devastating earthquake and tsunami in northeastern Japan in March, 2011, however, has created new economic challenges. The need to fund a recovery of the affected areas may well forestall prospects for the enactment of significant tax cuts in the near future and, in fact, may require increased taxes.

Notes

1. These reports are available in Keidanren shūhō, 1951-1994, 2006. CD ROM set. Tokyo: Marubeni Kabushiki Kaisha.
2. *Yomiuri shinbun* 1990–1996. Available in the Yomidasu database. Available from: http: database.yomiuri.co.jp/rekishikan/ [Accessed at the Duke University Library].

References

Amyx, J.A., 2004. *Japan's financial crisis: institutional rigidity and reluctant change*. Princeton: Princeton University Press.

Beason, D. and Patterson, D., 2004. *The Japan that never was: explaining the rise and decline of a misunderstood country*. Albany: State University of New York Press.

Flath, D., 2005. *The Japanese economy*. Second Edition New York: Oxford University Press.

Grimes, W., 2001. *Unmaking the Japanese miracle: macroeconomic politics, 1985–2000*. Ithaca, NY: Cornell University Press.

Ito, O., 2007. *Nihon no keizai: reikishi, genjō, ronten*. Tokyo: Chūō Shinsho.

Johnson, C.A., 1982. *MITI and the Japanese miracle: the growth of industrial policy, 1925–1975*. Stanford: Stanford University Press.

Katz, R., 1998. *Japan, the system that soured: the rise and fall of the Japanese economic miracle*. Armonk, NY: M.E. Sharpe.

Keidanren hōkoku, 1995. October. Nihon sangyō no chūki tenbō to kongo no kadai.

Keidanren shūhō, 1985. 'Nihon keizai no tenbō to kadai' o kengi. No. 1744, 23 May, pp. 2–10.

Keidanren shūhō, 1988a. Ketsugi: sekai keizai katsuseika ni kōken suru Nihon no yakuwari to wareware no ketsui. No. 1901, 6 June, pp. 4–6.

Keidanren shūhō, 1988b. Zeisei bappon kaikaku no suishin to Shōwa 64 nendo zeisei ni kansuru kengi. No. 1920, 17 October, pp. 2–6.

Keidanren shūhō, 1989a. Bukka antei no iji to naigai kakakusa zesei o yōbō–Aino Keizai Kikakuchō chōkan to iken kōkan. No. 1950, 1 May, pp. 2–3.

Keidanren shūhō, 1989b. Keiki wa hikitsuzuki kakudai, sakiyuki no pointo wa bukka. No. 1979, 20 November, pp. 5–6.

Keidanren shūhō, 1991. '1990 nendai no Nihon keizai no tenbō to kadai–chōwa aru shijō keizai o mokushi shite' o happyō. No. 2047, 11 March, pp. 1–26.

Keidanren shūhō, 2006. CD ROM set. Tokyo: Marubeni Kabushiki Kaisha.

Keizai Dantai Rengōkai, 1999. *Keizai Dantai Rengōkai gojū nen shi*. Tokyo: Keizai Dantai Rengōkai.

Kikkawa, T., 2005. Keizai kikki no honshitsu. *In*: Tokyo Daigaku Shakaikagaku Kenkyūjo, ed. *'Ushinawareta jūnen'o koete [I]: keizai kikki no kyōjun*. Tokyo: Tokyo Daigaku Shuppankai, 15–39.

Lincoln, E.J., 2001. *Arthritic Japan: the slow pace of economic reform*. Washington, DC: Brookings Institution Press.

Metzler, M., 2008. Toward a financial history of Japan's long stagnation, 1990–2003. *Journal of Asian studies*, 67 (2), 653–666.

Ogawa, A. and Matsumura, T., 2005. Kisei kaikaku no seika to sono kadai. *In*: Tokyo Daigaku Shakaikagaku Kenkyūjo, ed. *'Ushinawareta jūnen' o koete [1]: keizai kikki no kyōjun*. Tokyo: Tokyo Daigaku Shuppankai, 105–143.

Rosenbluth, F.M. and Thies, M.F., 2010. *Japan transformed: political change and economic restructuring*. Princeton University Press.

Schaede, U., Forthcoming. The strategic inflection point in Japanese business. *Asia Pacific business review*.

Vogel, E., 1979. *Japan as number one: lessons for America*. Cambridge, MA: Harvard University Press.

von Staden, P., Forthcoming. Fettered by the past in the march forward: ideology as an explanation for the malaise in today's Japan. *Asia Pacific business review*.

Warner, M., 2011. Commentary: whither Japan? Economy, management and society. *Asia Pacific business review*, 17 (1), 1–5.

Yomiuri shinbun, 1990. Zenkoku Shōkōkairen mo daitenhō no kaihai hantai o ketsuji. 20 March, p.6. Tokyo morning edition.

Yomiuri shinbun, 1991a. Tōgin no kashishutsu zandaka nobi ōhaba donka, kinyū hikishime han'ei, 90 nendo wa 6.1% ni. 10 April, p.7. Tokyo morning edition.

Yomiuri shinbun, 1991b. Kinyū seisaku no henkō hitsuyō nashi, Suematsu Zenginkyō kaichō ga shūnin kisha kaiken. 24 April, p.7. Tokyo morning edition.

Yomiuri shinbun, 1991c. Yūbin chōkin ni kansuru chōsa kenkyūkai hōkoku ni yūchō gyōmu no kakudai o kennen, Suematsu Zenginkyō kaichō. 22 May, p.9. Tokyo morning edition.

Yomiuri shinbun, 1991d. Zenkoku 154 ginkō no 3-gatsu ki kessan, yokin, sōshisan ga hajime no genshō, keijō rieki mo renzoku gen'eki. 28 June, p.6. Tokyo morning edition.

Yomiuri shinbun, 1991e. Baburu 'chinseika' ni wa sara ni kanshi ga hitsuyō, Suematsu Zenginkyō kaichō ga kenkai. 03, July, p.6. Tokyo morning edition.

Yomiuri shinbun, 1991f. Zenkoku ginkō no heisei 3 nendo chūkan kessan, zennen dōki hi de gyōmu jun'eki 6.4% zō. 27 December, p.6. Tokyo morning edition.

Yomiuri shinbun, 1991g. Kōtei buai sage, keizaikai wa jinsoku na ketsudan to kangei, issō no sage nozomu koe mo. 31 December, p.7. Tokyo morning edition.

Yomiuri shinbun, 1992a. Keiki shissoku o kannen, Suematsu Zenginkyō kaichō. 19 February, p.7. Tokyo morning edition.

Yomiuri shinbun, 1992b. Kabuka 2 manen ware, zaikai=shōshūhō kaisei o, tekkō=gensan ni hakusha mo, shōsha=yunyū kakō shinpai. 17 March, p.6. Tokyo morning edition.

Yomiuri shinbun, 1992c. Kōtei buai hikisage, keizaikai toppu ni kiku. 28 July, p. 10. Tokyo morning edition.

Yomiuri shinbun, 1992d. Sōgō keizai taisaku, sangyōkai nado keiki fuyō ni rakkan to kaigi, shotoku genzei nao tsuyoi yōbō. 29 August, p.6. Tokyo morning edition.

Yomiuri shinbun, 1992e. 'Kansōkyoku' 'baburu seisan' munetsuki hatchō, nayamu Zenginkyō no don, Iwai Kaichō. 25 October, p.9. Tokyo morning edition.

Yomiuri shinbun, 1993a. Genzei taisaku de akaji kokuseki no hakkō yōnin hajimete hyōmei, Iwai Zenginkyō kaichō. 17 February, p.7. Tokyo morning edition.

Yomiuri shinbun, 1993b. Kinkyū keizai taisaku, keizaikai ni wa fuman no koe, 'sobanateki, kitai motezu.' 17 September, p.6. Tokyo morning edition.

Yomiuri shinbun, 1993c. Seifu zeichō chūki toshin, zaikai, shōhizei age ni sanpi, sangyōkai wa keiki e no hairyō yōbō. 20 November, p.6. Tokyo morning edition.

Yomiuri shinbun, 1994. 'Keizai seminaa' furyō saiken, shōkyaku okure ga ginkō keiei no appaku, keiki kaifuku no ashikase ni. 17 January, p. 13. Tokyo morning edition.

Yomiuri shinbun, 1995a. Furyō saiken shōri, kōteki shikkin dōnyū wa kokuminteki giron ga hitsuyō, Hashimoto Zenginkyō kaichō. 14 June, p.7. Tokyo morning edition.

Yomiuri shinbun, 1995b. Hatan kinyū kikan shōri kōteki shikkin dōnyū subeki, Hashimoto Zenginkyō kaichō ga yokin hoken kikkō de kenkai, 6 September, p.7. Tokyo morning edition.

Yomiuri shinbun, 1995c. 'Daitenhō haishi' teigen ni nanshoku, Inaba Nishōkai tō. 21 September, p.9. Tokyo morning edition.

Yomiuri shinbun, 1995d. Jūsen sonshitsu no shōkyaku, bunkatsu shōri kentō o, Zenginkyō kaichō. 8 November, p.7. Tokyo morning edition.

Yomiuri shinbun, 1995e. Ōte ginkō, jūsen sonshitsu o ikkatsu shōkyaku e, furyō saiken shōri no tōmeido takame shinyō kaifuku narau. 10 November, p.6. Tokyo morning edition.

Yomiuri shinbun, 1995f. Kisei kanwa shōin hōkoku, daitenhō nado chūshō kigyō uchigeki mo, purasu men ikasu taisaku. 8 December, p. 10. Tokyo morning edition.

Yomiuri shinbun, 1995g. 96 nendo yōsan Ōkurashō gen'an, kōchoku haibun, sangyōkai ni fuman, kakukai no hankyō. 21 December, p.8. Tokyo morning edition.

Yomiuri shinbun, 1996a. Keidanren ga 2020 nen e 'shinkeizai keikaku', shōhi zeiritsu o 2005 nendo 10–12% ni. 19 January, p.6. Tokyo morning edition.

Yomiuri shinbun, 1996b. Jūsen e zaisei shikkin yōnin, kokumin no nōtoku jōken ni, YIES kōenkai de Toyoda Keidanren kaichō. 8 February, p.2. Tokyo morning edition.

Yomiuri shinbun, 1996c. Jūsen shōri yōsan an, zaisei tōnyū yamu nashi, Toyoda Shōichirō, Keidanren kaichō ga hyōmei, Hiroshima. 7 March, p.7. Osaka morning edition.

Yomiuri shinbun, 1996d. 97 nendo irai no shōhi zeiritsu age o yōnin, Keidanren zeiseiin ga teigen. 20 March, p.8. Tokyo morning edition.

Yomiuri shinbun, 2010a. Seichō senryaku no suishin semaru, Keidanren teigen, Seifu no torikumi ni fuman. 10 April, p.9. Tokyo morning edition.

Yomiuri shinbun, 2010b. Shōhi zeiritsu, Keidanren kaichō '10% teido' ni sōkyū na hikiage motomeru. 13 April, p.9. Tokyo morning edition.

Yomiuri shinbun, 2010c. Keidanren kaichō 'defure dakkyaku ni wa keizai seichō,' shin shushō to betsu rosen,' 8 June, 8. Tokyo morning edition.

Yomiuri shinbun, 2010d. Keidanren kaichō, shōhizei age shiji, shushō, keizai 3 dantai kondan. 18 June, p.4. Tokyo morning edition.

Yomiuri shinbun, 2010e. Keidanren 'hōjinzei 5% sage o.' 4 August, p.9. Tokyo morning edition.

Yomiuri shinbun, 2010f. Keidanren 'hōjinzei 30% ni,' 11 nendo zeisei kaisei teigen, kankyōzei hantai. 4 September, p.2, Tokyo evening edition.

From developmental state to the 'New Japan': the strategic inflection point in Japanese business

Ulrike Schaede

School of International Relations and Pacific Studies, University of California at San Diego, USA

Between 1998–2006, Japan's political economy underwent a strategic inflection point, anchored on legal changes so profound that they are irreversible. These reforms sought to enable large companies to shift from the post-war priority on sales and market share toward a new focus on profitability. The arrival of powerful low-cost Asian competitors in assembled goods, and a drastic change in the shareholder structure in Japan brought the end of the 'developmental state' approach and necessitated repositioning into innovative, high-margin sectors. The congruence model posits that a successful shift in critical tasks requires a realignment of formal organization, people and culture. For Japan's highly diversified companies, to compete as efficient innovators meant making clear choices what businesses to compete in, and then to restructure to focus on winning in those few businesses. For Japan as a country, the shift in formal organization came through a wholesale change in the underlying approach to law-making and regulation, as well as corporate law. The 1990s were not so much a 'lost decade' for Japan as one of renewal and repositioning.

Introduction

How can the 'developmental state' reconfigure once development has been accomplished and the competitive environment has completely changed? The rapid rise of Japan as an economic success story in the post-war period (1950s–1980s) made the country's export-oriented growth policies a model for many other Asian nations. As Japan has struggled to revise its domestic political economy in response to global economic changes in the twenty-first century, we have gained insights into the processes of a country finding a new congruence that may also shed light on future tasks for other nations. The congruence model (Nadler and Tushman 1997, Tushman and O'Reilly 2002) hypothesizes that for an organization to be successful, an alignment of critical tasks, formal organization, people and culture is necessary. The tighter this alignment, the more successful the organization. Ironically, however, over time and with success, inertia and size also make the organization less likely to change effectively in response to disruptive technologies (O'Reilly and Tushman 2008). In the face of a major disruption, organizations must 'unlearn' and realign. It often takes a major crisis to increase willingness to change; it always takes strong leadership to orchestrate renewal; and it can take over a decade for the transition to be accomplished.

This study argues that Japan underwent such a transformation between the years 1998–2006. The logic of the congruence model helps interpret Japan's 'lost decade' of the 1990s rather as one of reform and adjustment to the new global competitive environment. Staying with the business corollary, not only is Japan no longer a hungry 'startup', but the globalization of trade and the end of Japan's cost advantage in manufacturing high-quality consumer end products has rendered Japan's post-war growth strategy outdated. Thus, the critical tasks for twenty-first century Japan have to be redefined. During the post-war period, Japan's political economy was anchored on the idea of export-led growth by a set of champion industries and companies, picked and supported by a strong state system that relied on situational regulation by the bureaucracy to guide the allocation of resources. Described as a 'developmental state' system (Johnson 1982), or an 'iron triangle' set-up between the Liberal Democratic Party, bureaucracy and business, this system created strong vested interests as well as entry barriers for any type of competitor, in politics or business.

From the corporate perspective, what it took to 'win' in this industrial policy set-up was size, which was measured in sales and/or market share, as larger firms were granted easier access to government 'goodies' such as trade quotas (Abegglen and Stalk 1985). This created incentives for companies to diversify continuously, as any sale was a good sale regardless of profits. Over the four decades after WWII, Japan's largest companies morphed into unwieldy conglomerates, and investment and growth decisions were often predicated not on sound business strategy, but to scale with competitors.

A combination of factors reversed these incentives in the 1990s, in particular rising labor costs and a changing global trade regime. In the twenty-first century, facing competition by its Asian neighbors, Japanese companies have to win through higher margins based on higher rates of innovation and specialization in areas where others cannot compete. Japan's conglomerates with their large labor force, widespread 'also-run' business activities and slow bureaucracies can no longer match their Asian neighbors in mass-producing consumer end products (see Warner 2011). Globalization also coincided with the arrival of institutional and foreign investors in Japan that value profitability more than size. Moreover, the recognition that new firm entry was needed to push Japan to the next level of an affluent society cast doubt on the wisdom of ironclad business networks and running the economy on conglomerates. Deregulation and the rise of mavericks, such as in the retailing industry, were propelled by the arrival of imported goods on Japanese markets, which greatly changed the nature of competition within Japan.

The 1990s earned the nickname 'lost decade', for Japan seemed unwilling to embrace reform. One major reason why the country was slow to respond was inertia: the old system had served the country well and had created a resistance to change, perhaps due to an attitude of 'we have always done it this way' and an engrained culture of risk averseness and an unwillingness to stand out by doing some new and different. It was precisely because the system had worked so perfectly that it took so long to launch change and respond to the arrival of Taiwanese, Korean and Chinese competitors.

However, for those who saw the disruption in Japan's external environment, the 1990s became a period of transformation. The business catchphrase at the turn of the century was 'choose and focus' (*sentaku to shūchū*). This referred to a focus on the core business and the shedding of all activities that are not profitable or not central to the company's revised corporate strategy. Thus, companies needed to retrench, slim down, exit non-profitable businesses, spin off unrelated businesses, and lay off excess workers. Yet, Japan's business laws of the post-war years formed a straightjacket that did not allow for easy reorganization. It took the major crisis year of 1998 to trigger a wave of reforms aimed at enabling Japanese firms to compete in a changed global economy through corporate repositioning.

This study chronicles this period of change from 1998–2006, and argues that the reforms were so deep and profound that they are irreversible. Therefore, this period marks a *strategic inflection* point for Japanese business. The reforms aimed at a 'turn toward the market' by rewriting literally all business laws, to afford companies greater liberties in strategy, and by increasing rights of shareholders and stakeholders, to heighten managerial accountability. The standing of politicians and the law and courts has increased, while that of the bureaucracies has greatly declined, as situational regulation through the 'carrot-and-stick' mechanisms of administrative guidance was phased out. Of course, laggards remained within business and government, as many preferred to hold on to the status quo. Vested interests are difficult to destruct in corporations, and even more so in countries. Old system vestiges and pockets of reform resistance notwithstanding, however, Japan's reform period of 1998–2006 offers a remarkable case study of large-scale, country-based realignment.

Theory and hypotheses: congruence model

The congruence model (Nadler and Tushman 1997, Tushman and O'Reilly 2002) hypothesized that for effective implementation of a given strategy, four key organizational elements have to be fully aligned: (1) the recognition of what it takes to 'win', that is, the translation of corporate strategy into executable critical tasks; (2) a formal organization that incentivizes and rewards employees toward these tasks; (3) employees selected and/or trained for ability to accomplish these tasks efficiently and effectively; and (4) a corporate culture that sets strong norms and values toward these tasks. If any one of these elements is not fully aligned, the company will operate at suboptimal levels. For example, if the goal is to be a leading innovative company, yet corporate culture disallows taking action and people are rewarded for risk averseness (not making mistakes), the company will most likely fail. If a company's success is predicated on employees making extra efforts to save costs through teamwork (helping wherever there is a need), yet if employees are not selected or trained for being team players, the company will not fare as well as it otherwise might.

Studies for the US have shown that the most successful companies stand out for purposeful alignment and constant efforts at maintaining this alignment (Southwest Airlines, IBM, Wal-Mart). This stance is a recipe for success, unless things suddenly change. New technological innovations – such as the arrival of telephony, the semiconductor, or the internet – cause punctuated equilibria that disrupt otherwise incremental growth. Whereas a good strategic alignment can be modified at the margin to respond to incremental change, a disruption of the equilibrium path typically demands a reformulation of critical tasks, which in turn requires reorganization of rewards, people and culture. The challenge is that the tighter alignment, and thus the more successful the organization in the previous setting, the more difficult the renewal and repositioning, as engrained best practices and success habits have to be altered (Harreld *et al.* 2007)

For companies, such punctuations are typically subsumed under the header 'disruptive technologies'; for entire industries or economies, they cause 'strategic inflection points' (Burgelman and Grove 1996). A strategic inflection demarcates a point in time when the balance of forces shifts completely, away from previous structures to new ways of doing things, and therefore fundamentally alters the ways in which companies compete.[1] For an inflection to be strategic, it has to be irreversible.

The congruence model is typically employed to identify performance gaps in a single corporation. However, this is also helpful in guiding analysis at the much higher level of country strategy. For Japan as a country, the arrival of South Korea, Taiwan and, eventually, China as *bona fide* competitors in high-quality mass production pulled the rug away from under the post-war period strategy of large-scale manufacturing groups. Japan's success in the post-war period (1950s–1980s) was based on the strategic goals of fast export-led growth and technological catch-up with the West. This was translated into the critical tasks of: (a) government policies to support the growth of leading companies in strategic industries, to be executed by a strong bureaucracy; (b) controls of technology imports, research activities, and other corporate activities; and (c) incentives for companies to grow and employ workers on a long-term (lifetime) basis to focus government efforts on infrastructure growth policies by reducing the need to build a large-scale social security system. The idea was to catch up through hard work in producing high. Employees were rewarded for working long hours, doing precisely as told, and not causing a disruption. One result was the world's leading manufacturing system in terms of product quality and value of the twentieth century.

In organizational terms, the biggest heritage from the post-war era was a set of incentives that drove companies to grow, at any cost. Between the 1960s–1980s, when domestic markets were shielded from most foreign influence, corporate competition was primarily for access to desired items that the government controlled. Access to industrial policy allocations (trade quotas, raw materials, technology licenses) was based on industry rankings by firm size, measured in sales. Access to talent was also based on size, as the largest companies had the first-round pick of university graduates, and working for a large company was the predominant aspiration. Main banks also competed for size and supported company expansion; they were willing to tolerate very high debt levels as size was also an insurance against bankruptcy, because the lifetime employment system made companies 'too big to fail'. Size made corporate managers important players in the political economy (Fletcher 2012). Thus, aggressive growth was expected by stakeholders, supported by shareholders (other firms and banks), and pushed by government policy (Schaede 2008, chap. 3).

Empirical studies of Japan's post-war industrial organization confirm this trend towards increasing diversification among large Japanese firms (see Goto 1981, Yoshihara *et al.* 1981, Fukui and Ushijima 2007). Onto four decades of continuously rising diversification, the bubble economy from 1987–1991 added exuberant, unrelated diversification – be that by steel companies into semiconductors and amusement parks, shipbuilders into finance, or construction firms into golf courses. Rampant unrelated diversification ultimately challenged organizational capabilities. When the bubble burst, Japanese companies found themselves with what came to be called the 'three excesses' of equity, capacity, and labor.

Research on the performance consequences of diversification for the United States has shown that whereas strategic diversification around the core competence of a company may well improve performance, unrelated diversification will decrease performance over time (Palich *et al.* 2000). As studied in a large body of research, the United States underwent a shift from diversification to focus in the 1980s (cf. Schaede 2008, chap. 4). Major triggers for refocusing included: increased uncertainty and volatility through globalization, and a new understanding that large conglomerates were too slow in their adjustment to competitive changes; a new regulatory stance by the Reagan Administration's antitrust team that allowed within-industry consolidation; the arrival of the efficient market hypothesis in finance that shifted the previous emphasis on risk diversification through a given company toward specialization by the company and diversification of investment portfolios; the emergence of institutional investors that hunted for profit, and of a new type of financial intermediaries such as leveraged buyout funds that specialized in bust-up deals; and the arrival of corporate raiders who increased the threat of hostile takeovers and triggered voluntary restructuring as a preemptive move. Finally, excessive diversification posed great challenges to organizational design and management: the larger the organization, the more likely are internal resource allocations are subjected to opportunism, bureaucracy, corporate politics and similar obstacles of human nature that undermine the initial efficiency consequences of the multi-product firm (Williamson 1975, 1985). Business units that should have been shut down were not, due to vested interests, and new businesses in unrelated areas were opened to reward successful managers.

A very similar scenario played itself out in Japan in the 1990s. Globalization undermined the previous advantages associated with size; the arrival of foreign investors in Japan during the 1990s banking crisis (including institutional investors and private equity and hedge funds) shifted managerial attention toward profitability; and the large flagship concerns of the Old Japan were bogged down by politics, vested interests, and an inability to react to the new challenges of the 1990s. As a result of encrusted structures and restrictions on laying off workers, restructuring or reorganizing, the average profitability of Japanese stock exchange-listed companies showed a continuing decline. Figure 1 shows the unweighted average of several profitability indicators for 1414 companies listed on the Tokyo Stock Exchange without interruption between 1980–2009 (author's calculation based on Nikkei Needs data, unconsolidated, 1980–2009). Return on assets declined from an average of 10% in the 1980s to approximately 3%; operating profit and ordinary profit (operating and ordinary income, respectively, over revenues) fell from an average of 7% to 3.5%; and return on equity, showing high variation over time, has hovered below the 5%

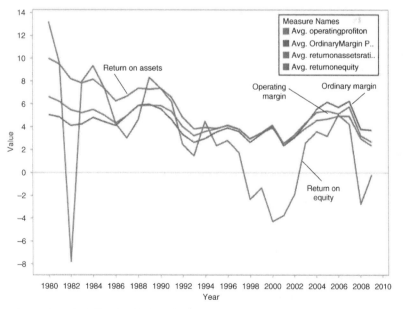

Figure 1. Average profitability data by listed Japanese companies, 1980–2009. Note: ROE data for 1982 are an outlier due to a reporting inconsistency. Source: Constructed from the Nikkei Needs database, unconsolidated, for 1414 companies listed in all 30 years.

line since the 1990s. In international comparison, these are dismal numbers. About one quarter of all listed companies earned no profits at all during the 2000s, even though the years 2003–2007 marked the longest boom period in Japanese record-keeping history. Japan had stopped growing, and it stopped being successful at what it was doing. The strategic goal of the post-war period developmental state was no longer accomplishable. The crisis of the 1990s forced Japan toward strategic repositioning.

Applying the congruence model to the situation of Japanese companies, and of Japan's economy overall, *we can hypothesize that for change to result in a new viable system, it needs to occur at a number of levels.*

- First, to survive against Asian competitors, Japanese companies have to reposition strategically into higher margin sectors, that is, they have to focus on technological leadership. This requires a reformulation of critical tasks toward innovation, risk-taking and individual contribution.
- Second, this means employees (and at the higher level, companies) have to be rewarded for the true contribution they make, not just for being there or being large. This requires people (and companies) to think on their own feet, as opposed to walking lockstep toward the previous goal of export-led growth or 'also-run'.
- Finally, culture (norms and values) need to shift to an emphasis on individual contribution, variety and risk-taking. For companies with over 100,000 employees such a shift can easily take a decade; for a country it may take a generation.

In what follows, I argue that the 1990s laid the groundwork for precisely this transition. Because this transition is far from being completed, this contribution discusses the accomplishment made, as of 2011, in the first step, strategic refocusing. An analysis of changing employment patterns, and the societal shift toward individualism, performance pay and growing income differentials, as well as individual career paths and work-life balance are left for further research.

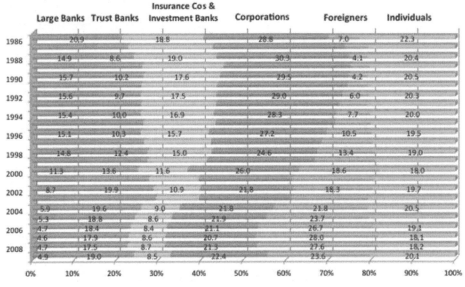

Figure 2. Ownership percentages, by type of investor. Source: TSE (2009); in percentage of total market capitalization, as of March each year.

The 1998 tipping point

Performance struggles by Japan's largest companies were exacerbated by three events that came together in the 1990s: globalization, the banking crisis, and social distress. Thus, the 1990s became a decade of repositioning and renewal, for the crisis was exploited by Prime Ministers Hashimoto (1996–1998) and Koizumi (2001–2006) to push for fundamental reforms in the corporate sector.

Globalization and new owners

Globalization occurs at four different levels: in manufacturing as separate from finance, and flowing out of an economy ('in-out' foreign direct investment, for example) as well as flowing in ('out-in'). Japanese manufacturing had begun moving abroad in full speed during the 1980s, when globalization was discussed in terms of how the location of manufacturing elsewhere affected domestic industries, and this trend continued into the twenty-first century. However, until the 1990s, domestic markets remained relatively shielded, both in manufacturing and finance.

In the 1990s, however, globalization hit Japan's domestic markets with full force. By 2004, the import penetration ratio in manufactured goods had doubled from the previous 7% of total sales to 13% (CAO 2004, figure 3-2-1). Suddenly, price competition reached intermediate product markets, just as a shift to global parts procurement threatened previously tight-knit subcontractor relations.

In financial markets, in 1998 the old 'Foreign Exchange and Foreign Trade Control Law' was replaced by a new 'Foreign Exchange Law' that liberalized cross-border financial transactions and removed most of the remaining barriers to investment in Japanese companies. This facilitated entry for foreign equity funds and other investors that had developed an appetite for assets sold by Japanese banks cleaning up their bad loans, with fire sales of golf courses, hotels and office buildings. Figure 2 shows that the percentage of foreign ownership in companies listed in the first section of the Tokyo Stock Exchange (TSE) more than quintupled, from 5% in 1991 to 28% in 2008. More than 50 of the leading TSE-listed companies had foreign ownership exceeding 50%. The fact that a significant portion of foreign investments were sourced from within Japan only underscores that strategies pursuing higher return on investment had become popular, at the expense of the post-war period of long-term stable intergroup shareholdings.

At the same time, the share held by trust banks – institutional investors that act as custodians for investment funds, pension funds, and so forth – doubled from less than 10% to 19%. Trust banks include investment and pension funds as well as so-called 're-trusts', wholesale investors that administer corporate pensions and other large-scale funds. In other words, these are newly emerging institutional investors that compete, in the final analysis, through higher returns on investment. Thus, Japan's combined share of institutional investors interested in superior corporate profitability increased from about 20% in 1996 to 47% in 2006. No Japanese manager could afford to ignore this new investor category.

Banking crisis

The collapse of Japan's bubble economy (1987–1991) caused a serious banking crisis in the mid-1990s. Scandals that had begun at commercial and investment banks engulfed the bureaucracy in 1995. In 1997, another round of widespread bank accounting fraud eventually revealed the true extent of the non-performing loan crisis and the abysmal situation of the financial system (Hoshi and Kashyap 2001, Amyx 2004). Bank failures began in 1995 and culminated, in November 1997, in the collapse of a first-tier bank and a leading investment bank. And while the Asian financial crisis of 1997 did not hit Japan directly, it caused great losses for Japanese banks actively involved in Asian trade finance and investment.

In rapid succession, more trouble came to the fore. In September 1998, the collapse of Japanese Leasing, a subsidiary of the Long-Term Credit Bank, with debt of ¥2.2 trillion (almost $20 billion) was the biggest failure of a Japanese firm to that date. A month later, the government nationalized LTCB and another specialized long-term credit bank that had been main contributors to the post-war growth plan (later sold to foreign funds and restructured into Shinsei and Aozora Banks). The banking crisis was so severe that between March 1998 and March 1999, the government had to infuse ¥9.3 trillion (about $90 billion) into the largest banks (Hoshi and Kashyap 2001, Takeuchi 2003). A revision of the antitrust restriction on holding companies allowed large banks to merge, and major consolidation reduced the number of leading banks from 13 to four.

Long planned by former Prime Minister Hashimoto, 1998 also was also the year of the financial 'Big Bang'. This reform package brought a revision of almost all laws relating to the financial industry, in particular accounting and disclosure. Mandatory consolidated reporting meant that banks and corporations could no longer hide their non-performing loans in undisclosed subsidiaries, and cross-subsidization within diversified companies also had to be declared. It is difficult to exaggerate the implications of this reform, for it invalidated the financial advantage of building large conglomerates. A company's core and affiliated

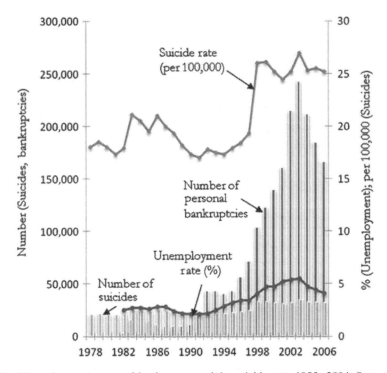

Figure 3. Unemployment, personal bankruptcy, and the suicide rate, 1955–2004. Sources: www. stat.go.jp/data/roudou/2.htm, http://www.npa.go.jp/toukei/index.htm, http://www.courts.go.jp/search/ jtsp0010?

businesses and their separate performances were now regularly reported, finally allowing a meaningful evaluation and comparison of the financial health of Japanese companies.

In the mid-1990s, scandals involving ministry officials led to first revisions of administrative guidance that placed stricter limits on personal connections between firms and ministries. In 1998, the Ministry of Finance was stripped of most of its supervisory role in the financial sector. In its stead, the newly created Financial Services Agency (FSA) soon became a prime example of how regulatory processes had begun to change. For the first time, the 1999 'Inspection Manual' introduced a detailed and binding rulebook on bank inspections. In defining what constituted a 'non-performing loan', the FSA wiped out decades of banks' convenient self-reporting. The banking crisis afforded the FSA heightened authority, as banks were facing failure and the government's capital infusion had triggered public scrutiny.[2] In 2002, Prime Minister Koizumi issued an aggressive program for structural change, based on financial system reform and the clean-up of non-performing loans by 2004. This was indeed accomplished, as the ratio of non-performing loans at major banks declined from 8.4% in 2002, to 2.9% in 2005. Even though problems remained at the smaller banks, by 2006 the loan portfolios of Japan's major banks had improved and profits had resumed.

Social crisis

Unprecedented social crisis in the late 1990s showed that post-war period policy tools had been rendered ineffective in addressing the new economic hardship and social suffering. In 1998, indicators of social distress all hit new record highs, including unemployment, bankruptcies by small firms, homelessness, crime, divorce rates, child abuse, and suicides (see Figure 3). Remarkably, these social indicators were directly related to economic hardship. A US–Japan comparison of the relation between economic data (growth, unemployment) and private distress (personal debt, bankruptcy, suicide) showed a much more direct association for Japan than for the US (Schaede 2006). This was attributed to the fact that during the post-war period Japan had little need for comprehensive government programs of unemployment support, public assistance and poverty relief. During the years of post-war economic growth, building a system of long-term unemployment insurance was not considered necessary given the system of lifetime employment, and the working poor had usually been able to find jobs. Families were expected to be the first and last resort for people in need but in the 1990s, families often found themselves unable to help. For Japan, one of the most affluent countries in the world that prides itself of social stability and security, these shocking events increased the general willingness to embark on drastic change.

Japan's strategic inflection, 1998–2006

As the domestic crisis increased eagerness to 'do something', and external changes and the continuing recession required that 'something be done', a window of opportunity for true reform in the business sector opened up. Between 1998–2006, Japan underwent changes in laws and regulation, regulatory processes, and domestic and global competition so fundamental that these define a strategic inflection point.

Regulatory change: post-remedy regulation and 'leave it to the market'

Even though Prime Minister Koizumi made postal privatization his major platform – and later was evaluated based mainly on that one initiative – it is in denouncing risk socialization, and not intervening in the bankruptcies of a number of large failing firms, that he made his mark with the reforms 'toward the market'. His line 'leave to the private sector what the private sector can do' (*minkan ni dekiru koto wa minkan ni yudaneru*) became the core message of the 2002 Financial Revival Program, and his relentless insistence convinced business that they could no longer sit and wait for the government to bail them out (Koizumi 2002). Throughout the post-war period, companies had hedged against failure by asking for approval from the regulating ministry, to count on that ministry for support should the investment run afoul. This exchange of information was private and closely-held, greatly empowering the ministries. Koizumi's new stance curbed this informal decision-making, transferring the discussion of business decisions to companies and their shareholders, and leaving ministries with open and transparent regulatory decision-making powers. As one official of the Ministry of the Economy, Trade and Industry (METI) put it in an anonymous interview in 2007, 'It is no longer fun to be a METI official.'

One foundation for this shift 'toward the market' through privatization, deregulation, and clear corporate accountability was the 2001 government reorganization. In addition to a streamlining of ministries to reduce the size of government and clarify responsibilities, this reform concentrated decision-making power in the Prime Minister's Office. A strong prime minister – such as Koizumi between 2001–2006 – could now pull reform deliberation away from the ministries and into his own discussion group, the Council on Economic and Fiscal Policy (CEFP), thus curtailing the role of ministries in the policy-making process. During the post-war period, ministry-based deliberation councils (*shingikai*) had played an important role in reinforcing the power of the various ministries and their vested industry interests (Schwartz 1998, von Staden 2012). A council's final report was often written by bureaucrats and frequently turned into law. Under the new system, the Prime Minister, who is also a member of the CEFP, can choose to pull a policy deliberation away from the ministry to open it for broader discussion, thereby overriding vested interests.

Situational regulation was further reduced with the 1998 revocation of controls over foreign trade through the new Foreign Exchange Law, and the phasing out of a series of specialized industry laws. The post-war system had placed great emphasis on entry regulation, whereby the regulator (the ministry in charge, which was also tasked with protecting and nurturing an industry) decided which companies were allowed to engage in what business activities. Process regulation – the monitoring of firms once they were 'in' – had been left to informal agreements, implemented through frequent contacts between companies and ministries (Schaede 2000, 2003). An important tool of informal regulation was administrative guidance, which allowed for situational application as it rested on a carrot-and-stick mechanism. Those who cooperated were rewarded whereas mavericks were punished. In addition to entry licenses and permits in the ministries' discretion, until the 1980s the Ministry of Economics, Trade and Industry greatly relied on trade controls to evoke business cooperation in informal *quid pro quo* regulation. Removing these controls deprived the ministries of their most powerful carrots.

These changes were followed by a series of other new laws that shifted the regulatory focus away from the actor (an industry or company) and toward the action itself (a market or transaction). This de-personalized the act of regulation and undercut the value of personal relations among businesses and bureaucrats, which had been the core of ministerial power in the post-war period. The post-war period informal regulatory processes, based on the fact that a ministry in charge of nurturing an industry was also tasked with its regulation, was undermined by a shift to legal processes and a turn to the courts.

This transition came with a fundamental reorientation in Japan's legal philosophy. Japanese corporate law, as it existed through the 1990s, dated back to nineteenth century Civil Law logic of 'pre-regulation': if not explicitly spelled out in a law, an activity was not allowed. For corporations, the law outlined most corporate activities *ex ante* and imposed detailed restrictions on management, while also reducing the threat for managers to be held liable by shareholders. However, the inherent limitations had become too much of an obstacle for reform, and in 2001 the Ministry of Justice announced a reorientation toward a 'post-remedy' approach, as used in Common Law countries, under which everything is possible unless it is specifically prohibited (Ministry of Justice 2001). Corporate law was to be the test case for this new approach to law-writing.

As Milhaupt and Pistor (2008) argue, the practical differences between common and civil law applications are not nearly as stark as typically characterized. In reality, codes are insufficiently specific, making the courts' interpretations powerful in shaping corporate rules. Rather, the critical difference between pre- and post-regulation lies in the incentives they offer to invest in legal innovation, and the access they provide to lawmaking. A corporate example of this is stock options. In the US with a common-law approach, a company can freely issue a right, written as a simple document; the financial, accounting and legal ramifications of this document are to be decided by the courts later. Thus, the company has just influenced law design. In contrast, civil law systems used to have no room for a stock option, so companies could not just introduce them; rather, they either had to develop functional equivalents (such as perquisites), or they had to lobby politicians to rewrite the law.

Japan's switch to post-remedy adjudication was cemented in easier access to the courts, by streamlining court processes, reducing fees, and helping courts specialize in certain areas such as bankruptcy. Both have resulted in a new demand for law in Japan. What this means is a shift away from centralized lawmaking as well as away from post-war informal problem resolution – both between regulators and companies, and among companies – and towards a larger circle of participants and therefore a market for ideas and innovation in the legal process.

Corporate change: reorganization and restructuring

The biggest challenge faced by proactive companies that aimed to address the 'three excesses' of the bubble economy – equity, capacity, and labor – and adjust to the new global competitive environment was a lack of structure for the processes of corporate reorganization. The tipping point of 1998 had brought to the fore the need for large companies to 'choose and focus' in order to compete more nimbly against rising competitors in Asia. 'Choose' meant the identification of core businesses in which to compete and 'focus' meant concentrating corporate resources in these few business segments, and exiting all non-core activities – be that through shutting down business units, spinning them out into independent small companies, or selling them off to competitors or hedge funds.

Beginning in 1997, Japan began to revise the Commercial Code annually for a decade, until, in 2006, the new Corporation Law (*Kaisha-hō*) superseded previous laws regarding company creation, restructuring, and corporate governance. Related laws such as those on labor, finance, taxation, and bankruptcy were also amended at a rapid rate. Reflecting the new legal philosophy of post-remedy adjudication, these revisions increased managerial flexibility and choice but also brought new regulations toward a level playing field, particularly in the form of transparency and accountability. In the decade following 1998, Japan literally revised every single law pertaining to commerce, and in the process succeeded in clarifying and concretizing the legal situation. As a result, somebody who knew Japan well in the 1980s but has not looked since might not recognize the new legal environment (for a list of legal changes in this period, see Schaede 2008, pp. 34–35).

While these laws enabled change, new accounting rules pushed for reorganization beginning in 2000. In particular, mandatory consolidated accounting raised the cost of carrying non-performing subsidiaries, which suddenly reduced profitability data, forcing a move to refocusing even in slow reformers. Moreover, companies had to report mark-to-market valuations (as opposed to book or purchase prices) of their assets. Whereas those who had acquired assets in the early post-war period could report a windfall gain by switching to present values, most companies had bought shares and real estate during the bubble period. If they did not want to report huge losses, they needed to sell these off. Beginning in 2001, mark-to-market valuation also applied to cross-shareholdings, which contributed greatly to the unraveling of cross-shareholdings (Schaede 2008, chap. 5).

Pressure on banks to clean up non-performing loans increased demand for easier ways 'out', such as through bankruptcy-based restructuring and outright liquidation. In the post-war period, banks had addressed business failures by working out informal debt restructuring that left the loans on the books, to be covered by loss reserves taken from bank profits. The goal was to save the company and recoup the loans in the long run, all the while maintaining employment; the government had been very supportive of such rescue operations. However, several large-scale bankruptcies in the late 1990s were a harbinger that the government had revised its stance on the 'too-big-to-fail' rule, and Koizumi's end of business risk socialization greatly affected turnaround strategies. Moreover, most banks could no longer afford to bail out failing clients, as bank profits were too slim to cover loss reverses. The main bank system of old, with its quasi-automated rescue function for all clients, had come to an end (Hoshi *et al.* 2011).

Instead, in order to clean up their non-performing loan portfolio expeditiously, banks switched to direct bad-loan disposals, whereby the bank suffers a one-time extraordinary loss, then initiates bankruptcy procedures or a turnaround event, and sells off non-core assets. To facilitate such actions, the 2000 Civil Rehabilitation Law (*Minji saisei-hō*) replaced a clumsy and rarely used law of 1927 to design new bankruptcy procedures for corporations and individuals. In 2003, the revised Corporate Reorganization Law *(Kaisha kōsei-hō)* allowed 'Chapter 11'-type turnarounds adjudicated in courts. Moreover, a 2001 Guideline for Out-of-Court Workouts addressed bank-led workouts by stipulating how debt forgiveness should be organized in cases with multiple lenders but uncertain claims (Takeuchi 2003, Higashino 2004a). In 2004, the old Liquidation Law *(Hasan-hō)* was revised to simplify legal procedures for shutdown and fair distribution of assets.

To facilitate reorganization and increase speed in liquidation, court reforms allowed banks and companies to file a reorganization petition with a court in Tokyo or Osaka even if the failing firm or its lenders are located elsewhere. These two district courts established special reorganization departments to handle bankruptcy cases promptly and efficiently. Data by Teikoku Databank show that bankruptcy procedures skyrocketed with the adoption of these measures. In the period between April 2000 and March 2005, a total of 86,972 bankruptcies were reported (with liabilities of ¥73 trillion), the vast majority of which were under the Corporate Reorganization Law (see Takagi 2003).

Short of shutting down a non-profitable business unit, companies could spin it out or sell it off. Between 1998–2000 laws were rewritten to facilitate mergers and acquisitions (M&A), as well as spin-offs. New stock swap and stock transfer systems allowed companies to sell off parts of the organization or merge with another firm through a stock swap. Companies were allowed to repurchase their own stock (to reduce excess equity generated during the bubble period), and a 2001 revision lifted restrictions on what companies could do with their own 'treasury stock', including allowing stock swaps to acquire other companies. In addition to deregulating stock options, the introduction of new stock categories and new rules on transactions offered unprecedented flexibility in refinancing, compensation, corporate restructuring, and takeover defense. Together with the lifting of the ban on holding companies in 1997, this opened new venues for companies to reorganize. Subsequent reforms offered a new set of deals in terms of asset transfers, leveraged or management buyouts and takeovers (Hashimoto 2002, Higashino 2004a, 2004b). New rules on internal oversight made members of the Board of Directors liable for mismanagement and increased pressures to attach clear responsibilities to business units. Companies can now think strategically about their business portfolio – which business units to keep, which to spin off, and which to close down – and then execute these strategies in completely new ways.

As part of its Revival Program, the Koizumi government also began to revise labor rules. Prior to 2000, a spin-off or transfer of operations required the consent of labor, yet workers often resisted because in Japan smaller companies tend to pay significantly lower wages. In addition, around 2000, the courts softened their stance on what constituted a 'fair' dismissal of a regular employee, by allowing that one of four conditions (as opposed to all four) was sufficient grounds: the company was in distress, the person to be dismissed was incompetent, part-time workers had already been cut, and the unions had agreed. Previously, fulfilling all four conditions meant, for example, that a company had to be facing bankruptcy before it could let go of ineffective workers; now companies could reduce employees for proactive adjustment measures, to prevent bankruptcy (Schaede 2008, chap. 9). While it is still difficult to dismiss workers in Japan, it is no longer impossible. This shift undermined previous expectations of work relations and began a long-term change in the social contract between the government, companies and employees that is likely to extend for a generation.[3]

New legislation also aimed to open the door for hostile takeovers. These had long been hindered by cross-shareholdings and a lack of rules regarding minority owners. New rules beginning in 2000, which were further revised and codified in the Corporation Law of 2006, allow for a 'squeeze-out' in which minority owners must submit their stakes if the takeover is offered at a fair price. In contrast to other countries, the threshold where such a squeeze-out can begin in Japan may in some cases be as low as 66% of ownership, even though 85% may be the more usual boundary (Nakayama 2010). Suddenly, the Old Japan horizontal business groups (*keiretsu*) where each member owned a small stake in each other no longer offered reliable protection against raiders. This further undermined the logic of cross-shareholdings. To allow companies to search for different measures of protection – similar to those granted in the US and Europe – the Ministry of Justice and METI released a Takeover Guideline in 2005 that validated a 'poison pill' (a mechanism that makes a hostile bid prohibitively expensive) in the form of new warrant issues that dilute the raider's stake (Milhaupt 2005, CVSG 2006). This Guideline was incorporated into the new Corporation Law of 2006, and it clarified the rights of owners in defense situations by giving shareholders a choice to issue a carte blanche for such mechanisms, or to insist on ratification each time new defense schemes are introduced.

One concern at the time was that Japanese firms would use the new hostile takeover guideline to formulate a plethora of defense mechanisms. However, whereas a poll of June 2006 revealed that 27% of listed companies were considering the introduction of such measures – by October 2007, only some 10% of listed firms had in fact adopted poison-pills (*Nikkei* 19 June 2006, 15 October 2007). Perhaps most importantly, the possibility of hostile takeovers in and of itself pushed management towards 'choose and focus'. In addition to pressure to maintain stock price and market cap at a high level, the best defense against a hostile takeover is to do by oneself what an incoming raider would do to an underperforming company: replace ineffective management, revise the business model, and improve performance. Thus, the mere threat of a hostile takeover greatly increased managerial discipline.

In 2007, the new Financial Instruments and Exchange Law (FIEL, *Kinyū shōhin torihiki-hō*) greatly revised regulations on corporate disclosure, internal auditing and compliance, in addition to governing financial transactions and disclosure associated with takeover bids. Perhaps the biggest contribution of this law to the strategic inflection point was to further push for transparency and managerial accountability. First, it made quarterly earnings reports statutory for all listed companies. Second, it contained a section referred to as 'J-SOX' – the Japanese version of the US Sarbanes-Oxley Act that prescribes internal controls and independent audits, including liability of members of the board of directors (FSA 2006, Konishi and Shimizu 2006).

Other legal revisions in line with 'leaving it to the market' included reforms of antitrust (to enforce cartel rules more forcefully), intellectual property rights, and company formation rules in an effort to spur venture activities (Schaede 2008). At the end of the decade-long process, the legal and financial setting within which Japanese companies operate had completely changed. The new settings undercut previous sources of power (such as personal networks, access to regulators, and company size), and demand a new skill set of management leadership, clear strategic positioning, and the pursuit of long-term profit.

Implications

As Figure 2 showed, whereas in the 1980s some 75% of shares at the Tokyo Stock Exchange were held by stable, friendly shareholders such as banks and corporations, by 2008 almost 50% of shares were owned by institutional (including foreign) investors. For better or worse, these new investors are much more short-term oriented than the previous stable shareholders: they will buy high-performing stocks that raise their return on investment over that of other funds but they are likely to sell low-performing stocks, thereby depressing a company's stock price and increasing the threat of a takeover. To impress these investors, Japan's leading large conglomerates embarked on a slimming-down diet. While an easy fist step to increase profitability was to simply exit non-profitable businesses, the most aggressive reformers, such as Panasonic, completely reorganized their core businesses and shed hundreds of subsidiaries.

This refocusing on the core businesses occurred through three main measures: (a) reorganizing the company to create clear profit and loss centers around the core businesses; (b) strengthening the core by consolidating with (acquiring) competitors; and (c) exiting non-core businesses. During the refocusing wave of the 1980s in the United States, it was estimated that about half of the county's Fortune 500 firms engaged in at least one of these activities (Markides 1995). To evaluate the extent of Japanese refocusing, Schaede (2008) counted activities in these three categories by Japan's Nikkei 500 firms during 2000–2006. During that period, 75% of Japanese companies declared at least one act of corporate reorganization, consolidation, or exit. One third of Japan's leading firms adopted multiple measures of 'choose and focus', such as turning the company into a holding (to focus the business units as stand-alone companies), merging non-core units with a competitors' entity, or selling off or shutting down activities no longer considered relevant. Thus, just in terms of simple numbers the Japanese refocusing wave of the early 2000s was perhaps even larger than that in the US in the 1980s.

Of course, not all Japanese companies were eager reformers. Many laggards remained, even among the large Japanese household names, and cultural reasons were often cited to explain their unwillingness or inability to move beyond a mere lip service of 'choose and focus'. One common obstacle was the long-standing HR practice of appointing to the president position of a subsidiary those managers that were not promoted into top ranks at the mother company. These presidents of subsidiaries were often classmates of the managers at the mother company, and given limited mobility in Japan's executive labor market, it was allegedly difficult to close down businesses run by classmates. Thus, while some large companies charged ahead and completely repositioned, others stumbled along, often faring exceedingly poorly.

The plurality in how Japanese companies have reacted to the strategic inflection point can be explained with the help of the congruence model, applied to both the corporate and country level. The most basic insight is that the transition from an existing alignment to a new one is a time-consuming process. Even though Figure 1 above showed a strong upward trend in average profitability of listed firms for the early 2000s, so far systemic empirical studies of the effects of 'choose and focus' have found either no increase in average profit indicators, or remained ambiguous (Asaba 2006). This is not surprising. First, average profit data may be misleading, as for every proactively refocusing company there was at least one slow mover. More importantly, these studies used data only until 2002, and better results can be expected from future research. This is because true organizational renewal entails more than simply spinning off non-profitable business units. In order to translate strategic repositioning and new critical tasks into results, formal organization, people and culture have to be realigned, and for large organizations this process can last well over one decade.

Another insight gained from the application of the congruence model is that strategic positioning alone will not bring true change, and not all companies may appreciate this or go at it at the same pace. The first step, of course, must be the identification of new critical tasks. With the possible exception of a handful of industries, for most Japanese manufacturing companies the assignment can no longer be to mass-produce high-quality end products. Rather they must compete in upstream components and materials that earn higher margins, and feed into intermediate products made in Taiwan and South Korea, which in turn feed into end products assembled in China. The only way for Japanese manufacturers to earn profits in competition with Asian countries is through technology leadership and constant innovation. This insight has led competitive companies to change their human resource management practices: rewards had to shift from working hard to working efficiently and effectively; people had to be selected for individual talent as opposed to not making mistakes; and culture had to change to speed and risk-taking. The celebrated turnaround president of Panasonic, Kunio Nakamura, described the changes in his company as akin to a 'cultural revolution'. A full evaluation of Japan's 'choose and focus' wave will have to be based on data after 2010.

Finally, the application of the congruence model to Japan as a country reveals that an even longer wait is necessary, as a repositioning here may require a generational change. For Japan, the critical tasks have shifted from fast export-led growth and catching up with the West, to building structures that support a rapidly ageing society and a shrinking workforce, at a time when government debt exceeds 200% of GDP. Rather than interfering with corporate strategies, like the erstwhile developmental state used to do, the new government role is to build a level playing field that supports innovation and new company formation while refocusing on societal tasks. The country culture has to shift away from expecting government to socialize risk, and toward a system that supports individual effort and variation, be that in career or pension planning. Given the shrinking workforce, people have to be more efficient to earn the revenues needed to support the country, and rewards in society are shifting towards career differentiation, work-life balance, and a new appreciation for risk and return. Japan's society will adjust to these new tasks much more slowly than even the largest companies, but it is already apparent that the next generation of workers is undergoing this change. Voices that doubt the glory of the fabled 'salary-man' work ethic have become louder; societal and family structures are changing; and the lockstep motion of Japan's society, perhaps always exaggerated, is visibly breaking open. This is not easy, as underscored by the vivid discourse within Japan of the increasingly 'unequal society' (*kakusa shakai*, the growing differential between the rich and poor) of the early 2000s. As of 2010, even though at the corporate level the strategic inflection point has irreversibly occurred, it may take Japan as a country another decade to make this transition.

Conclusions

The stronger the alignment between critical tasks, formal organization, people and culture, the more successful is the organization, yet the more difficult it is to change. In the 1990s, global shifts in the competitive environment and the replacement of Japan as the world leader in mass-manufacturing high-quality consumer goods by China, Taiwan and South Korea brought an end to the 'developmental state' model. In the twenty-first century, Japan must compete through technological leadership. To enable Japan's companies to 'choose and focus' on innovation in materials and components, the country as a whole needed to realign (see Warner 2011). The legal system, regulatory processes and incentives for people and companies in the political economy have been overhauled. Corporate ownership structures and business networks have changed. What it takes to win in the New Japan is fundamentally different from what it took in the post-war period, and it requires a shift to new motivations, processes and strategic approaches, for individuals, corporations and the country as a whole. The 1990s were not a lost decade for Japan but a painful realignment away from old, successful habits toward new and still emerging processes.

As of 2010, Japan is still in the progress of repositioning, both at the corporate level and as a country. The reforms of the 1990s and early 2000s have allowed forward-looking companies to change into new world competitors. These companies are world leaders in electronic components and input materials that other Asian companies cannot mimic. According to one study, even though Japan has relinquished its erstwhile dominant position in high-end consumer electronics end products, Japanese companies combine to a dominant world market share in components needed to make those products (METI *et al.* 2005). As of 2010, the contribution to overall economic activity by these leading firms was still fairly small. To unleash the energy that exists in Japan's entrepreneurial firms, the country as a whole has to find a new alignment.

Notes

1. In mathematics, an inflection point is reached when the first derivative (the slope of the trajectory) becomes zero, and the second trajectory (the rate of change) reverses its sign.
2. The FSA published inspection results on the internet, including the difference with the banks' own claims. Initially, the 15 largest banks understated non-performing loans by 36% (five banks

underreported by more than 50%). Yet, by 2002, average underreporting had declined to 5.5%. See FSA Sept 16, 2004, press release, available from: www.fsa.go.jp/news/ newse/e20040916-1.html

3. By 2008, 80% of Japan's listed companies had switched to performance pay and promotion, and perhaps half of these used promotions as outright incentives to attract and retain talent. See Schaede (2008) for an analysis of changing employment practices in the context of Japan's strategic inflection point until 2008.

References

Abegglen, J.C. and Stalk, G. Jr., 1985. *Kaisha–the Japanese corporation: how marketing, money, and manpower strategy, not management style, make the Japanese world pace-setters*. New York: Basic Books.

Amyx, J., 2004. *Japan's financial crisis: institutional rigidity and reluctant change*. Princeton University Press.

Asaba, S., 2006. Jigyō no 'sentaku to shūchū' to keiei seika ['Choose and focus' and corporate performance]. *In*: *Kigyō katsudō kihon chōsa paneru deeta o katsuyō shita Waga-kuni kigyō katsudō no takakuka kōdō to pafo-mansu ni kan suru chōsa kenkyū*. [Analyzing diversifcation and performance of Japanese companies, based on panel data from the Basic Survey of Corporate Activities]. Tokyo: METI Keizai sangyō seisaku-kyoku, 105–120.

Burgelman, R.A. and Grove, A.S., 1996. Strategic dissonance. *California management review*, 38, 8–38.

Cabinet Office, Government of Japan, 2004. Annual report on the Japanese economy and public finance 2003–2004: no gains without reforms IV [Translation of the *Keizai Zaisei Hakusho* 2004], Tokyo.

CAO, *See* Cabinet Office, Government of Japan.

Corporate Value Study Group, 2006. Corporate value report 2006: toward the firm establishment of fair rules in the corporate community, Ministry of Economy, Trade and Industry, Tokyo.

CVSG, *See* Corporate Value Study Group.

Financial Services Agency, ed., 2006. New legislative framework for investor protection: 'Financial Instruments and Exchange Law'. Financial Services Agency, Tokyo.

Fletcher, M., 2011. Dreams of economic transformation and the reality of economic crisis: *Keidanren* in the era of the 'bubble' and the onset of the 'lost decade,' from the mid-1980s to the mid-1990s. *Asia Pacific business review*, 18 (2), 149–165.

FSA, *See* Financial Services Agency.

Fukui, Y. and Ushijima, T., 2007. Corporate diversification, performance and restructuring in the largest Japanese manufacturers. *Journal of the Japanese and international economies*, 21, 303–323.

Goto, A., 1981. Statistical evidence on the diversification of Japanese large firms. *Journal of industrial economics*, 29, 271–278.

Harreld, J.B., O'Reilly, C. and Tushman, M., 2007. Dynamic capabilities at IBM: driving strategy into action. *California management review*, 21–43.

Hashimoto, M., 2002. Commercial code revisions: promoting the evolution of Japanese companies. *NRI Studys*, Nomura Research Institute.

Higashino, D., 2004a. The business of rehabilitating companies in Japan (NPLs and corporate restructuring, part 2) [online]. *Japan Economic Monthly*. Available from: www.jetro.go.jp/en/m arket/trend/special/index.html/pdf/jem0405-1e.pdf.

Higashino, D., 2004b. Corporate reorganization picks up steam in Japan: part 1. Improved legal provisions [online]. *Japan Economic Monthly*. Available from: www.jetro.go.jp/en/market/trend/special/index.html/pdf/jem0411-1e.pdf.

Hoshi, T. and Kashyap, A., 2001. *Corporate financing and corporate governance in Japan: the road to the future*. Boston: MIT Press.

Hoshi, T., Koibuchi, S. and Schaede, U., 2011. Corporate Restructuring in Japan during the Lost Decade. *In*: K. Hamada, A. Kashyap and D. Weinstein eds. *Japan's bubble, deflation, and long-term stagnation*. Cambridge, MA: MIT Press, 343–373.

Johnson, C., 1982. *MITI and the Japanese miracle – the growth of industrial policy, 1925–1975*. Stanford University Press.

Koizumi, J., 2002. *Policy speech to the 154th session of the Diet*, 4 February. Available from: http://www.kantei.go.jp/foreign/koizumispeech/2002/02/04sisei_e.html.

Konishi, M. and Shimizu, K., 2006. Japan's new financial instruments and exchange law. *Asia Law & Practice Japan Review*. Available from: www.asialaw.com.

Markides, C.C., 1995. Diversification, restructuring and economic performance. *Strategic management journal*, 16, 101–118.

METI, MHLW and MEXT, 2005. *2005nenpan Monozukuri Hakusho*, [2005 White paper on the manufacturing industries]. Tokyo. Available from: www.meti.go.jp/report/data/g51115aj.html.

Milhaupt, C.J., 2005. In the shadow of Delaware? The rise of hostile takeovers in Japan. *Columbia law review*, 105, 2171–2216.

Milhaupt, C.J. and Pistor, K., 2008. *Law and capitalism*. Chicago University Press.

Ministry of Justice of Japan, 2001. Japanese corporate law: drastic changes in 2000–2001 and the future [online], Available from: www.moj.go.jp/ENGLISH/information/jcld-01.html.

Nadler, D. and Tushman, M., 1997. *Competing by design: the power of organizational architecture*. Oxford University Press.

Nakayama, R., 2010. *Japan squeeze-out guide*, International Bar Association, IBA Corporate and M&A Law Committee 2010. Available from: www.ibanet.org.

O'Reilly, C.A. and Tushman, M.L., 2008. Ambidexterity as a dynamic capability: resolving the innovator's dilemma. *Research in organizational behavior*, 28, 185–206.

Palich, L.E., Cardinal, L.B. and Miller, C.C., 2000. Curvilinearity in the diversification–performance linkage: an examination of over three decades of research. *Strategic management journal*, 21, 155–174.

Schaede, U., 2000. *Cooperative capitalism: self-regulation, trade associations, and the antimonopoly lw in Japan*. Oxford University Press.

Schaede, U., 2003. Industry rules: from deregulation to self-regulation. *In*: U. Schaede and W.W. Grimes eds. *Japan's managed globalization: adapting to the 21st century*. Armonk, NY: M.E. Sharpe, 191–214.

Schaede, U., 2006. Privatverschuldung and Sozialhilfe in Japan: Kredithaie, das 'Mittelmarket-Loch' und der japanische Sozialvertrag [Private debt and social welfare in Japan loan sharks, the 'middle-risk gap' and Japan's social contract]. *Zeitschrift fuer Betriebswirtschaftslehre*, 87–108.

Schaede, U., 2008. *Choose and focus: Japanese business strategies for the 21st centuries*. Ithaca, NY: Cornell University Press.

Schwartz, F.J., 1998. *Advice and consent: the politics of consultation in Japan*. Cambridge University Press.

Takagi, S., 2003. *Kigyō saisei no kiso chishiki*. [The bbasics of corporate rehabilitation]. Tokyo: Iwanami Shoten.

Takeuchi, K., 2003. Japan has revamped its corporate insolvency system by creating new procedural rules and substantive provisions. Available: www.sakuralaw.gr.jp/publication/takeuchi/59.pdf.

Tokyo Stock Exchange, 2009. *Heisei 20nendo kabushiki bunpu jōkyō no chōsa kekka ni tsuite*, [Results of the 2009 Survey on Shareholdings].Tokyo.

Tushman, M.L. and O'Reilly, C., 2002. *Winning through innovation: a practical guide to leading organizational change and renewal*. Boston: Harvard Business School Press.

von Staden, P., 2012. Fettered by the past in the march forward: ideology as an explanation for the malaise in today's Japan. *Asia Pacific business review*, 18 (2), 185–200.

Warner, M., 2011. Commentary: whither Japan? Economy, management and society. *Asia Pacific business review*, 17 (1), 1–5.

Williamson, O.E., 1975. *Markets and hierarchies: analysis and antitrust implications*. New York: The Free Press.

Williamson, O.E., 1985. *The economic institutions of capitalism: firms, markets, and relational contracting*. New York: Free Press.

Yoshihara, H., Sakuma, A., Itami, H. and Kagono, T., 1981. *Nihon kigyō no takakuka-senryaku - keieishigen aproochi*. [Diversification strategies by Japanese firms: a resource-based approach]. Tokyo: Nihon Keizai Shinbun-sha.

Fettered by the past in the march forward: ideology as an explanation for today's malaise in Japan

Peter von Staden

Bristol Business School, The University of the West of England, Bristol BS16 1QY, UK

Japan's 'lost decade' of the 1990s is more than 10 years of economic downturn. The fact that a further decade later the malaise continues suggests that this is more than just an extended bad patch. Measures have been implemented to revitalize the economy however, the Japanese economy continues to wither. Why is this the case? This is an historical institutionalist's argument drawn from D.C. North's work that reform measures fall short of their aims if they are not underpinned by a complementary ideology. And, effectively, Japan is a case in point. Japanese-language records of debates between policy makers in 1999, after a decade of reform, show that they continued hold to a 'mental model' of a political economy that was of the preceeding high growth period and, indeed, much further in Japan's past. Such key figures as Prime Minister Obuchi Keizō argued both for the inculcation of greater market competition and, at the same time, lamented the loss of Japan's former 'virtuous capitalism'. In other words, fettered by the past, they prepared Japan for the future.

Introduction

Accounts of the 'lost decade' identify that Japan's economy reached a critical point at the end of the 1990s when the effects of key reforms began to be realized (Amyx 2004, Schaede 2008). Turning to this juncture, this study focuses on the Japanese-language records of debates in 1999 between government and business during *shingikai*, or Council of Deliberation, meetings over proposed reform measures. This analysis is part of a larger longitudinal study of the linkages between how key stakeholders conceptualize and reconceptualize policy and the ramifications for Japan's current politico-economic transition. While much of the literature focuses on reform measures and their impact, the historical institutionalist interpretation provided here sees the lost decade as more than just an economic downturn. Drawing on D.C. North's work on the socio-cognitive underpinning of political economy, answers based on ideological grounds are provided to questions raised in the literature as to why reform measures in the 1990s fell short of their intended outcome. And, we extend the implications of these findings to the present. Notwithstanding whatever gains may be achieved by the reform measures to date, the prognosis is that Japan's economy will continue, at least in the short-run, to do poorly.

The malaise of the 1990s brought an end to Japan's remarkable post-war economic rise (see Fletcher forthcoming, Schaede forthcoming). For a decade, government and business debated alternative solutions and implemented policies to revitalize the economy.

Nonetheless, today, some 20 years after the onset of the lost decade, Japan has not yet found its way (see Warner 2011). To be sure, Japan has changed and continues to change. However, in as much as Japan had struck upon an effective politico-economic framework to channel its drive for catch-up, it continues to look for a replacement. The transition for a nation engrossed in catching up to the 'what next' after having caught up is not necessarily easy or smooth. After all, what is at stake is not merely the rejigging of a few market institutions – which in itself is difficult enough – but rather something more profound and all encompassing.

From all quarters, Japan has been urged to find a way to rejuvenate itself. Yet, its search continues. The bifurcation of its economy between globally competitive multinationals and cosseted domestic small and medium sized firms signals that Japan has the wherewithal to be innovative, flexible and competitive at the highest standards. But, at the same time, Japan tolerates the opposite among its domestic firms. Given these strengths, that still after some 20 years of economic restructuring and political reform Japan continues to stagnate suggests that the matter is of a deeper nature.

At its most elemental level – and where the crux of the matter lies – this transition is not about the creation of new institutions, or the adoption of new rules for old institutions or the reconfiguration of their matrix. Analysis at this level is epiphenomal. Ultimately, what fetters Japan's resurgence is not its rules of operation that govern the market but, in the Northian sense, the ideology that underpins these rules. To be sure, change in the rules themselves may increase competitiveness and lead to growth but, as the last 20 years have shown, this is not enough. Japan's economy has lost its former vitality and tinkering on the edges will not cut the mustard.

It is telling that despite a decade of debate about reform measures, fundamental ideological conflict continued among key stakeholders about the very nature of Japan's future political economy. Among these discussions, a key concern was that of competition. Records of *shingikai* meetings in 1999 reflect their acceptance of the need to increase domestic market competition but also their concerns about some of the consequences. Before the participants stood a wide range of bills whose overarching aim was to put Japan on a new footing commensurate with the challenges, economic among others, of the new century. They accepted the need for change but framed it within a vision of a political economy inspired by the past. Underpinned by values more closely associated with a socioeconomic framework of the high growth period, this vision was significantly different than neo-liberalists would have hoped for. Japan's post-transition political economy was on the one hand to be more competitive than its forerunner and, on the other, inspired by the tenents of the very one that it was to replace. With one foot in the past it tried to move forward.

Fundamentally, what Japan needs is to decide how it wants its market to operate. A market is about the allocation of resources. The regulations which dictate how that allocation will be determined is not, however, preordained but a humanly devised construct. It reflects the values of the nation. As history shows, in the long run, agreement by a people on how their resources, capital and wealth are shared is essential. Expressed in Northian terms, the contestation of the rules of the game, formal and informal, is part of the process of a nation defining and redefining how its market will operate. In so doing, the market becomes a means through which a nation realizes its hopes and desires. In this sense, the lost decade was a period of reflection on what kind of market – and, indeed, nation – Japan wanted. This issue remains unresolved still today. And, until such time that this resolution is found, Japan will continue to wander through its 'valley of transition'.

Theory and hypotheses: ideology and institutional rigidity

The term 'lost decade' is somewhat of an unfortunate epithet. The word 'lost' suggests that something has gone astray, 'decade' tells us the time period and, through usage, we have come to associate it with economic crisis. But, this term fails to convey the sense of the pivotal role that the lost decade plays in Japan's history. That said, as part of the larger transition from the post-1945 high growth period's politico-economic (cum-socio) framework to its following reconfiguation, the lost decade is but 10 years within the long run. That the origins of the bursting of the real estate bubble in 1991 reach into the 1980s and that the ensuing downturn is two decades long points to the severity of Japan's *bouleversement*. The jigsaw has broken apart and its pieces are coming together in new ways ultimately producing a very different picture (Pempel 1998, Hook 2011). Although it is still unclear what this new institutional configuration will be, it is clear that research on the lost decade needs to appreciate the larger historical process at play.

The spectrum of approaches to instutional theory is vast spanning the social sciences, each offering a different vista on the process of institutional formation, continuity and change.[1] Similarly, the actor-structure issue remains a hotly contested issue. New Institutional Economics à la North (1990), New Institutional Organizational Theory (see Greenwood *et al.*, 2008), Structuration Theory (Giddens 1984), Critical Realism (Bhaskar 1989, Archer 1995) and a Darwinian approach (Hodgson 2004, Hodgson and Knudsen 2010) each contribute to this discourse. Notwithstanding difference that bedevils greater convergence, it is fair to say that there is agreement that both actor and structure are two parts of a mutually constitutive whole. The dynamics of that interaction though, are at the frontier of the literature. With respect to the lost decade, as will be seen, the dominant perspective in the literature is that of 'structure'. While it is not that the literature sees 'actors' as bereft of agency, it is rather by ommision that they have been rendered largely silent. This is, though, a shortcoming. The contribution by Fletcher here in this collection of contributions helps redress this and signals the importance of agency in decision making processes. By specifically looking at some of the very business actors who conceive and convey opinion, he underscores that reform measures are a result of previously conceived ideas and not the other way around. That said, one must be sensitive to the actor-structure dialectic and recognize that the very reforms that actors create, in turn, provide new structures which both facilitate and shape further decision making. We seek here an understanding of institutional change in terms of a process worked out through time in order not to lose sight of the ongoing politico-economic meta-narrative and to draw into relief the trajectory of Japan's economy. And, it is thus, that we turn to historical institutionalism to frame the ensuing research and findings.

Historical institutionalism is often closely associated with path dependency, that is 'once a path [decision] is taken, previously viable alternatives become increasingly remote, as the relevant actors adjust the strategies to accommodate the prevailing pattern' (Thelen 2004, p. 27). The point of origin of the path dependent trajectory comes at 'critical junctures' when a particular institutional configuration sets (Thelen 2004). Although not necessarily impossible, later radical change is difficult to realize until a further turning point or 'crisis' is reached. While this theoretical approach may provide good explanations for why an economy persists along a sub-optimal path, it is less useful at predicting when change will occur (Peters 2005). However, in the case of the lost decade, the issue is understanding why, despite reform measures, little has changed. This, in turn, steers us towards the actors themselves to find answers raising questions about their motivation and ideas. The importance of the socio-cognitive in explaining institutional change and stasis has been recognized within institutional theory such as New Institutional Organizational Studies (DiMaggio 1997) and New Institutional Economics (North 1990, 2005). It is, however, the work of D.C. North that, in particular, provides theoretical underpinnings for answers to why political economies underperform and key insights come from his work on the socio-cognitive.

A focal point of the life's work of Nobel Laureate, Douglass C. North, is the limits of orthodox frameworks to explain economic underperformance. In his early work, he discerned that the rationality premise of neo-classical economics needed to be relaxed in order to better explain the rationale and motivations that drove political decision making which led to poor growth. Over time, his thinking has incorporated aspects of sociology and psychology to provide a more balanced appreciation of the actor-structure issue. Although for North the actor remains the main driver of institutional change, said agent is also located within and shaped by an ideological framework.

Ideology, we can hypothesize, informs the actor of how, for example, a market should operate and shapes how decision makers respond to the need for change. Although a dialectic exists between the actor and the structure that allows for one to effect the other, in the main, the ideological framework remains a constant in stable times. This constancy may give way in times of crisis when actors are forced to reflect on the very tenets that underpin their ideas of how things should operate. It is in such circumstances that opportunities emerge for fundamental shifts in thinking. While the door to radical change may be open, it is up to actors to grasp the opportunity.

North (2005) emphasized the institutional rigidities hypothesis as importantly linked to the grip of belief continuities and, in turn, path dependencies. In early work (notably North 1990, 1994, Denzau and North 1994), he laid the foundation stones for the explication of 'mental models' which were defined as the 'subjective perceptions (models, theories) all people possess to explain the world around them' (North 1990, p. 23). He identifies that subjectivity in human interpretation of reality is a key factor in understanding actor decisions (North 1990, p. 23). Accordingly, North (2005) provides an ideological context for economic choices; to wit, he delves into the very sociocognitive foundations of choice. As he puts it, 'we choose among alternatives that are themselves constructions of the human mind, (t)herefore how the mind works and understands the environment is the foundation of this study' (North 2005, p. 11).

Commencing with the central proposition that institutional change is the outcome of deliberate or intentional choices made by actors, North (2005) sets out to explain how humans come to make said choices. In so doing, he explicates the sociocognitive process by which intentionality emerges as humans construct beliefs that shape decisions to alter the process of institutional change. He posits that beliefs are mental constructs derived from learning, present and past, individual and cumulative, and embodied in a society's culture. As he says: 'The focus of our attention, therefore, must be on human learning – on what is learned and how it is shared among members of a society and on the incremental process by which the beliefs and preferences change, and on the way in which they shape the performance of economies through time' (North 2005, p. viii).

For North, institutions are not only part of our genetic evolution, but also part of our cultural evolution and so, institutional change derives from the complex interplay between genetic dispositions and widely varied human experience (North 2005, p. 42). Humankind's ceaseless efforts to gain control over their lives, to try and structure human interaction is constrained by the vestige of institutions accumulated from the past which 'give rise to organizations whose survival depends on the perpetuation of those institutions and which hence will devote resources to preventing any alteration that threatens their survival' (North 2005, pp. 51-52). But it is also 'that the belief system underlying the institutional matrix will deter radical change' (North 2005, p. 77). Understanding institutional change, then, necessitates an understanding of path dependence in order to appreciate the nature of the limits it imposes on change because 'at any moment of time the players are constrained by path dependence – the limits to choices arising from the combination of beliefs, institutions, and artifactual structure that have been inherited from the past' (North 2005, p. 80).

For North, then, to understand institutional change requires an understanding of beliefs which, he believes, are at the heart of human consciousness. As he says:

> We have not only a vision about the way an economy or society is working but a normative view of how it could be restructured to work better. Thus consciousness can lead to the construction of a set of beliefs that induce players to believe that revolution is a preferred alternative to a continuation of what is perceived as a deteriorating condition. At the other extreme, consciousness can lead to the construction of a set of beliefs in the 'legitimacy' of a society. We need to explore under what conditions beliefs get activated to produce order and disorder. (North 2005, p. 103)

Disorder can result from changes, such as political and economic crises, resulting in a dilution of coercive enforcement of formal rules or from a weakening of informal norms of cooperation, inducing individuals, organizations, or nation-states to attempt radical change to the 'rules of the game'. In short, in explaining both the emergence and change of institutions over time, North details a chain of causality from individual genetic architecture, through to sociocultural heritage/context of cognition and belief formation, and finally to deliberate choice in changing formal and informal rules to convert uncertainty to risk. North emphasizes that the differential performance of societies makes it abundantly clear that the cultural component of the institutional scaffolding humans erect is central to the success or otherwise of societies (North 2005). These observations are crucial to our understanding of why Japan finds the transition from its politico-economic framework to the next so difficult.

A key characteristic of realizing change in Japan is the relationship between state and society. For much of post-war Japan, an implicit pact existed between the Japanese people and government that, as long as they delivered economic growth, political matters would be left to politicians and bureaucrats. As Daniel Okimoto has argued, Japan is 'without question a societal state' (Okimoto 1989, p. 226). At the top of this interlocked relationship between how the market operates, how policy is formed and the support of society is the state. In its focal role, as Maruyama Masao (1963) has argued, the state embodies the collective will of the people and, through the instruments at its disposal, it harnesses that will to achieve goals shared by society. By extension, then, the 'economy is of importance in providing the instrumental means of achieving larger, collective goals set forth by the polity' (Okimoto 1989, p. 226). Taking this further, Okimoto argues that the 'secret to the power of the Japanese state is thus embedded in the structure of its relationship with the rest of society' (1989, p. 226). Although corruption prior to and throughout the lost decade had sullied the reputation of the state's leading actors, to wit politicians, bureaucrats and big business, these actors continue today to play an essential representative, coordinative and directorial function in Japan.

Literature in the field

Their tripartite role is seen both as the recipe for Japan's impressive post-war growth record (Johnson 1982) and an important factor in explaining Japan's lacklustre reform implementation (Katz 1998, Ihori 2003, Amyx 2004, Vogel 2006). These two positions are not mutually exclusive. They are, effectively, part of a historical institutionalist's explanation for path dependency and continuity. Dependent on conditions and the stage of economic development, networks may either facilitate or hinder. As a fetter to change, coordinative roles over time tend to become embedded and key stakeholders' interests do not necessarily correspond to the imperatives of change. Current economic reform in Japan is one part of a larger picture and, given the extent of the requisite reform, necessarily requires adjustment elsewhere in the institutional matrix. Two important edited volumes both published following the lost decade in 2005 attempt to draw together the multiple strands of Japan's transformation to provide a comprehensive overview. The first of these, *Beyond the lost 10 years* (Tokyo Daigaku Shakai Kagaku Kenkūjo 2005) focuses on explanations for the economic crisis and the reform years under Prime Minister Koizumi Junichirō (2001–2006). The second, *Reviving Japan's Economy: Problems and Prescriptions*, addresses the 'profound transformation process', which the lost decade was one stage of, in terms of its 'economic, demographic, social, and political' facets (Ito and Patrick 2005, p. 1). The multi-disciplinary approach of these volumes underscores that the lost decade can not be understood only in terms of its economic or financial dimensions. The multi-facted nature of Japan's long run economic malaise argues, in turn, that actors in coordinative roles fulfill key functions in steering the nation through the transition. Because their interests are shaped, in part, by their own beliefs of what should be, reform measures may fall short of expectations and needs.

Certainly, change did occur but it also clear that after a decade of downturn, far more was necessary to raise the economy from its moribund state (Katz 1998, Amyx 2004, Vogel 2006). As Edward Lincoln questions:

> Is Japan really forging ahead with major economic restructuring, institutional reform, and deregulation? This study argues that the surface image of change is misleading. That 'something' is changing cannot be denied, and the pace of change has clearly increased from the stasis of the preceding two decades. (Lincoln 2001, p. 5)

He follows then by outlining some of the essential characteristics of what he sees Japan's political economy to hold for the future. Among others, government in Japan will continue to be 'intrusive in the economy', general 'mistrust of markets' will remain and social considerations will 'temper the drive for efficiency' (Lincoln 2001, p. 5). Japan will continue to adhere to the fundamental values that underpinned the social capitalist framework of the high growth period. This tendency is reflected, he continues, in the fact that though '*structural* change' has occurred, this is 'quite different from *systemic* change' (Lincoln 2001, p. 5, emphasis in original). And without this radical – as opposed to incremental – change, Japan's economy can not regain its former vitality.

In Lincoln's assessment of Japan's reform initiatives, he says that there is a widely held 'belief in the value of the existing system' (Lincoln 2001, p.8). Although growth on average throughout the 1990s was barely 1%, it was growth nonetheless. For stakeholders, as long as growth continues, belief in the economic system outweighs economic underperformance. The cautious voice argues that old ways 'should not be carelessly abandoned in hopes of a better performance' (Lincoln 2001, p. 221). Reflecting Japan's network economy, Steven Vogel posits that:

> If we want to know why the Japanese government made critical errors in fiscal policy, monetary policy, and banking regulation, then we must begin with the bureaucrats who oversee these policies and whose ideologies inform the substance of these policies. If we want to understand the politics shaping those reforms with the greatest potential to alter Japan's economic model ... then we must look to industry preferences and how these preferences are

aggregated by industry associations, political parties, and government ministries. (Vogel 2006, p. 50)

James Lincoln and Michael Gerlach argue that in the absence of the requisite political will, the 'trajectory of change [in Japan] is shaped by legacies of the past: idealized images of how business should be conducted, the slow and haphazard process of deregulation, and the residue of historicial affiliations' (Lincoln and Gerlach 2004, p. 299). If a nation is incapable of mustering the will to realize reform, it falls on political leadership to lead (Katz 1998, Ihori 2003, Kumei 2003, Amyx 2004, Vogel 2006). Thus it is not reform, *per se*, that is the issue but rather did the Japanese political and corporate elites really want to change?

Empirical evidence

In January 1999, *shingikai* members were convened in preparation for deliberations on a wide spectrum of bills[2] which, ostensibly, would lead to sweeping change. This institution has a long-standing presence in Japan's policy formulation process whose role is to provide a formal, legislated forum for discussion. Membership varies according to the issue at hand often drawing on government, the ministries, business and academe for participants.[3] This *shingikai* was made up of 40 individuals some of whom, as we shall see, came from the highest ranks of government. As their discussions show, they believed that Japan stood at a critical point in its history and, reflecting the breadth of the bills before them, their task was no less than to bring about national transformative change. They argued that Japan remained a country of great promise but had become derailed in its pursuit of economic gain. It was thus their task, through these bills, to bring back the virtues (*toku*) that had formerly underpinned Japan and, in so doing, revitalize the nation. In this sense, the *shingikai* forum for them was not just a place to hash out the bills' details – that would come later – but also an opportunity to delve into and expose the very essence of Japan's malaise.

The fact that these discussions came at the end of the lost decade is significant. The participants' reflective, if not confessorial, dialogues suggest that they understood that solutions to what ailed Japan would not be found in just passing more reform measures. As the literature suggests, the alteration of rules to bring about change amounts to little without a commitment to realize them not only in letter but also in spirit. As North argues, rules frame how institutions operate and, by extension, if this is at variance with actor beliefs, problems of compliance may arise.

In May, *shingikai* members reconvened and so began discussions led by Ōta Seiichi, Director-General of the Management and Coordination Agency. Established in 1984, this institution's central aim was to restructure the organizations and functions of the Prime Minister's Office. Setting the tone for the deliberations, he turned to the first matter on the agenda, namely the revision of the Cabinet Law. The proposed changes, he argued, were based on four reasons:

1. the need to strengthen political leadership;
2. to reduce the 'evils' of interministerial rivalry;
3. to reduce the size of government; and
4. to enhance political transparency and efficiency. (*Shingikai* number 3, 1999, p. 4).

In its aim, the strengthening of the Prime Minister's Office was a direct challenge to the norms of Japan's political decision making. During the Liberal Democratic Party's (LDP) sustained post-war dominance, power was diffuse and spread across political factions, bureaucrats and business. Similarly, Ōta's emphasis on the importance of Prime Ministerial leadership signalled fundamental change. Responsive to the electorate which both raised him to power and whose trust was essential to the functioning of the Diet underscores the new realities brought by reform in the election process (see *Shingikai* number 3, 1999, p. 4, Rosenbluth and Thies 2010). This, combined with the call for greater transparency in political decision making, signals that transformative change was in their sights.

This gravity was reflected by the poignant historical references made by participants. These deliberations were seen as more than an opportunity to implement changes to lift Japan out of its decade-long rut. One surmises that if that were the case then the thrust of discussions would have been related to economic issues. Rather, they spoke in expansive terms of the truly momentous point at which they stood in Japan's history. At this juncture, theirs was to recast, not just the economy, but their nation. Ibuki Bunmei, former LDP Minister of Labour, believed that their decisions spelled change as portentous as those made by Bakumatsu leaders in the mid-nineteenth century to end Japan's isolationist policy or as transformative as the effect of the reforms of the Allied occupation after World War II. However, whereas change was previously forced upon Japan by foreigners, at this watershed point, the Japanese had the responsibility for and opportunity provided by self-determination (*Shingikai* number 4, 1999, pp. 9, 29). One participant characterized change as a matter of survival, warning that as dinosaurs found it impossible to adapt to their changing environment and so became extinct, Japan too must evolve (*Shingikai* number 4, 1999, p. 30). A different perspective was taken by Prime Minister Obuchi Keizō who argued that this was not just another turning point but a third in a series of steps towards the restructuring of the relationship between central and local government. Steps in this process of decentralization had been achieved under the guidance of occuption forces but now Japan must finish the work (*Shingikai number 4, 1999, p. 11*). Ultimately, as Chairman of the Democratic Party of Japan and later Prime Minister Hatoyama Yukio reflected, discussion on the need for change was fine but the time had come to answer the question 'what form should Japan take?' (*Shingikai number 4, 1999, p. 44*).

Although never fully elaborated, in broad brush terms participants spoke of the need to recreate their society as one that would be 'free, fair and open' with the implication that Japan did not now have those characteristics (*Shingikai number 4, 1999, p. 41*). What is clearer though is that among these law makers, bureaucrats and businessmen there was a need for a 'new system' (*Shingikai* number 4, 1999, p. 30). That which ailed Japan was, for these participants at least, not a matter that could be dealt with through economic reform measures. The roots of the malaise were deeper and a manifestation of something much more fundamental which had gone wrong. As Obuchi put it, the creation of Japan's wealth enjoyed by its people was thanks to the efforts of those who came before. However, the world had changed and the values of the Japanese people too had 'dramatically diversified' (*Shingikai* number 4, 1999, p. 30). The issue remains whose values had changed and whether they could be reconciled with the imperatives of enhanced economic competitiveness.

The *shingikai* records reflect that the overarching sentiment expressed by participants was that Japan had lost its way. It had achieved wealth but, in its pursuit, had lost something far greater: virtue (*toku*). What is meant by this term is never explained. Whose virtue? What virtues? These are questions that were never squarely addressed. By the same token, though, participants neither questioned what they meant by the term. One surmises that however this term was interpreted by *shingikai* members, they believed that they shared a common understanding. Moreover, it was accepted that, indeed, Japan lost its 'virtue' in the pursuit of wealth. Prime Minister Obuchi saw the problem as one of a balancing act as economic gain carried the seeds of mammonism and if left unchecked would be a country's undoing.

> The pursuit of economic wealth is natural however, this can not be done at the sacrifice of the spirit [*kokoro*]. A balance needs to be maintained. To be frank, there is a problem of spirit in Japan and it stems from education. The critical issue is what that balance should be. Among our forefathers of the Meiji Period, Shibuzawa Eiichi stands out.... I was told that students of his time were taught how to use the abacus and, at the same time, the Annalects of Confucious [*rongo*]. In other words, students were made to understand the inherent conflicts between the pursuit of money and remaining a virtuous person. Students studied how to balance these two opposing ends which was extremely important. (*Shingikai* number 4, 1999, pp. 14–15)

This invocation of Viscount Shibusawa, perhaps modern Japan's greatest entrepreneurial pioneer, and his Confucian credo is significant. Beyond mere symbolic value, it is his role in Japanese history that gives this reference such weight. As entrepreneur-cum-reformer, he was a leading figure during an earlier watershed point in Japan's history, namely that of the Meiji Restoration (1868). In response to the Western threat, Restoration leaders introduced sweeping institutional changes that placed Japan's capitalism on a modern footing to help realise the aim of industrialization. Johannes Hirschmeier makes the point that by the start of this transformative period, the traditional prejudice against the merchant class had diminished. But, he adds, these gains were lost during its initial years due to the 'total disregard of the public interest' by the former merchant class in pursuit of personal financial gain (Hirschmeier 1964, p. 163). Shibusawa and Fukuzawa Yukichi, another leading figure of this time, recognized that in order to foster entrepreneurship in Japan a new public image had to be created, distinct from that of the tainted political merchant. Although he himself benefited from close political contacts, Shibusawa remains characterized as an entrepreneur who rose above personal financial gain to show how capitalism was a virtuous means to serve the nation.

Echoing North's views on learning and its crucial role in shaping a political economy, participants believed that the root of Japan's malaise, then, was socio-cognitive. They understood that the solution was found in the very formative process of not only just shaping the mind in order to become an effective actor in the market but in the making of one who is also virtuous. In this sense, virtue is not just about obeying market rules of competition, for example, but to remain vituous in that pursuit. One surmizes that this was an oblique attack at the evils of consumerism and unbridled capitalism. Although North does not specifically draw a link between 'virtue' and economic performance, he does make clear that another widely accepted 'evil,' to wit, corruption, can have detrimental effects. He observes, for example, that notwithstanding gains achieved through Russia's recent market reforms, corruption remains endemic in its economy. North makes the point that corruption has not only hindered Russia's growth but also, in its endemism, points to something more important, namely ideology. History afforded Russia the opportunity to implement reform however a corresponding ideological shift not did occur and, in turn, the full economic gains from these measures have not been realized (North 2005). Similarly, his research on Castillian Spain shows that regardless of how 'virtuous' market transactions may be, it is also necessary that the laws that shape the transactions be aimed at promoting national growth as opposed to furthering the personal aims of key policy makers (North and Thomas 1973). While point number 4 of the Cabinet Law addresses the problem of the non-transparency of decision making and was discussed in the *shingikai* meetings, there is little evidence to suggest that they saw 'corruption' as the worm at the core of why Japan's capitalism had gone bad.

Regardless, the point is that *shingikai* participants understood that the promotion of effective – as they defined it – market operation was not just about passing appropriate reform bills but about engendering an ideology embraced by actors that corresponded with approved values. In other words, their foremost task was to create an ideological underpinning in order to create a political economy as they deemed appropriate. By implication, if they limited themselves to just passing competition enhancing measures without concern the return of lost virtue, then Japan would dangerously slip into neo-liberalism.

Whatever form the disease may have taken, for Hatoyama 'Japan's illness manifested itself at the national, firm, and individual levels and resulted in the loss of Japan's spirit, economic strength, self-reliance and self-respect' (*Shingikai* number 4, 1999, p. 43). He lamented that the evils of capitalism were eating away the very fabric of Japan's society as evidenced by the fact that ' the community spirit [*kyōdōtai*] has been greatly weakened [and] so too its relationship with the family unit, regional community... and the relationship between the individual and the nation' (*Shingikai* number 4, 1999, p. 15). In short, the concern of *shingikai* participants was at the ideological level of who *homo economicus* had become and before any serious discussion of economic reform could be take place, it was necessary to understand the illness that had given rise to the lost decade.

It is critical to understand what the participants characterized as good and bad among the various activities and consequences of market-based accumulation of economic wealth. To be sure, their discussions do not suggest that they thought the market or capitalism was bad, *per se*. After all, theirs was the post-war generation that had through sacrifice and labor pulled Japanese society from poverty to affluence. But, they also recognized that in the reconfiguration of their politico-economic framework, they must reincorporate that which they had lost, namely, virtue. In short, they sought to recreate a 'virtuous capitalism' – one inspired by the past.

There was little further discussion about the reconciliation of these often conflicting ends. But, it was clear that the accent of discussions fell on this topic which, indeed, seemed a preoccuption for some participants. A similarly emotive debate arose when the talks focused on the more specific issue of competition. In terms of national cases, Europe's continental economies did not figure in their discussions. In what was tantamount to a rejection of neoliberalism, Ibuki turned to what he considered Japan's exemplars of alternate political economies, namely those under former President Ronald Reagan and Prime Minister Margaret Thatcher. Acknowledging that under strong leadership their nations' economies had grown, ultimately Ibuki deemed that the ideological tenets of how their market operated were unsuitable for Japan. He opined that the '1000, nay 1500 years of Japanese history had cultivated a sense of joint responsibility, family and a sense of unity of and sacrifice for the nation' (*Shingikai* number 4, 1999, p. 13). He accepted that though Japan's market needed deregulation, 'the principle of competition and the omnipotence of market economics for the survival of the fittist and mammonism leads to a spiritually desolate society' (*Shingikai* number 4, 1999, p. 13). Prime Minister Obuchi echoed these sentiments in his acknowledgement of the importance of market reform and his fears over the social problems from hypercompetition. Striking a middle ground, he urged reformers to find rules to ensure fair competition, a second chance for those who fail and a social security net to ensure that all enjoy a minimum standard of living. He exhorted those participating in *shingikai* meetings on economic reform that whatever shape the political economy may take, they must ensure that these criteria are maintained (*Shingikai* number 4, 1999, p. 13).

Although reform measures that were introduced did bring greater competition, there was little sign at the end of the decade that the economy would return to growth rates similar to the benchmark of developed Western nations. Reform legistation was passed – the need was too pressing to be ignored – but implementation, as we know, is another matter. Without political will and the acceptance of the Japanese people to accept the attendant pains, change was contained within the framework of a political economy that reflected existing values. Authors have argued for greater competition but the records show a strong fear that what was perceived as unbridled competition in the US and Britain would undermine the fabric of Japanese society. It is argued here that the reason why reform was less efficacious than one would expect is because the full implementation of market reform cut across the beliefs held by political decision makers and the Japanese people.

Implications for Japan today

With the announcement on 7 September 2008 that the two US government-supported firms *Fannie Mae* and *Freddie Mac* would be nationalized, the global financial crisis was brought squarely into the forefront of the business world. For Japan, this came at a time when its economy was beginning to show signs of recovery from the 1990s downturn and the LDP was in turmoil from its rapid succussion of prime ministers following the retirement of Prime Minister Koizumi in 2006. Although the in-house 'cleansing' of Japan's banks placed them in a comparatively healthy and less exposed position to weather the global storm, the economy as a whole was weak (Grimes 2009, p. 107). The stimulus measures that followed have helped prevent what would have been far worse. But, the expenditures have also rendered further market restructuring politically unviable until, at least, economic recovery is in swing. This prospect is increasingly difficult given Japan's tightening fiscal noose.

A legacy of Japan's post-war growth strategy reliant on US bound exports is the current tepid domestic demand. Although this asymmetric trade relationship is changing with Japan seeking to stimulate consumers' spending, declining real wages suggest that in the near future domestic demand will not be able to take up the slack. If the long-term forecast of 0.5–1% GDP growth is correct, then not only will government have to walk a tight-rope to be able to pay back its largesse but it will also have to find new ways of expanding economic output. Richard Katz argues that without fundamental restructuring of the domestic market, Japan cannot achieve strong sustained growth (Katz 2010). If growth is sought by freeing up the domestic market, a rise in unemployment would follow which potentially would be tolerable if new jobs were generated and government could afford the costs of dislocation and, at the same time, increase household income, support the aging population and pay back debt. This possibility is – at least for the moment – unrealistic. Under current economic conditions, firms will more likely continue to keep worker numbers above efficiency levels and fund construction firms that otherwise would be forced to fold. Here, business and government need each other – as does this nation as whole – for this 'catch-22' relationship is a key aspect of Japan's informal social safety-net (Murphy 2009). As long as gains from restructuring are less than the political backlash to change, the relationship will at least keep a foot in its past ways of the high growth period.

That said, the Japan at the outset of the lost decade and that of some 20 years later are different. In 1998, T.J. Pempel wrote that the 'socio-economic, institutional, and policy underpinnings of the old regime have shifted, and the change is irreversible... [but] no clear agenda commands comprehensive support' (Pempel 1998, p. 212). Three years later, Prime Minister Koizumi Junichrō came into power bringing hope for the seemingly moribund state. Being mediagenic and a consummate political tactician, he rose on a platform of reform assuring the electorate that Japan would be better for the attendant pains. Time will tell what his legacy will be. However, it is clear that following Koizumi's departure, neither the Liberal Democratic Party or the Democratic Party of Japan have demonstrated the ability to lead the nation through the painful change. Rather, the rapid succession of new prime ministers underscores the seeming absence of strong political leaders from which the parties can draw.

Part of the problem may be an issue of age. As the evidence here shows, there was reluctance among *shingikai* members whose values were formed during the high growth period – years of considerable personal sacrifice – to sweep them aside for something new. Attuned to this generational issue, a survey conducted in 2005 among 480 elected members of the House of Representative, the lower house of Japan's bicameral legislature, suggests that though attitudinal difference exist between generations, they are not radical. The authors point out that the 'younger cohorts may indicate an openness to neo-liberal policies … this result is not evidence that these younger generations have adopted such views to the same degree and extent as have leaders in Washington or London (Boyd and Samuels 2008, p. 48). On the basis of this assessment, regardless of how diverse public discourse may become, future politicians will follow a path of incremental change.

> However much the Japanese media associates the rise of right-wing nationalism and cultural conservatism in Japan with an angry and alienated youthful generation, this connection is not reflected in the distribution of preferences among Diet members. To the contrary this study finds that the distribution of preferences is far less extreme than many fear. Though democratic discourse remains active and vibrant in Japan, we find little evidence that either the midcareer generation or the youngest generation will stake out a radically new course for the nation. (Boyd and Samuels 2008, p. 51)

Takanaka Heizō, academic and reform czar under Prime Minister Koizumi, argues in his recent book *What happened to 'reform'? Is this the chance for the Democratic Party of Japan?*(Takanaka 2009) characterizes the nation today with the words 'hope' (kibō) and 'despair' (zetsubō). His central point is that while fundamentally the economy is strong (senzai teki ni tsuyoi), the impetus for reform has dangerously waned in the last years. Although there are numerous impediments, vested interests among others, which hinder change, the responsibility for driving the reform process, nonetheless, rests with politicians. The implication is that short of strong leadership a la Koizumi, it will be difficult for Japan to realize fundamental transformative change. He also suggests that part of the problem is that, despite its prolonged nature, the economic malaise has not been so bad as to galvanize public demand for change (Takanaka 2009, p. 4). This, in turn, raises the issue whether Japan really did experience a 'crisis' and what this term means. As Colin Hay argues:

> [A] crisis is not merely a property of a system, it is a lived experience; it is a politically mediated moment of decisive intervention and structural transformation. Moreover, it involves the active display of agency by actors or bodies which have some autonomy *at the level at which the crisis is identified*. What this in turn suggests is that the very identification of a moment of crisis is an integral aspect of the process of state transformation (Hay 1999, p. 323; emphasis in the original).

Thus, as an opportunity for transformative change, a crisis is not the point where the reading of economic indicators merely says so but the point when actors experience it as such. The distinction is important. The first assumes an automatic and direct causality link between economic conditions and human reaction; and the second argues that it is when stakeholders believe that the economy is in crisis that is it in crisis. As Blyth (2002) argues, a crisis occurs when stakeholders have run out of ideas on how to mend the economic problem so that they are prepared to accept a new ideational paradigm. In the case of the Great Depression, US government and big business found themselves at the edge of the road map, as it were, and, in turn, embraced Keynesian economics. In abandoning a laissez-faire approach to market intervention and the acceptance that it was good and appropriate for government to be interventionist, stakeholders embraced the new values that underpinned the New Deal.

In the case of Japan, however, on the cusp of the new millennium, after a decade of economic decline, reform, and much reflection on 'what next', Japanese political and corporate leaders still showed few signs of having found their way. A paradox arises: given the once vaunted coordinative capacity of Japan's economy and the pressing need for change, why did Japan not rise to the challenge this time? Vested interests and weak political will played its part, as authors have noted, but these factors do not bring us to the nub of the matter. They are, rather, indicators that answers lie elsewhere.

Conclusions

North's concept of a 'mental model' is key to understanding why reform initiatives during the lost decade fell short of what observers thought they should achieve. It is also critical in interpreting the trajectory of Japan's economy. As he hypothesized, we live in a non-ergodic world and institutions act as mechanisms by which we reduce uncertainty. As humanly conceived, they are also reflections of how we perceive the world should be. The institutions of a political economy are, in this sense, indeed constructs to organize the activities that lead to economic growth. And, by extension, their matrix is not only a macro level politico-economic framework but also a reflection of the values, or beliefs, of the policy makers. North is also very conscious of and, indeed, pointedly argues that key stakeholders implement policies that do not necessarily lead to economic growth either because their interests lie elsewhere or that they hold beliefs in how their political economy should operate, resulting in lesser growth.

Research on the government and business elites' response to the 1990s economic turmoil raises the question whether they really wanted to change. Recognizing the imperatives of the time, reform measures were implemented and have shaped how the market operates. But, as authors note, there was a lack of political will. The debates of key policy makers in 1999, after a decade of economic turmoil, show that they continued to hold on to values and beliefs of a political economy that resembled that of the high growth period. Indeed, in defence of these beliefs, speakers reached for examples of what they considered to be hypercompetition and invoked stories of Japan's past to buttress their positions.

The point to be made is not that the values of Japan's social capitalist system are wrong but that, if policy makers wish to hold on to this model of its political economy, they must find within this framework a solution that squares its particular circle of conflicting problems and, at the same time, achieve sustainable growth. Whatever the solution, Japan will need to accept the attendant pains which, in the foreseeable future is politically unrealistic. Expressed differently, at this juncture in Japan's history, the opportunity exists to reconceptualize its political economy. This is not merely a technical matter of reform measures but, fundamentally, about how political and market related institutions enmesh to produce growth and share the gains. To achieve this, policy makers need to decide what values they wish to hold on to and what ones to let go of in order to forge a political economy for tomorrow.

Japan is a 'sleeping giant'. Among its manifold assets most important is the dynamism and discipline of its people. As much as this was true of Japan as it emerged from the ashes of World War II, it remains true today. The politico-economic framework of the 'economic miracle' harnessed the national desire for 'catch up'. The attendant sacrifice was accepted as it resulted in economic growth and that, critically, the sharing of the gains were considered by and large fair. A deal was struck. This deal was underpinned by shared beliefs and values that governed that distribution of wealth. Similarly, Japan today must come upon a new way of aligning the strength of its people with a new politico-economic system, one that is rooted in the past but also one that carries it into the future.

Former Chairman of *Toyoda* Motor Corporation (1992–1999) and Chairman of Japan Business Federation (1994–1998), or *Keidanren*, Toyoda Shoichiro struck a similar cord in his popular book *The Creation of a Japan with Charm* (Toyoda 1996). Writing during the lost decade, he lamented the current state of affairs and outlined, as he saw it, the multifaceted problem that confronted Japan. The economic, political and social framework which had served Japan well in its period of catch-up now required revamping from the ground up. And, importantly, this framework needed to be located within a new a 'vision' for the nation – one, he suggested, that had not yet been found (Toyoda 1996, p. 2). Still, 15 years later, one is pressed to find that 'vision'.

Notes

1. For an overview of institutional theory in political science see Peters (2005) and for the field of political economy consult Weingast and Wittman (2006).
2. The list included the following bills:

   - Partial Revision of the Cabinet Law (Naikaku Hō no Ichibu wo Kaisei Hōritsuan)
   - Partial Revision of the National Administrative Law (Kokka Gyōsei Soshikihō no Ichibu wo Kaisei Suru Hōritsuan)
   - Establishment of the Cabinet Office (Naikakufu Setchhi Hōan)
   - Local Government Reform (Chūōshōfutō Kaiaku no tame no Kuni no Gyōsei Soshiki Kankei Hōritsu no Setsubitō ni kan suru Hōritsuan)

Also, bills were submitted that deal with or the creation of the following ministries or agencies:

   - Ministry of Internal Affairs and Communication (Sōmushō Setchi Hōan)
   - Postal Services Agency (Yūsei Jigyōfu Setchi Hōan)
   - Ministry of Justice (Hōmushō Setchi Hōan)
   - Ministry of Foreign Affairs (Gaimushō Setchi Hōan)
   - Ministry of Finance (Zaimushō Setchi Hōan)
   - Ministry of Education, Sports, Science and Technology (Bunbu Kagakushō Setchi Hōan)
   - Ministry of Health, Labor and Welfare (Kōsei Rōdōshō Setchi Hōan)
   - Ministry of Agriculture, Forestry and Fisheries (Nōrin Suisanshō Setchi Hōan)
   - Ministry of Economy, Trade and Industry (Keizai Sangyōshō Setchi Hōan)
   - Ministry of Land, Infrastructure, Transport and Tourism (Kokudō Kōtsūshō Setchi Hōan)
   - Ministry of Environment (Kankyōshō Setchi Hōan)
   - Independent Administrative Cooperative Body (Dokuritsu Gyōsei Hōjin Tsūsoku Hōan)
3. For further details on post-1945 *shingikai*, see Schwartz (1998).

References

Amyx, J.A., 2004. *Japan's financial crisis: institutional rigidity and reluctant change*. Princeton University Press.

Archer, M., 1995. *Realist social theory: the morphogenetic approach*. Cambridge University Press.

Bhaskar, R., 1989. *The possibility of naturalism: a philosophic critique of the contemporary human sciences*. 2nd ed. Brighton: Harvester.

Blyth, M., 2002. *Great transformations: economic ideas and institutional change in the twentieth century*. New York: Cambridge University Press.

Boyd, J.P. and Samuels, R., 2008. Prosperity's children: generational change and Japan's future leadership. *Asia policy*, 6 (July), 15–51.

Denzau, A.T. and North, D.C., 1994. Shared mental models: ideologies and institutions. *Kyklos*, 47, 3–31.

DiMaggio, P., 1997. Culture and cognition. *Annual review of sociology*, 23, 263–287.

Fletcher, W.M., forthcoming. Dreams of economic transformation and the reality of economic crisis: Keidanran in the era of the 'bubble' and the 'lost decade'. *Asia Pacific business review*.

Giddens, A., 1984. *The constitution of society: outline of the theory of structuration*. Cambridge: Polity Press.

Greenwood, R. *et al.*, eds, 2008. *The SAGE handbook of organizational institutionalism*. London: SAGE Publications.

Grimes, W.W., 2009. Japan, the global financial crisis, and the stability of East Asia. *In*: A.J. Tellis, A. Marble and T. Tanner eds. *Strategic Asia 2009–2010: economic meltdown and geopolitical stability*. Washington: The National Bureau of Asian Research, 105–129.

Hay, C., 1999. Crisis and the structural transformation of the state: interrogating the process of change. *British journal of politics and international relations*, 1 (3), 317–344.

Hirschmeier, J., 1964. *The origins of entrepreneurship in Meiji Japan*. 2nd ed. Cambridge, MA: Harvard University Press.

Hodgson, G.M., 2004. *The evolution of institutional economics: agency, structure and Darwinism in American institutionalism*. London: Routledge.

Hodgson, G.M. and Knudsen, T., 2010. *Darwin's conjecture: the search for general principles of social and economic evolution*. London: University of Chicago Press.

Hook, G.D., ed., 2011. *Decoding boundaries in contemporary Japan: the Koizumi administration and beyond*. London: Routledge.

Ihori, T., 2003. Analysis of the phenomenon of postponement (Sakiokuri Genshō). *In*: M. Muramatsu and M. Okuno, eds. *Research on the development of the bubble: the depression after the collapse and the handling of bad loans*. [Seisei Baberu no Kenkyū: Hōkai no Fukyō to Fuyō Saiken Shori]. Vol 2. 5th ed. Tokyo: Tōyō Keizai Shinpōsha, 51–82.

Ito, T. and Patrick, H., 2005. Problems and prescriptions for the Japanese economy: an overview. *In*: T. Ito, H. Patrick and D. Weinstein, eds. *Reviving Japan's economy: problems and prescriptions*. Cambridge, MA: MIT Press, 1–37.

Johnson, C., 1982. *MITI and the Japanese miracle: the growth of industrial policy, 1925–1975*. Stanford University Press.

Katz, R., 1998. *Japan the system that soured: the rise and fall of the economic miracle*. Armonk, NY: M.E. Sharpe.

Katz, R., 2010. Japan's fake economic reforms: more creative destruction. *Foreign policy*, 8 January. Available from: http://www.foreignpolicy.com/studys/2010/01/08/japans_economic_reforms [Accessed 27 December 2010].

Kumei, I., 2003. *Public opinion and politics: public capital investment* [Kōteki tōshi tōnyū wo meguru seiron to seiji]. *In*: M. Muramatsu and M. Okuno eds. *Research on the development of the bubble: the depression after the collapse and the handling of bad loans*. [Seisei Baberu no Kenkyū: Hōkai no Fukyō to Fuyō Saiken Shori]. Vol 2. 5th ed. Tokyo: Tōyō Keizai Shinpōsha, 109–156.

Lincoln, E.J., 2001. *Arthritic Japan: the slow pace of economic growth*. Washington, DC: Brookings Institution Press.

Lincoln, J.R. and Gerlach, M.L., 2004. *Japan's network economy: structure persistence and change*. Cambridge University Press.

Masao, M., 1963. *In*: I. Morris, eds. *Thought and behaviour in modern Japanese politics*. New York: Oxford University Press.

Murphy, R.T., 2009. The financial crisis and the tectonic shifts in the US–Japan Relationship. *The Asia-Pacific journal: Japan focus*, 32 (2) Available from: http://japanfocus.org/-R_Taggart-Murphy/3200 [Accessed 27 December 2010].

North, D.C., 1990. *Institutions, institutional change, and economic performance*. New York: Cambridge University Press.

North, D.C., 1994. Economic performance through time. *American economic review*, 84 (3), 359–368.

North, D.C., 2005. *Understanding the process of economic change*. Princeton University Press.

North, D.C. and Thomas, R.P., 1973. *The rise of the western world: a new economic history*. New York: Cambridge University Press.

Okimoto, D., 1989. *Between MITI and the market: Japanese industrial policy for high technology*. Stanford University Press.

Pempel, T.J., 1998. *Regime shift: comparative dynamics of the Japanese political economy*. Cornell University Press.

Peters, B.G., 2005. *Institutional theory in political science: the 'new institutionalism'*. 2nd ed. London: Continuum.

Rosenbluth, F.M. and Thies, M.F., 2010. *Japan transformed: political change and economic restructuring*. Princeton University Press.

Schaede, U., 2008. *Choose and focus: Japanese business strategies for the 21st century*. Ithaca, NY: Cornell University Press.

Schaede, U., forthcoming. The strategic inflection point in Japanese business. *Asia Pacific business review*.

Schwartz, F.J., 1998. *Advice and consent: the politics of consultation in Japan*. Cambridge University Press.

Shingikai Records, 1999. Number 3 (Dai 3 Gō), 19 May.

Shingikai Records, 1999. Number 4 (Dai 4 Gō), 25 May.

Takanaka, H., 2009. *What happened to 'reform'? Is this the chance for the Democratic Party of Japan?*. ['Kaikaku' wa doko ei itta? Minshūtō ni chansu wa aru ka?]. Tokyo: Toyo Keizai Shinpo Sha.

Thelen, K., 2004. *How institutions evolve: the political economy of skills in Germany, Britain, the United States, and Japan*. Cambridge University Press.

Tokyo Daigaku Shakai Kagaku Kenkūjo, ed, 2005. *Beyond the lost 10 years*. [Ushinawareta 10 Nen wo Koete]. Vols 1 and 2. Tokyo: Tokyo Daigaku Shuppankai.

Toyoda, S., 1996. *The creation of a Japan with charm*. ['Miryoku aru Nihon' no Sōzō]. Tokyo: Toyo Keizai Shinpo Sha.

Vogel, S.K., 2006. *Japan remodeled: how government and industry are reforming Japanese capitalism*. Ithaca, NY: Cornell University Press.

Warner, M., 2011. Commentary: whither Japan? Economy, management and society. *Asia Pacific business review*, 17 (1), 1–5.

Weingast, B.R. and Wittman, D.A., 2006. *The Oxford handbook of political economy*. Oxford University Press.

Family and non-family business resilience in an economic downturn

Bruno Amann[a] and Jacques Jaussaud[b]

[a]Université de Toulouse, Université Paul Sabatier Toulouse 3, France; [b]Université de Pau et des Pays de l'Adour, France

As widely documented in academic literature, family businesses perform better and enjoy a sounder financial structure than non-family businesses, a trend that applies to Japan as well, which is the context of this paper. Therefore, conventional wisdom suggests that family businesses should recover better or more easily from an economic downturn and persist in their stronger performance. This study tests this hypothesis, especially in reference to the current global economic crisis, by drawing lessons from the Asian crisis of 1997, for which relevant data are available. The study pertains specifically to the case of Japanese family and non-family companies. The empirical investigation uses a matched pair methodology, which allows for strong controls of size and industry variables. The sample consists of 98 carefully selected pairs (one family and one non-family) of firms that are of the same size and from the same industry. According to the results, family businesses achieve stronger resilience both during and after an economic crisis, compared with non-family businesses. They resist the downturn better, recover faster, and continue exhibiting higher performance and stronger financial structures over time.

Introduction

Research on family businesses suggests that they perform better and enjoy a sounder financial structure than do non-family businesses. Recent investigations in Japan confirm this conclusion (Kurashina 2003, Allouche *et al.* 2008). The strong performance of family businesses aligns with several theoretical perspectives, which imply that family businesses should recover better in the face of an economic downturn. In particular, the theory regarding the concept of organizational resilience suggests that a resilient firm can take situation-specific, robust and transformative actions when confronted with unexpected and powerful events, such as economic recessions (Lengnick-Hall and Beck 2009).

Japan is of particular interest in this setting because of its long tradition of family businesses, beginning even before the country opened its borders to the rest of the world at the end of the nineteenth century. During the feudal *Tokugawa* period (1603–1868), Japanese firms were owned entirely by families or, perhaps more properly, by clans (Morck and Nakamura 2007). Following the *Meiji* Restoration of 1868, rapid industrialization in Japan promoted the development of *Zaibatsu*, defined as pyramidal groups controlled by families, such as the Mitsui family's control over the Mitsubishi group. During the first decades of the twentieth century, prior to World War II, the Japanese economy remained structured around such *Zaibatsu*.

However, by the second half of the twentieth century, the dominant position of family businesses in Japan began to falter. First, allied forces dismantled *Zaibatsu*, and when *Keiretsu* emerged in the 1950s and 1960s as a new form of inter-firm cooperation, companies had lost the family dimension (Miyashita and Russell 1994). In addition, according to Morikawa (1996) and Morck and Yeung (2003), Japanese enterprise ownership has undergone dramatic changes in recent decades, mainly at the expense of family businesses.

This history raises some key questions for the modern day (see Allouche *et al.* 2008): Do family businesses remain a significant force in the Japanese economy? How do they perform and financially structure themselves compared with non-family businesses? Are they comparable to parallel firms in Western countries?

A study by Kurashina (2003) found that 42.68%, or 1074, of Japanese listed companies (1st sector) in 2003 were family businesses. Saito (2008) gives the same percentage. Another study by the *Nihon Keizai Shimbun* (2006), shows that, between 29 December 1989 and 15 January 2003, 99 enterprises increased capitalization, and of the top 10 firms, eight were family businesses. In most countries in the world, family businesses account for a major share of business, employ a significant portion of total employees and record significant amounts of turnover, added value, investments, and accumulated capital (Allouche *et al.* 2008). Beyond that, the question of being a significant force in an economy is closely related to the comparative performance of family businesses vs. non-family businesses. In the case of Japan, Allouche *et al.* (2008) confirm that family businesses in Japan achieve better performance than non-family businesses, for both profitability and financial structures. Empirical results from Saito (2008) indicate that family businesses slightly outperform non-family businesses in Japan, but the family business premium mainly results from the active founders. After the retirement of the founders, the results become mixed (Saito 2008). Even if some factors can mitigate the family business premium (founders for Saito 2008, importance of family control for Allouche *et al.* 2008) globally speaking, despite the huge and radical changes in the Japanese economy, family businesses in Japan, as in Western economies, globally outperform non-family businesses.

Furthermore, the evolution of the Japanese economy and its effects on family businesses may provide an insight into global economies. For example, without data regarding the current global economic crisis, we cannot test the effects of the modern recession. Instead, this study compares the performance of family and non-family businesses during and after the 1997 Asian financial crisis. The crisis caused the financial and real estate bubbles to burst, leaving the ailing Japanese economy unable to recover fully until the 1990s, this period became known as Japan's 'lost decade'. By 2003 the Japanese economy had fully recovered. Therefore, this context provides a long-range view of the effects of an economic crisis on family and non-family businesses. In Japan, it implies that family businesses are particularly resilient, both during and after the crisis.

In the next section, we provide an overview of broadly accepted interpretations of why family businesses tend to enjoy better performance and stronger financial structures than do non-family businesses. We also extend these interpretations to recovery situations during and after economic downturns, such as the Asian financial crisis of 1997. Methodology and data collection are then described, we conclude with test results and a discussion of the pertinent findings.

Background and hypothesis

As in any emerging field of research, some fundamental questions, both theoretical and practical, remain unsolved for family business studies. For example, how can we define a family business precisely, and to what extent do family businesses differ from non-family businesses? For this study, we apply the concept of organizational resilience to family businesses, using the context of the 1997 Asian crisis to structure our empirical investigation.

Family business and performance

Defining family business

Academic literature includes family business definitions based on both single and multiple criteria. The former focuses on ownership or control through management; the latter feature both these dimensions (Rosenblatt *et al.* 1985, Handler 1989). For example, Miller and Le Breton-Miller (2003, p. 127) define a family business as 'one in which a family has enough ownership to determine the composition of the board, where the CEO and at least one other executive is a family member, and where the intent is to pass the firm on to the next generation'.

Regarding the availability of several definitions, without a consensus on any one in particular, Villalonga and Amit (2004) note that many include three key dimensions:

- A significant part of the capital is held by one or several families.
- Family members retain significant control over the company through the distribution of capital among non-family shareholders and voting rights, with possible statutory or legal restrictions.
- Family members hold top management positions.

For this study, in line with prior literature (Kurashina 2003, Villalonga and Amit 2004, Alllouche *et al.* 2008), we define a family business as one in which family members hold top management positions, such as chief executive officer, or sit on the board of directors, and are among the main shareholders.

Varied interpretations of performance

Most empirical investigations find better performance among family businesses compared with non-family businesses, largely according to their financial performance (Monsen *et al.* 1968, Monsen 1969, Charreaux 1991, Gallo and Vilaseca 1996), though some investigations also consider non-financial performance dimensions such as growth. Accordingly the better performance by family businesses may be interpreted in several ways.

One explanation relies on agency theory, following Berle and Means (1932) and Galbraith (1967). According to this perspective, family businesses perform better because they reduce agency costs by minimizing the separation between ownership and management. The objectives of owners and managers are similar in family businesses, which allows for less control over managers (Fama and Jensen 1983).

However, this approach suffers some limits (Arrègle *et al.* 2004). For example, family businesses may suffer other costs, such as a premium needed to balance the risk for minority investors and prevent owners from exploiting the business only for their own profit (Shleifer and Vishny 1997; La Porta *et al.* 1999). Scholars also have identified several additional agency costs (Barclay and Holderness 1989, Kets de Vries 1993, Schulze *et al.* 2001, 2003, McConaughy *et al.* 2001, Burkart *et al.* 2003, Morck 2003, Morck and Yeung 2003, Chrisman *et al.* 2005). Therefore, we cannot exclusively assert that agency costs are lower or higher for family businesses compared with non-family businesses. Rather, agency costs vary and must be specified precisely in each case (Morck and Yeung 2003). Carney (2005) highlights three propensities of a family-based governance system that could mitigate agency costs: parsimony (capital deployed sparingly and used intensively), personalism (unification of ownership and control in the owner) and particularism (families can employ decision criteria other than those based on pure economic rationality).

Another explanation takes the perspective of stewardship theory and argues that family members act as stewards because they strongly identify with the firm (Davis *et al.* 1997). According to Miller and Le Breton-Miller (2009), stewardship can take three forms. First, stewardship over continuity means that family members want to ensure the longevity of the company and therefore invest to create conditions for the long-lasting benefit of all family members. Second, stewardship over employees implies that family businesses attempt to nurture the workforce through motivation and training, as well as by transmitting a set of constructive values to employees. Third, stewardship over customers means that family businesses strengthen their connections with customers to sustain their prosperity and survival.

The better performance of family businesses results from the long-term orientation of family shareholders. This argument stems from Porter (1986), although he underlines that pressure from financial markets leads to short-term management by listed companies. Pressures from financial markets are less for family business, which reduces 'managerial myopia' (Stein 1988, 1989). Perhaps family businesses dominate as a form of organization because family managers have longer prospects than managers in non-family companies (Harvey 1999).

Additional interpretations rely on a neo-institutional perspective, in which the enterprise is a social construction. Therefore, success draws on the set of values that family members share, such as trust (Fukuyama 1995, Chami 1999) and altruism (Van den Berghe and Carchon 2003). Finally, family businesses might achieve increased efficiency through their intricate connections, according to the concept of 'familiness'[1] (Habbershon and Williams 1999). Such connections can provide additional resources and competencies, which eventually should strengthen the firm's potential competitive advantage (Habbershon and Williams 1999, Habbershon *et al.* 2003, Arrègle *et al.* 2004, Chrisman *et al.* 2005).

Financial structure

Research also emphasises differences in the financial structure between family and non-family businesses, such that the former tend to take more cautious attitudes toward debt. The main challenge for family businesses is to promote growth without challenging the permanence of family control (Goffee 1996, Abdellatif *et al.* 2010). This approach is consistent with the proposed longer-term perspectives adopted by family businesses, according to stewardship theory.

A contingency-based view also suggests the possibility of varied risk preferences (Gomez-Mejia *et al.* 2007, Abdellatif *et al.* 2010). For example, socio-emotional wealth may be a key goal for family businesses, which would be more likely to perpetuate the owner's direct control over the firm's affairs (Gomez-Mejia *et al.* 2007). Although owners want to preserve their socio-emotional wealth and diversification, a strategic choice such as going international, implies a loss of socio-emotional wealth therefore family owners are likely to avoid that strategic choice, even if it would confer some risk protection to the company (Gomez-Mejia *et al.* 2010). Finally, family businesses in general are developed and managed for the benefit of current and future generations, therefore, their strategic decisions are not limited to purely economic considerations.

Organizational resilience and family businesses

The question of organizational resilience involves the relationship between crisis planning and effective adaptive behaviours during a crisis.

Definition

The concept of organizational resilience is a generalization of the concept of resilience from psychology. It refers to a fundamental quality in people, groups, organizations or systems to respond to a significant change that disrupts the expected pattern of events without engaging in an extended period of regressive behaviour (Horne and Orr 1998). Although organizational research lacks a clear consensus about its meaning, resilience captures the firm's ability to take situation-specific, robust and transformative actions when it confronts unexpected and powerful events that have the potential to jeopardize its long-term survival (Lengnick-Hall and Beck 2009).

Coutu (2002) highlights three characteristics of resilient organizations:

(1) Facing down reality. These organizations are pragmatic, even optimistic, as long as their optimism does not distort their sense of reality.
(2) The search for meaning, or a propensity to make meaning of terrible times.
(3) Ritualized ingenuity, which is the ability to suffice using whatever is at hand. Coutu clearly links this characteristic to the French term 'bricolage'. (This concept comes from the French anthropologist Claude Levi-Strauss and relates closely to the concept of resilience.) The term, in its modern sense, means a form of inventiveness or the ability to improvise a solution to a problem without proper or obvious tools or materials.

Bridge to family business

The various interpretations of the stronger performance of family businesses clearly link to the resilient organizations characteristics (Coutu 2002). Because the intrinsic characteristics of family businesses are quite similar to the features that mark resilient organizations, we expect family businesses to be more resilient than other organizational forms, as Table 1 shows. From these interpretations, we derive three hypotheses:

H1: Family businesses resist economic downturns better than non-family businesses.
H2: In economic downturns, family businesses are better able to mobilize their resources than non-family businesses.

Table 1.   Resilient and family business characteristics.

Argument #	Resilient organizations' characteristics	Family businesses' characteristics
1	Facing down reality	- Long-term orientation (Stein 1988, 1989, Miller 2005) - Familiness (Habbershon and Williams 1999, Chrisman *et al.* 2003)
2	The search for meaning	- Familiness (Habbershon and Williams 1999, Chrisman *et al.* 2003) - Stewardship theory (Davis *et al.*, 1997, Miller *et al.* 2006, 2009 - Social capital (Arregle *et al.* 2007)
3	Ritualised ingenuity	- Parsimony - Personalism - Particularism (Carney 2005) - Socio-emotional wealth (Gomez-Mejia *et al.* 2010)

H3: In economic downturns, family businesses have stronger financial structures than non-family businesses.

Resilience and economic downturns

To study the specific impact of an economic downturn on family and non-family businesses, we split the Asian crisis into three significant periods:

- 1998, the worst year in economic terms. This year provides a basis for investigating the behaviour of firms in an economic downturn and thereby determining if family businesses offer a greater resistance to the crisis.
- 2003, the year of confirmed recovery in Japan. With this timing, we study the behaviour of companies at the end of the economic downturn and thus determine if family businesses have a greater ability to exit the crisis.
- 2007, or a few years after the confirmation of the recovery. This period enables us to investigate the behaviour of companies and whether family businesses perform better, even after an economic downturn.

To test our three hypotheses accurately, we translate them into sub-hypotheses related to each period, 1998, 2003 and 2007, as follows:

H1: Family businesses resist economic downturns better than non-family businesses.

H1a: During an economic downturn, family businesses enjoy better financial performance than non-family businesses.

H1b: After an economic downturn, family businesses recover better in terms of financial performance than non-family businesses.

H1c: After recovery from an economic downturn, family businesses keep their advantages in term of financial performance over non-family businesses.

H2: In economic downturns, family businesses are better able to mobilize their resources than non-family businesses.

H2a: During an economic downturn, family businesses better mobilize their resources than non-family businesses.

H2b: Family businesses mobilize their resources better than non-family businesses at the end of an economic downturn.

H2c: Family businesses mobilize their resources better than non-family businesses after the end of an economic downturn.

H3. In economic downturns, family businesses have stronger financial structures than non-family businesses.

H3a: During an economic downturn, family businesses have stronger financial structures than non-family businesses.

H3b: Family businesses have stronger financial structures than non-family businesses at the end of an economic downturn.

H3c: Family businesses have stronger financial structures than non-family businesses after the end of an economic downturn.

The conceptual model in Figure 1 displays this set of hypotheses.

The 1997 Asian crisis

The Asian currency crisis in 1997 affected not only Asia but the whole world until 1998. It began in Thailand and other South-East Asian countries (e.g. Indonesia, Malaysia) and

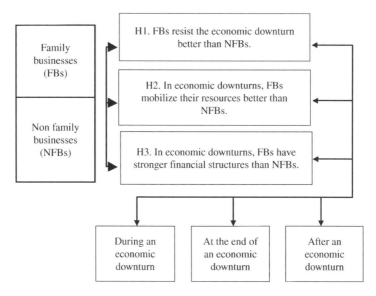

Figure 1.   Conceptual model.

quickly spread to Korea as a financial and currency crisis (Stiglitz 2003). The gross domestic product (GDP) of most countries decreased in 1998, including those of the United States (− 0.4%), the European Union (− 0.4%), and elsewhere (*Japan Economic Almanac 1999*). Japan was especially affected, compared to most other industrialized nations, with a − 1.3% decrease in its 1998 GDP. As a consequence, this setting is particularly relevant for comparing how Japanese family and non-family businesses recovered from the downturn.

It took several years for many Asian countries to recover, mostly under the aegis of the international monetary fund (IMF) (cf. Malaysia, which did not accept the IMF's conditions for support). As Table 2 shows, the Japanese economy enjoyed significant growth again as soon as 2000, but it then faced difficulties in 2001 and 2002. Only after 2003 was the economy officially recovered.

Although it is beyond the scope of this paper to analyze the Asian crisis mechanisms, it is important to recognize that in Japan, the crisis led to a massive banking and financial sector rescue; this sector would not have been able to recover on its own from the burden of bad loans from the beginning of the 1990s. Japanese authorities encouraged the main financial institutions to merge and take over the weaker institutions, although some went bankrupt. The whole process took several years and ended in 2005 with the merger of Tokyo Mitsubishi Bank and the UFJ group. This reorganization process in the financial industry is generally regarded as just one more difficulty that Japanese enterprises must confront in order to receive funds from banks and other financial institutions.

Table 2.   GDP growth rate of Japan (in real terms), by civil year.

Year	1996	1997	1998	1999	2000	2001
GDP	3.9%	0.8%	− 1.3%	0.1%	2.8%	0.2%
Year	2002	2003	2004	2005	2006	2007
GDP	− 0.3%	1.4%	2.7%	1.9%	2.2%	

Source: Keizai Koho Center (1999, 2004, 2006, 2008).

Methodology and data

Matched pair methodology

When comparing the performance and financial structures of family and non-family businesses, even industry by industry (Kurashina 2003), external sources of influence might affect them differently, such as historical reasons. In this case, it is difficult to ensure that the true reason for performance differences is related to the family or non-family nature of the business. A matched pair methodology, as applied by Allouche and Amann (1998, 2000) to the French case and Allouche *et al.* (2008) and Abdellatif *et al.* (2010) to the Japanese case, addresses this question; we use it for this contribution as well.

The idea behind our application of the approach is to compare systematically family and non-family businesses with the same profiles, in the same industry, and of nearly the same size. We first set up pairs of business (one family business, one non-family business) in the same industry and of approximately the same size (in terms of sales or number of employees). This approach helps mitigate two key reasons for performance and financial structure variance and thereby sheds more light on the influence of family control on both performance and financial structure.

To identify the firms' industries, we use the four-digit standard industrial classification (SIC). Using this widely adopted classification ensures that companies in each pair conduct similar activities. Our measures of the size of the business reflect sales and number of employees. Two companies in the same industry are regarded as similar in size if their sales or number of employees are within 20% of each other.

Assuming a sufficient number of such pairs of family and non-family businesses, we can compare their performance, financial structure, and other indicators, having controlled for size and industry. We therefore compute the following indicators: return on assets (ROA), return on equity (ROE), return on investments (ROI), long-term debt to total capital, cash to current assets and so on. For each indicator, we compute the difference between family and non-family businesses as averages. Then for each indicator, we test (t-test, paired sample) whether the difference is significant at a 5% threshold; if it is not, we also consider whether it is significant at a 10% threshold. We assessed these comparisons in all three years under investigation, 1998, 2003 and 2007.

Data

We collected data from two sources, the well-known *Worldscope* database (1998, 2003, 2007) for financial indicators and the list of family and non-family businesses in Japan from Kurashina (2003). To identify family and non-family businesses, Kurashina (2003) used various published materials, including directories, and relied on the help of several financial institutions, such as brokerage firms and others, as well as the companies themselves.

Worldscope (2003) provides a wide range of financial and non-financial data, including SIC codes, for 3194 Japanese companies, which constitute almost all of those listed. Cross-referencing the data from *Worldscope* and Kurashina (2003) to build the sample of pairs, represented a massive undertaking, so we limited our investigation to first-section firms on the Tokyo Stock Exchange. From the 1638 companies listed in the first section in 2003, we excluded purely financial firms and companies with too many missing values in *Worldscope*. Therefore, our sample includes 1271 companies, 491 of which were family businesses. In most cases (416, or 84.72%), family control encompassed both capital (family members are among the largest shareholders) and management (family members hold influential positions, such as CEO).

On the basis of this sample (1271 companies, 416 family businesses), we built our pairs for companies for which we had data in *Worldscope* for all three years (1998, 2003 and 2007). We thus had a sample of 98 pairs of companies that we investigated over three years. Using a consistent sample across all three years ensured that we compare the ability of specific family and non-family-businesses to recover.

Major findings

Hypothesis 1: even in a downturn, family businesses achieve better performance

We base H1 on extant literature and divide our analysis into periods of time, that is, during the crisis, immediately after the downturn, and subsequently. In all cases, we predict that family businesses perform better than non-family businesses.

With regard to our performance metrics (i.e. ROA, ROE, ROI and net income indicators), the results in Table 3 indicate that in 1998, family businesses enjoyed greater profitability than non-family businesses. However, only ROI is significantly different at a 5% threshold; at 10% (a threshold considered in some settings and that requires great care) ROE and net income are also significantly different between family and non-family businesses, and the former has the advantage. Therefore, we cautiously regard H1a as validated.

In 2003, the contrasts grow more evident. The differences are greater than they were in 1998 and more often significant at the 5% threshold. The ROA and ROI, as well as the pretax margin, indicate that family businesses perform significantly better; at the threshold of 10%, the ROE is also significant. We thus consider H2b validated.

Family businesses recover better than non-family businesses, then they retain that advantage. The reason, as previously stated, may involve family businesses' greater investments and ability to mobilize their resources to recover, as tested with H2. Alternatively, the advantage may reflect the links between the characteristics of resilient organizations and those of family businesses.

H2: Even in a downturn, family businesses can mobilize their resources

We again consider our hypothesis across three different periods: during the downturn (1998, H2a), during the recovery period (2003, H2b), and after recovery (2007, H2c).

According to the data in Table 5, in 1998, family businesses invested more than non-family businesses, which shows the family businesses' apparent willingness to prepare for the future, even in an adverse situation. Two ratios that reflect funds used to acquire fixed assets, namely, the capital expenditure-to-fixed assets and capital expenditures-to-total assets ratios, are significant at the 5% level and indicate the greater determination of family businesses.

The ability of family businesses to mobilize their resources both during an economic downturn and after (H2) may explain their stronger performance (H1) and their ability to recover. The financial structures of both kinds of businesses also may play a role.

H3: Even in a downturn, family businesses have stronger financial structures

To confirm our claim that during the downturn, the recovery process, and thereafter, family businesses maintain stronger financial structures than do non-family businesses, we again test three sub-hypotheses, distinguished by the period to which they refer. Table 7 provides the results related to H3a and H3b. Table 8 contains the comparison pertinent to H3c.

Table 3. Profitability of family and non-family businesses in an economic downturn.

Indicators	1998						2003					
		Average						Average				
	Number of pairs	Non Family Businesses	Family Businesses	Différence	Signification	% of pairs in favor of family businesses	Number of pairs	Non Family Businesses	Family Businesses	Différence	Signification	% of pairs in favor of family businesses
Return on Assets	91	0.869	1.060	0.191	0.521	56.94%	93	1.878	3.440	1.562	0.002	61.29%
Return on Equity	94	0.881	3.067	2.185	0.073	60.81%	95	3.147	6.642	3.495	0.057	47.36%
Return on Invested capital	95	0.906	1.788	0.881	0.049	55.40%	95	3.029	5.136	2.107	0.002	60.02%
Net income	95	1844.57	5104.30	3259.73	0.06	0.60	95.00	4389.79	5396.06	1006.27	0.269	46.31%
Pretax margin	94	2.142	2.262	0.120	0.974	53.33%	94	3.505	6.228	2.723	0.007	58.51%

Table 4. Profitability of family and non-family businesses after economic downturn.

Indicators	2003						2007					
	Number of pairs	Average		Différence	Signification	% of pairs in favor of family businesses	Number of pairs	Average		Différence	Signification	% of pairs in favor of family businesses
		Non Family Businesses	Family Businesses					Non Family Businesses	Family Businesses			
Return on Assets	93	1.878	3.440	1.562	0.002	61.29%	89	3.344	4.337	0.994	0.059	60.60%
Return on Equity	95	3.147	6.642	3.495	0.057	47.36	89	5.868	7.728	1.859	0.08	58.81%
Return on Equity	95	3.029	5.136	2.107	0.002	60.02%	88	4.418	5.716	1.298	0.047	67.04%
Net income	95	4389.79	5396.06	1006.27	0.269	46.31%	87	10557.43	15951.20	5393.77	0.475	48.27%
Pre tax margin	94	3.505	6.228	2.723	0.007	58.51%	94	4.352	8.295	3.943	0.001	63.83%

Table 5. Mobilization of resources in an economic downturn.

Indicators	1998						2003					
	Number of pairs	Average		Différence	Signification	% of pairs in favor of family businesses	Number of pairs	Average		Différence	Signification	% of pairs in favor of family businesses
		Non Family Businesses	Family Businesses					Non Family Businesses	Family Businesses			
Capital Expenditures / fixed Assets	92	3.327	5.272	1.945	0.003	59.78%	94	3.858	6.397	2.539	0.002	63.44%
Capital Expenditures / sales	94	2.196	2.707	0.511	0.237	50.71%	94	2.279	3.704	1.425	0	64.51%
Capital Expenditures / Total Assets	96	1.736	3.590	1.854	0.035	58.60%	94	2.397	3.248	0.541	0.002	56.38%
Reinvestment rate per share	92	0.052	0.970	0.919	0.241	53.35%	92	1.907	5.211	3.304	0.003	56.52%
Retained Earnings PctEquity	Shortage of data						95	37.172	51.878	14.706	0.007	63.15%
Research&dev to sales	Shortage of data						65	1.238	2.254	1.017	0.002	48.38%
Cash/current assets	94	27.890	34.202	6.312	0.004	62.16%	92	24.205	35.523	11.318	0.001	56.69%
Cost of goods/ sales	70	70.610	70.581	−0.029	0.988	56.12%	92	73.348	65.277	−8.071	0.001	76.08%
Foreign assets/ tot Assets	57	3.581	7.328	3.747	0.007	63.42%	68	8.312	11.547	3.235	0.034	55.88%
Foreign Sales/tot Sales	65	6.604	10.354	3.750	0.025	61.35%	72	10.799	15.266	4.467	0.033	55.56%

Table 6. Mobilization of resources after an economic downturn.

Indicators	2003						2007					
	Number of pairs	Average		Différence	Signification	% of pairs in favor of family businesses	Number of pairs	Average		Différence	Signification	% of pairs in favor of family businesses
		Non Family Businesses	Family Businesses					Non Family Businesses	Family Businesses			
Capital Expenditures / fixed Assets	94	3.858	6.397	2.539	0.002	63.44%	93	4.848	7.696	2.847	0.003	59.13%
Capital Expenditures / sales	94	2.279	3.704	1.425	0	64.51%	93	2.798	4.407	1.609	0.004	55.78%
Capital Expenditures / Total Assets	94	2.397	3.248	0.541	0.002	56.38	92	2.977	4.027	1.05	0.009	59.97%
Reinvestment rate per share	92	1.907	5.211	3.304	0.003	56.52%	84	3.535	5.389	1.854	0.057	61.90%
Retained Earnings PctEquity	95	37.172	51.878	14.706	0.007	63.15%	98	44.029	56.559	12.530	0.001	59.60%
Research&dev to sales	65	1.238	2.254	1.017	0.002	48.38%	62	2.039	3.446	1.406	0.027	60.29%
Cash/current assets	92	24.205	35.523	11.318	0.001	56.69%	96	23.794	32.025	8.231	0.001	70.83%
Cost of goods/sales	92	73.348	65.277	−8.071	0.001	76.08%	97	71.633	66.561	−5.072	0.009	64.94%
Foreign assets/tot Assets	68	8.312	11.547	3.235	0.034	55.88%	50	11.097	18.170	7.074	0.007	60.00%
Foreign Sales/tot Sales	72	10.799	15.266	4.467	0.033	55.56%	58	14.318	23.088	8.770	0.006	56.89%

Table 7. Financial structures in an economic downturn.

| Indicators | 1998 | | | | | | 2003 | | | | | |
| | Number of pairs | Average | | | | % of pairs in favor of family businesses | Number of pairs | Average | | | | % of pairs in favor of family businesses |
		Non Family Businesses	Family Businesses	Différence	Signification			Non Family Businesses	Family Businesses	Différence	Signification	
Long Term Debt / Total Capital	93	19.656	20.056	0.400	0.257	50.70%	95	16.406	15.700	−0.705	0.795	57.85%
Tot Debts/ Tot Common equity	94	85.235	67.041	−18.195	0.266	56.16%	95	117.177	49.267	−67.910	0.069	62.10%
Equity/Total Common equity	95	74.895	80.624	5.729	0.032	64.21%	95	76.718	84.333	7.615	0.011	61.05%
Current ratio	93	1.514	2.039	0.525	0.002	66.66%	95	1.100	1.862	0.762	0.008	56.84%
Quick ratio	95	1.052	1.577	0.525	0.001	63.20%	95	1.233	1.780	0.548	0.003	63.15%
Fixed Charge Coverage Ratio	89	9.282	40.940	31.658	0.039	58.41%	94	185.385	398.835	213.450	0.269	58.51%

Table 8. Financial structures after an economic downturn.

Indicators	2003						2007					
	Number of pairs	Average		Différence	Signification	% of pairs in favor of family businesses	Number of pairs	Average		Différence	Signification	% of pairs in favor of family businesses
		Non Family Businesses	Family Businesses					Non Family Businesses	Family Businesses			
Long Term Debt / Total Capital	95	16.406	15.700	−0.705	0.795	57.85%	85	14.633	9.953	−4.680	0.047	58.82%
Tot Debts/ Tot Common equity	95	117.177	49.267	−67.910	0.069	62.10%	85	65.852	36.777	−29.075	0.05	67.05%
Equity/Total capital	95	76.718	84.333	7.615	0.011	61.05%	86	82.483	87.884	5.401	0.375	59.30%
Current ratio	95	1.100	1.862	0.762	0.008	56.84%	93	1.772	2.402	0.631	0.004	60.41%
Quick ratio	95	1.233	1.780	0.548	0.003	63.15%	91	1.306	1.860	0.554	0.004	59.78%
Fixed Charge Coverage Ratio	94	185.385	398.835	213.450	0.269	58.51%	74	50.079	215.590	165.511	0.027	58.10%

In 1998, we found no significant difference between family and non-family businesses in terms of debts (both long-term and total). However, family businesses enjoyed better liquidity than non-family businesses, according to the current ratio and quick ratio, which implies greater flexibility. In addition, the fixed charge coverage ratio is significantly different at the 5% threshold, in favour of family businesses, which also indicates their greater flexibility. These results partially validate H3a; however, we find no difference with regard to long-term or total debt.

In 2003, the picture is almost the same, except the long-term debt-to-total capital ratio improves for both kinds of businesses, still without significant differences between them. In addition, the ratio of total debts to total common equity diverges, deteriorating for non-family businesses and improving for family ones. Therefore, we draw the same conclusion for H3b, namely, that it is partially validated.

In 2007, family businesses revealed sounder financial structures, in terms of both debts and liquidity. All the ratios except equity to total capital indicate significant differences in favour of family businesses at a 5% threshold. Thus, we regard H3c as validated.

Discussion

Family business performance in a downturn (H1)

The wider differences between family and non-family businesses in 2003, at the end of the downturn, compared with those in 1998 indicate that family businesses recovered better from the recession than did non-family businesses. Is this recovery success just a matter of time – such that non-family businesses eventually catch up to family businesses on the path to recovery? In H1c, we predict instead, that family businesses maintain at least some of their advantage, and in Table 4, we show that the differences between the types of business persisted in 2007, still in favour of family businesses. All businesses achieved better performance than in 2003. However, at the 5% threshold, the ROI and pretax margin of family businesses were significantly stronger than those of non-family businesses, and at the 10% threshold, ROA and ROE also significantly supported the benefits of family businesses. We thus find support for H1c.

The finding supports our hypothesis that family businesses resist economic downturns better than non-family businesses. In a clear reflection of the ability of family businesses to face down reality, these firms achieve their success because of both their long-term orientation (Stein 1988, 1989, Miller 2005) and their so-called 'familiness' (Habbershon and Williams 1999, Chrisman *et al.* 2003). This fundamental quality – which may appear in individual people, groups, organizations or systems – to respond to significant change that disrupts the expected pattern of events without behavioural regressions (Horne and Orr 1998) strongly suggests the greater organizational resilience of family businesses.

Family business and mobilisation of resources in a downturn (H2)

Family businesses adopt long-term orientations. Even during a crisis, compared with non-family businesses, family firms 'invest for the future or undertake initiatives with significant short-term costs' (Miller and Le Breton-Miller 2006, p. 78). In addition, the cash-to-current assets ratio is significant (5%), which indicates greater flexibility among family businesses. More so than non-family businesses, these companies also are keen to exploit opportunities abroad. Their ratios of both foreign assets to total assets and foreign sales to total sales differ significantly at a 5% threshold, in support of H2a.

Similar findings pertaining to the superiority of family businesses in 2003 indicate that by this point every ratio in Table 5 significantly favours (5%) family businesses. They invest more, conduct more research and development, take the lead in overseas markets and control costs better, all in support of H2b. In addition, our findings show that during this immediate post-crisis period, investment in innovation (in a broad sense) offers firms an effective means to resist. The organizational resilience of family businesses emerges in the form of 'ritualized ingenuity'.

Because the differences are greater in 2003 than in 1998, as well as more systematically significant, we can assert that family businesses moving from a crisis into a recovery phase can better mobilize their resources than can non-family businesses. Even well after the recovery, family businesses continue to display a better ability to mobilize their resources; in Table 6 every ratio remains at nearly the same levels, with significant differences between family and non-family businesses in 2007. Thus we also have support for H2c.

Family business and stronger financial structures in a downturn (H3)

The interpretation of these results rests on two previously mentioned explanations. First, academic research notes that family businesses tend to adopt more cautious attitudes toward debt. Second, some interpretations suggest varied risk preferences for family versus non-family businesses (Gomez-Mejia et al. 2007). We posit that during an economic downturn, family businesses renounce their traditional or classical debt-related behaviour and acknowledge the need to vary their risk preferences. After the crisis, they re-adopt their traditional behaviours. The results clearly support our first argument, with regard to facing down reality, and our third claim, pertaining to the translation of ritualized ingenuity into socio-emotional wealth.

A contingency-based view suggests the possibility of varied risk preferences (Gomez-Mejia et al. 2007, Abdellatif et al. 2010), such that socio-emotional wealth may be a key goal for family businesses. Accordingly, firms with these goals are more likely to perpetuate the owner's direct control over the firm's affairs (Gomez-Mejia et al. 2007). Because owners want to preserve their socio-emotional wealth, which they cannot do through diversification (e.g. going international), family owners likely avoid that strategic choice, even if it would confer some risk protection on the company (Gomez-Mejia et al. 2010). However, during a downturn, family businesses are flexible enough to temporarily accept changes to their traditional goals.

Implications

By addressing three different periods (in the crisis, the end of the crisis and after the crisis), this contribution makes a threefold contribution to extant literature, particularly with regard to the organizational resilience of family businesses in a Japanese context:

- First, during the crisis, family businesses, compared with non-family businesses, achieve better performance (H1), have a greater ability to mobilize their resources (H2) and are able to alter or adapt their behaviour when it comes to debt (H3). In short, they resist better.
- Second, at the end of the crisis, these businesses still enjoy better performance than non-family businesses; the differences between the two groups even increases, granting greater favour to the family business. On the two other points, the findings are quite similar. In short, they recover faster.

- Third, after the crisis, the differences in the performance of family versus non-family businesses again increase, in support of the superiority of family businesses. We find similar results pertaining to their ability to mobilize their resources. Regarding their recourse to debt, we show that family businesses go back to their classical behaviours. In short, they still outperform non-family businesses.

This study thus contributes to the broad research stream that addresses questions related to the performance and financial structure of family businesses; we find consistent results in contexts of both economic downturn and recovery. In addition, our study takes a step toward integrating the concept of organizational resilience with family business studies and understanding (and explaining) the behaviours of various businesses in economic downturns. These two points represent original contributions. Moreover, by gleaning lessons from the 1997 Asian financial crisis, this study provides some potentially helpful insights for dealing with the current global economic crisis. Thus, although it has scarcely been used to refer to family business settings, the concept of organizational resilience should be of greater interest in this field.

Several unexplored questions remain however, in relation to the concept of resilience. Our findings suggest a general debate: Is the resilience displayed by family businesses a matter of nature (i.e. their innate qualities) or nurture (i.e. experience)? This argument is quite well documented in entrepreneurship literature (Roderick *et al.* 2007) but insufficiently considered in family business literature. Without taking any position in this debate, we note that the managerial implications of our findings likely support the nurture position. We have also not addressed the question of how to measure organizational resilience, a topic that demands greater research attention (see Somers 2009). Both questions should be at the top of the research agenda for the family business field.

Conclusion

By carefully investigating how Japanese family and non-family businesses weathered the 1997 Asian crisis, we have revealed that family businesses achieved stronger resistance than non-family businesses, recovered faster, and eventually persisted in enjoying higher performance and sounder financial structures. In other words, they exhibited greater organizational resilience than non-family businesses.

However, even as we provide an in-depth analysis, we acknowledge some limitations to this research. First, we compare large family and non-family businesses, all of which are listed companies. However, most family firms, including those in Japan, are small and medium-sized enterprises. It is therefore necessary to keep this limitation in mind when considering the generalizability of our findings to other family businesses facing an economic downturn. Second, our research addresses only two of the three characteristics of resilient organizations (see Table 1; Coutu 2002): facing down reality and ritualized ingenuity. Data from this research cannot illustrate the implications of the search for meaning characteristic; a qualitative approach based on interviews of managers of both types of businesses would provide a means to address this point. Third, our study focuses solely on Japanese firms. Further studies should confirm if our results apply to other contexts, within and outside the Asia-Pacific rim, including North America, Europe and less developed areas.

Comparing the organizational resilience of family and non-family businesses to the 1997 Asian crisis against their resilience in the current economic crisis (once sufficient data become available) would provide an interesting basis for assessing the strength of our results. The two crises indicate similarities, particularly from a Japanese perspective: Both derive from financial challenges resulting from an excess of debts, both private and public, and both have caused significant harm to a wide range of industries. In accordance with our research and findings, it would be helpful to investigate the same hypotheses, using both a quantitative approach as we have and a qualitative approach that relies on interviews with a sample of carefully selected managers of both kinds of firms, especially if they have been able to retain their key positions throughout the crisis and recovery periods.

Acknowledgements

This research has benefitted from funding from the French National Agency for Research (ANR), under the auspices of the MNC Control program (2009–2011).

Note

1. According to Chrisman *et al.*, (2003), 'the family firm exists because of the reciprocal economic and non-economic value created through the combination of family and business systems. In other words, the confluence of the two systems leads to hard-to-duplicate capabilities of "familiness" that make family business particularly suited to survive and grow' p. 444.

References

Abdellatif, M., Amann, B., and Jaussaud, J., 2010. Family versus non-family business: a comparison of international strategies. *Journal of family business strategy*, 1 (2), 108–116.

Allouche, J., and Amann, B, 1998. Le retour triomphant du capitalisme familial, Harvard l'expansion.

Allouche, J., Amann, B., Jaussaud, J., and Kurashina, T., 2008. The impact of family control on the performance and financial characteristics of family versus non-family businesses in Japan: a matched–pair investigation. *Family business review*, 21 (4), 315–329.

Arrègle, J.–.L., Hitt, M.A., Sirmon, D.G., and Very, P., 2007. The development of organizational social capital: attributes of family firms. *Journal of management studies*, 44, 72–95.

Barclay, M., and Holderness, C., 1989. Private benefits from control of public corporations. *Journal of financial economics*, 25, 371–396.

Berle, A.A. and Means, G.C., 1932. *The modern corporation and private property*. New York: Macmillan.

Burkart, M., Panunzi, F., and Shleifer, A., 2003. Family firms. *Journal of finance*, 18 (5), 2167–2201.

Carney, M., 2005. Corporate governance and competitive advantage in family–controlled firms. *Entrepreneurship theory and practice*, 29 (3), 249–266.

Chami, R., 1999. What's different about family business? Working paper, University of Notre Dame.

Charreaux, G., 1991. Structures de propriété, relations d'agence et performances financières *Cahiers du CREGO*, IAE de Dijon.

Chrisman, J.J., Chua, J.H., and Steier, L.P., 2003. An introduction to theories of family business. *Journal of business venturing*, 18, 441–448.

Chrisman, J.J., Chua, J.H., and Sharma, P., 2005. Trends and directions in the development of a strategic management theory of the family firm. *Entrepreneurship theory and practice*, 29 (5), 555–576.

Coutu, L.D., 2002. How resilience works. *Harvard business review*, 80 (5), 46–55.

Davis, J.H., Schoorman, F.D., and Donaldson, L., 1997. Toward a stewardship theory of management. *Academy of management review*, 22 (1), 20–47.

Fama, E.F., and Jensen, M.C., 1983. Separation of ownership and control. *Journal of law and economic*, 26, 301–326.

Fukuyama, F., 1995. *Trust, the social virtues and the creation of prosperity*. London: Hamish Hamilton.

Galbraith, K., 1967. *The new industrial state*. Boston Houghton Mifflin College Division.

Gallo, M., and Vilaseca, A., 1996. Finance in family business. *Family business review*, 9 (4), 287–305.

Goffee, R., 1996. Understanding family business: issues for further research. *International journal of entrepreneurial behavior and research*, 2 (1), 36–48.

Gomez–Mejia, L.R., Makri, M.K., and Martin, L., 2010. Diversification decisions in family–controlled firms. *Journal of management studies*, 47 (2), 223–252.

Gomez–Mejia, L.R., Takacs, K.H., Núñez–Nickel, M., and Jacobson, K.J.L., 2007. Socioemotional wealth and business risks in family–controlled firms: evidence from Spanish olive oil mills. *Administrative science quarterly*, 52, 106–137.

Habbershon, T.G., and Williams, M., 1999. A resource–based framework for assessing the strategic advantage of family firms. *Family business review*, 12, 1–25.

Habbershon, T., Williams, M., and MacMillan, I.C., 2003. A unified systems perspective of family firm performance. *Journal of business venturing*, 18, 451–466.

Handler, W.C., 1989. Methodological issues and considerations in studying family businesses. *Family business review*, 2 (3), 257–276.

Harvey, S.J., 1999. Owner as manager, extended horizons and the family firm. *International journal of the economics of business*, 6 (1), 41–55.

Horne, J.F., III., and Orr, J.E., 1998. Assessing behaviors that create resilient organizations. *Employment relations today*, 24 (4), 29–39.

Japan Economic Almanac 1999, Tokyo: Nihon Keizai Shimbusha.

Keizai Koho Center, 1999, 2004, 2006, 2008. *Japan, an International Comparison*, Tokyo: Keizai Koho Center.

Kets de Vries, M., 1993. The dynamics of family controlled firms: the good and the bad news. *Organizational dynamics*, 21 (3), 59–71.

Kurashina, T., 2003. *Family Kigyô no Keieigaku, (Management studies on family business)*, Tokyo: Tôyô Keizai Shimbun Sha.

La Porta, R., Lopez–de–Silanes, F., and Shleifer, A., 1999. Corporate ownership around the world. *Journal of finance*, 54 (2), 471–519.

Lengnick–Hall, C.A., and Beck, T.E., 2009. Resilience capacity and strategic agility: prerequisites for thriving in a dynamic environment. Working Paper, University of Texas.

McConaughy, D.L., Matthews, C.H., and Fialko, A.S., 2001. Founding family controlled firms: performance, risk and value. *Journal of small business management*, 39 (1), 31–49.

Miller, D. and Le Breton–Miller, I., 2003. Challenge versus advantage in family business. *Strategic organization*, 1 (1), 127–134.

Miller, D. and Le Breton–Miller, I., 2006. Family governance and firm performance: agency, stewardship, and capabilities. *Family business review*, 19 (1), 73–87.

Miller, D. and Le Breton–Miller, I., 2009. Agency vs. stewardship in public family firms: a social embeddedness reconciliation. *Entrepreneurship: theory & practice*, 33 (6), 1169–1191.

Miyashita, K., and Russell, D., 1994. *Keiretsu: Inside the hidden Japanese conglomerates*, New York: McGraw-Hill.

Monsen, R.J., 1969. Ownership and management: the effect of separation on performance. *Business horizons*, 12, 46–52.

Monsen, R.J., Chiu, J., and Cooley, D., 1968. The effect of the separation of ownership and control on the performance of the large firm. *Quarterly journal economics*, 82 (3), 435–451.

Morck, R., 2003. Corporate governance and family control. *Global Corporate Governance Finance*, Special issue, Discussion Paper no.1. Available from: http://www.gcgf.org/library/Discussion_Papers_and_Focus%20Notes/Corporate%20Governance%20and%20Family%20Control,%20Morck%20–%20Nov%202003.pdf.

Morck, R., and Nakamura, M., 2007. Business Groups and the Big Push: Meiji Japan's Mass Privatization and Subsequent Growth. *Enterprise & Society*, 8 (3), 543–601.

Morck, R. and Yeung, B., 2003. Agency problems in large family business groups. *Entrepreneurship theory & practice*, 27 (4), 367–382.

Morikawa, H., 1996. *Toppu Managemento Keizai Shi, Keieisha Kigyo to Kazoku Kigyo (History of Top Management: Family Businesses versus Non-Family Businesses)*, Tokyo: Yuhikaku Corp.

Porter, M., 1986. Competition in global industries: a conceptual framework. *In*: M. Porter, ed. *Competition in global industries*. Boston, MA: Harvard Business School Press, chapter 1.

Roderick, E.W., Thornhill, S., and Hampson, E., 2007. A biosocial model of entrepreneurship: the combined effects of nurture and nature. *Journal of organizational behavior*, 28, 451–466.

Rosenblatt, P.C., de Mik, L., Anderson, R.M., and Johnson, P.A., 1985. *The family in business*. San Francisco, CA: Jossey–Bass.

Saito, T., 2008. Family firms and firm performance: evidence from Japan. *Journal of the Japanese & international economies*, 22 (4), 620–646.

Schulze, W.S., Lubatkin, M.H., Dino, R.N., and Buchholtz, A., 2001. Agency relationship in family: theory and evidence. *Organization science*, 12 (2), 99–116.

Schulze, W.S., Lubatkin, M.H., and Dino, R.N., 2003. Exploring the agency consequence of ownership dispersion among the directors of private firms. *Academy of management journal*, 46 (2), 179–194.

Shleifer, A. and Vishny, R.W., 1997. A survey of corporate governance. *Journal of finance*, 52 (2), 737–783.

Somers, S., 2009. Measuring resilience potential: an adaptive strategy for organizational crisis planning. *Journal of contingencies and crisis management*, 17 (1), 12–23.

Stein, J.C., 1988. Takeover threats and managerial myopia. *Journal of political economy*, 96, 61–80.

Stein, J.C., 1989. Efficient capital markets, inefficient firms: a model of myopic corporate behavior. *Quarterly journal of economics*, (November), 655–669.

Stiglitz, J., 2003. *Globalization and its discontents*. New York and London: Norton & Co.

Van den Berghe, L.A.A. and Carchon, S., 2003. Agency relations within the family business systems: an exploratory approach. *Corporate governance: an international review*, 11 (3), 171–179.

Villalonga, B. and Amit, R., 2004. *How do family ownership, control, and management affect firm value?* EFA 2004 Maastricht Meetings Paper No. 3620. Available from: http://ssrn.com/abstract=556032.

Characteristics of R&D expenditures in Japan's pharmaceutical industry

Sophie Nivoix[a] and Pascal Nguyen[b]

[a]Faculty of Law and Social Sciences, University of Poitiers, 2, rue Jean Carbonnier F-86000 Poitiers, France; [b]School of Finance and Economics, University of Technology Sydney, NSW 2007 Sydney, Australia

Characterized by a high level of R&D expenditure, pharmaceutical firms are also subject to specific risks that are reflected in their financial policies. In contrast to other firms, whose investments are directly related to internal cash flows, Japanese pharmaceutical companies do not appear to rely on this source of funds to undertake R&D investments. Our analysis reveals that R&D expenses largely depend on the firm's size and the strength of its balance sheet. More precisely, high levels of debt appear to hold back R&D expenditure, especially when debt has a short-term maturity. These results highlight the importance of funding risky investments with the adequate type of capital to avoid putting firms in financial distress. Despite the risk, R&D investments seem to be justified by the fact that they are generally associated with higher sales growth. However, the difficult conditions prevailing in Japan's pharmaceutical industry make these benefits less visible.

Introduction

The importance of intangible assets is well recognized. For instance, the studies of Griliches (1981), Hall (1993), Megna and Klock (1993), and others, show that R&D investments are associated with higher firm value. Lev *et al.* (2005) argue that firms invest in R&D to build competitive advantages that result in higher operating performance. Filatotchev and Piesse (2009) confirm that strong R&D capabilities contribute to the growth and internationalization of newly-listed firms. R&D investments can also be viewed as options to benefit from future technological or market developments (Schwartz 2004). Furthermore, it seems that R&D investments deliver greater benefits during economic crises. R&D intensive firms are probably less sensitive to external shocks since their products cannot easily be substituted with cheaper alternatives. Consistent with this argument, Nguyen *et al.* (2010) show that high R&D firms outperform in adverse market conditions whereas low R&D firms perform better in more favourable circumstances. Firms in financial distress also tend to implement extensive cost-cutting measures, but usually do their best to maintain their R&D investments.

The objective of this paper is to analyze the factors that affect R&D investments in Japan's pharmaceutical industry and to test whether R&D investments contribute to future growth. Our focus on pharmaceutical companies is justified by the fact that they present the highest level of R&D as well as an extremely high level of risk with very long pay-back periods generally extending over a decade. In Japan, the issues related to this industry are all the more pressing now that population ageing is occurring faster than in any other country, putting a tremendous burden on the public health system (Anderson and Hussey 2000, Jacobzone 2000). In addition, the saturation of the domestic market is forcing many firms to look for growth overseas or expand into new product areas. In that respect, R&D investments may provide the critical resources to break into new markets and successfully compete against incumbent firms (Lev *et al.*, 2005, Filatotchev and Piesse 2009).

In contrast to the case of US firms examined in Grabowski and Vernon (2000), the level of Japan's pharmaceutical R&D is difficult to explain. Mahlich and Roediger-Schluga (2006) argue that the tougher regulatory environment imposed by the Japanese health authorities reduces the expected payoff on R&D investments, and thus the incentives to undertake R&D activities. It follows that internal cash flows only play a minor role in explaining R&D expenditures. We extend their analysis by examining the role of funding and risk mitigation, and by evaluating the outcome in terms of future sales growth. The effect of accumulated debt on R&D expenditures and the role that the latter play in the development of newly-listed firms have recently been pointed out by Filatotchev and Piesse (2009).

Consistent with Mahlich and Roediger-Schluga (2006) we show that R&D expenses are weakly related to internal cash flows. Instead, our results suggest that they strongly depend on the firm's financial structure. In particular, debt is associated with lower R&D expenditures, especially when it has a short-term maturity. The use of the market-to-book value of assets as an indicator of investor sentiment suggests that R&D investments do not depend on market conditions in the pharmaceutical industry, contrary to the other sectors for which investor sentiment seems to have a stronger impact. Firm size also contributes to a higher R&D intensity, consistent with the argument that larger firms have greater access to product diversification and risk mitigation opportunities. Finally, the effect of R&D expenditure on future growth appears to be weak for pharmaceutical firms, perhaps because of their extended investment horizons, but is shown to be highly significant for the control group consisting of other firms with active R&D programmes.

The main implication of this study is to highlight the importance for firms to appropriately finance risky investments. In particular, providing sufficient equity capital is critical to fostering R&D activities considering the high level of uncertainty associated with their future payoffs (Sapienza *et al.*, 2006). The ability to pool projects and offset risks also gives large firms a greater incentive to undertake R&D investments. As a result, R&D intensive (and larger) firms tend to fare better in adverse market conditions because of their stronger balance sheets and their lesser reliance on short-term funding which may otherwise have devastating consequences during financial crises (Myers 1977). Another outcome of the study is to emphasize that R&D is not a guaranteed pathway towards future growth. While it is true that R&D tends to be associated with increasing sales, the overall conditions prevailing in a specific industry may blunt that relationship.

The rest of this paper is organized as follows. The next section explores the determinants of R&D investments and describes some aspects of Japan's pharmaceutical industry. The following sections present the methodology used in the study and the empirical results. The remaining sections provide a general discussion and conclusion.

The determinants of R&D investments

The pharmaceutical industry in Japan

Our focus on the Japanese pharmaceutical industry is justified for several reasons. First, like other high-tech sectors, the pharmaceutical industry is driven by innovation (Bottazzi *et al.*, 2001) which requires large and sustained amounts of R&D investment. On the whole, R&D expenditure represents about 3.39% of GDP in Japan compared to just 1.84% in Europe, according to national statistics for the year 2006.[1] However, the intensity of R&D expenditure relative to sales is by far the highest in the pharmaceutical industry, with an average greater than 10% over the period 1998–2007, compared to an average of 5.03% in the electrical appliances industry and an average of 3.13% for all the other industries (Nguyen *et al.*, 2010). The pharmaceutical industry also ranks highly in terms of R&D expenses per researcher, second only to telecommunications, and well ahead of the automobile industry which is often cited as an example.[2]

In recent years, the Japanese pharmaceutical industry has experienced a large number of mergers and restructuring, such as the fusion of Yamanouchi Pharmaceutical and Fujisawa Pharmaceutical to form Astellas Pharma, or the combination of Dainippon Pharmaceutical and Sumitomo Pharmaceutical, which gave birth to Dainippon Sumitomo Pharma (DSP), as well as the merger of Daiichi and Sankyo. Nevertheless, this sector is still fairly fragmented. From a total of about 1600 firms in 1990, nearly 1000 remained in 2005.[3] Meanwhile, most of the income is generated by a few dozen firms, which are generally listed, with the first five firms achieving nearly 30% of industry sales, the first 10 making close to 50%, and the first 50 accounting for more than 80% of total industry sales.

Several factors contribute to governing the pharmaceutical industry in Japan. The increased life expectancy of Japanese people is obviously a key driver of consumption, half all drug consumption is related to people over 65 years of age. People in that age category also spend five times more on their health compared to other countries (Oliver *et al.*, 1997). Another critical factor is the way prices are determined and the way products are distributed. Prices are set by the Central Social Insurance Medical Council (*chuikyo*), the distribution of drugs is mostly carried out through doctors rather than pharmacies. This creates an incentive for doctors to generously prescribe drugs, particularly those with a high profit margin. These profit margins (*yakka-saeki*) come from the difference between wholesale prices and the (higher) prices in the official list set up by the *chuikyo*, which determines the refunds provided by insurance companies to the doctors.

In an effort to curb escalating health costs, the Japanese Health Ministry regularly checks the accounts of pharmaceutical firms and drug wholesalers to determine the difference between market prices and those in the official list, and adjust the second to the first. This leads to semi-annual price cuts by sometimes more than 10% (Oliver *et al.*, 1997). These price reductions reduce the costs to the public health system, but have a significant effect on the drug market (Ikegami and Campbell 2004). Because of this negative trend in prices, the average lifespan of a drug is far shorter in Japan (less than 10 years) compared to other countries. This shorter life cycle inevitably reduces the incentives to undertake very risky and costly investments in innovative drugs, which require long periods of return on investment to recover the initial R&D expenses (Acemoglu and Linn 2004). Although a bonus scheme was introduced in 1992 to help cover the higher cost of developing innovative drugs, the situation has remained unchanged. Because the potential market for medical innovations is relatively weak, resolute marketing is therefore essential to achieve commercial success (Mahlich and Roediger-Schluga 2006).

In terms of organizational structure, it is useful to recall some characteristics of Japan's pharmaceutical industry. Since the beginning of the decade, Japanese firms have begun to outsource some of their activities, in order to optimize the use of their resources in light of increasing R&D costs.[4] The firms involved in this outsourcing process may receive R&D activities (*contract research organizations*), site management activities (*site management organizations*, which in biological activities mostly focus on finding patients, following the drug testing process on them, checking the ethical aspects of the experiments, or negotiating contracts), or marketing support activities (*contract sales organizations*, particularly active in biological activities, in order to enable laboratories to concentrate on the core of their activities).

Contract research organizations (CRO) appeared in the US and in Europe in the 1970s, and aim to develope products such as drugs, cosmetics and medical instruments. Site management organizations (SMO) help implement preparations related to clinical tests. In 1999 an analysis committee for clinical tests in Japan advised the use of such structures to help medical institutions. Since 2002 the demand for this type of services has increased (Mahlich and Roediger-Schluga 2006). Contract sales organizations (CSO) work on marketing tasks on behalf of pharmaceutical firms within a delegation contract. These structures emerged in Europe and then in the US in the 1980s, and have spawned in Japan since 2000. Now that R&D activities can be partially outsourced, it seems that establishing its optimum level is not simply an question for each firm to address, but should entail a broader industry response.

In a context of tighter controls of health expenditures (Oliver *et al.*, 1997, Ikegami and Campbell 2004), Japanese pharmaceutical companies clearly run the risk of falling behind their international competitors if they are not profitable enough. But if a high level of R&D expenditures is not a guarantee of future success or associated with higher returns (Nguyen *et al.*, 2010), why do firms maintain their R&D expenditure? The next sections will attempt to formulate answers to this question.

Determinants of pharmaceutical R&D investments

Explaining the performance of R&D-intensive firms can be quite difficult. Their revenue depends on new technologies and future products, which are characterized by a very long period for technological developments and a shorter period for the commercialization of products. In contrast to tangible assets, such as plants and equipment, R&D always involves the long term and generates seemingly random results. This is reflected in the high risk associated with the return on R&D-intensive firms (Scherer *et al.*, 2000, Bottazzi *et al.*, 2001). R&D expenditure is also different from other investments because it is intended to create intangible assets in the long run, and these assets are hard to evaluate. Not only does the expected return on R&D exhibit higher dispersion compared to other investments, but the distribution is highly asymmetric and characterized by heavy tails.

Because research involves a long and cumulative process of knowledge creation and the build-up of intangible assets, small firms have less capability to implement large scope R&D programmes. Even if it is frequently noted that start-up companies begin their activity with a total focus on a specific process or molecule, research diversification quickly becomes a necessity. This suggests that large firms invest more in R&D, despite the weight of their large scale structures.

Regarding the role of profitability, whilst one can expect a positive effect from R&D in the long run, there is no guarantee regarding the level and timing of future cash flows. Any type of relation may exist. Weak contemporary profits may not prevent firms from investing to ensure the development of new products. Conversely, high profitability stemming from existing products may not always lead to a higher level of R&D if the firm benefits from economic rents because of an effective portfolio of molecules. As a result, there should be no specific relationship between profitability and R&D intensity.

Knowing the potential impact that financing can make to value creation, one can expect that firms will try to tap the cheapest source of funds, which is normally debt. However, for funding R&D projects, firms tend to use equity mainly because future cash flows are highly uncertain and may not be available to pay back a long term debt (Filatotchev and Piesse 2004). Moreover, since their operating risk is already high, pharmaceutical firms should limit the use of debt to avoid the risk of default. Relating to the composition of debt, the long term horizon of R&D investments should induce firms to select a source of funds with a corresponding maturity when these projects cannot be funded internally. In that case, long-term debt should be used preferably to short-term debt.

Some studies have found a positive relation between R&D expenses and internal cash flows, which suggests the existence of financial constraints due to the difference between the costs of internal and external funds (Hubbard 1998, Hall 2002). This difference may also arise from information asymmetry (between the firm and its investors) or from moral hazard problems (over or under-investment in a project, depending on its high or low level of risk). Nevertheless, Japanese firms should far less depend on internal cash flows to finance their R&D projects as opposed to US firms because the Japanese financial system relies on bank financing rather than funding from the capital markets (Hoshi and Kashyap 2001). Bank loans represent a key aspect of the long term relationship between a bank and its customer, as the bank can check the firm's accounts in return for support in case of financial distress. This is particularly true inside the Japanese business groups (*keiretsu*), for which informational asymmetries between firms and lenders are considered to be lower.[5]

More generally, firms that can easily borrow because of lower informational asymmetry should have a lower cost of external funds. As a result, R&D investments should less depend on internal cash flows. Using a sample of 15 pharmaceutical firms, Mahlich and Roediger-Schluga (2006) found that R&D intensity is positively related to internal cash flows as well as expected return, as Grabowski and Vernon (2000) already observed. However, the role of cash flows appears to be weaker than in the US because, regardless of disparities in financing, new drugs do not significantly contribute to firm profitability in Japan as the government tries to rein in health expenses. But since the role of cash flows is not so important in Japan, firms do no need to retain their cash to finance future R&D projects. As a result, the association between R&D expenses and cash reserves is expected to be weak.

Taken together the above discussion suggests the following hypotheses concerning the determinants of R&D investments in Japan's pharmaceutical industry.

Hypothesis 1:   Firm size has a positive effect on R&D investments.

Hypothesis 2:   Strong funding has a positive effect on R&D investments.

Hypothesis 3:   R&D investments are unrelated to market conditions.

Hypothesis 4:   R&D investments are unrelated to internal cash flows.

Effect of R&D investments on firm growth

Because Japanese firms tend to pay less attention to current profits but prefer to build market share (representing a steady pathway to future profits), it is not surprising that studies looking at profitability ratios have failed to grasp the benefits that Japanese firms derive from their R&D investments. In this study, we articulate the view that Japanese firms invest in R&D to sustain their future growth measured by the increase in sales over the next period.

In this respect, it must be noted that the long operating cycle related to R&D projects is likely to induce persistence in growth. In other words, because R&D investments involve long term changes in the firm's activity, a high (low) sales growth in a given year is likely to be associated by a similar high (low) sales growth the following year. As a result of this persistence, it is theoretically possible for a firm to cut its R&D expenditures in a given year and still record an increase in sales the following year. Nonetheless, the most likely pattern is that R&D investments will be consistently sustained over time. Thus, we expect to find a positive association between R&D intensity and future growth in sales, even if the latter is measured after a short period of time (for instance, the following year).

Obviously, a number of factors can contribute to future sales and need to be controlled for. In the previous section, firm size was hypothesized to have a positive effect on the level of R&D expenditures, but since R&D investments do not always lead to higher sales, the relation between firm size and future growth cannot be determined from that angle. On the one hand, large firms have more resources and can more easily diversify their risks. This enables them to withstand poor economic conditions, but their reactivity is also weaker compared to smaller firms. On the other hand, small firms frequently suffer from a lack of resources even when they have good projects. Hence, it is difficult to anticipate the existence of a specific relation between firm size and sales growth.

The role of internal cash flows is also ambiguous. Mature firms exhibit low growth rates, but tend to generate abundant cash flows, while growth firms are usually characterized by the opposite. However, strong cash flows are likely to induce firms to increase their capital expenditures or make acquisitions, which are both expected to boost their sales growth. Besides, a high market to book value of assets is expected to be associated with higher sales growth, consistent with the typical interpretation of this ratio (as reflecting investors' anticipations of future growth).

Among the financing variables, leverage and cash are considered to have a negative effect on sales growth. The main argument is that highly leveraged firms are likely to face financial constraints which should curb their potential development; thus leading to lower sales growth. For similar reasons, firms with low cash balances are certain to experience greater difficulties in achieving their full development. Debt maturity, however, is expected to have a material effect only in the case where the firm is not able to roll over its short term debt. Although this problem has recently affected many firms as a result of the global financial crisis, it is not expected to have a significant impact during benign times.

Since the main objective of this section is to motivate the decision to invest in R&D, we formulate a single hypothesis regarding the determinants of firm growth.

Hypothesis 5:   R&D investments have a positive effect on future sales growth.

Methodology

The analysis is carried out using all pharmaceutical companies (Nikkei code 09) listed on the Tokyo Stock Exchange over the period 1998–2007. This sample contains 291 firm-year observations corresponding to 36 firms. It is likely to be representative of the pharmaceutical industry since the sales of these 36 firms correspond to nearly 75% of the sector's total sales. For the purpose of drawing comparisons, we use a control sample consisting of all Japanese firms that reported positive R&D expenditures, but excluding the above 36 pharmaceutical companies. A total of 10,182 firm-year observations were identified for the period 1998–2007. Firms with equity value below 10 billion yen (equivalent to about 80 million euros) were excluded from both samples. In order to avoid any size bias, the intensity of R&D expense was measured using the R&D/sales ratio. A ratio including fixed assets or total assets might not have been suitable as this expenditure does not appear in the balance sheet. As in Nguyen *et al.* (2010) the data is sourced from the Nikkei NEEDS corporate information database.

Figure 1 reveals that R&D intensity, measured by R&D expenses to sales, increased steadily between 1998 and 2007 in the pharmaceutical industry, but not in the other industries. This trend is similar to that observed by Mahlich and Roediger-Schluga (2006) for Japan's 15 largest listed pharmaceutical firms between 1987 and 1998. Despite the need for shorter term returns (because of the shorter drug lifespan) and the pressure on profit margins, as already pointed out, it appears that R&D intensity has not declined. This suggests that the necessity to create new drugs still dominates the potential proclivity to avoid some very long term and costly R&D investments. Hence, it is not surprising to observe a large, and even increasing, difference between the pharmaceutical industry (more than 17% in 2007) and the other R&D industries (less than 2.5% on average).

Since investments can only be justified if their payoffs are sufficiently high compared to the costs incurred, it is also important to consider the firms' operating performance. In this respect, the difference in ROA between the pharmaceutical industry and the other sectors appears to be smaller than for R&D expenses, with an average ROA about between 6% and 8% for the pharmaceutical industry against about 5% for the other sectors). Moreover, the decline in operating return for pharmaceutical firms between 2001 and 2007 may have alarmed investors regarding the industry's ability to find new growth drivers. One answer may come from the results of a study by consulting firm A.D. Little[6] indicating that future areas of development include emerging markets, and notably the

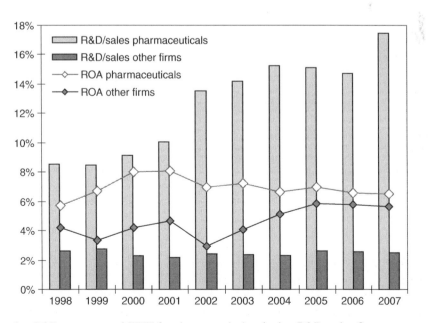

Figure 1.   R&D expenses and EBIT for pharmaceutical and other R&D-active firms.

BRIC countries (Brazil, Russia, India and China), with growth for pharmaceutical products estimated at about 15% per year, which is nearly three times the growth in the world pharmaceutical market. Regarding Japan, growth is precisely at the same level as the expected 5% world average for 2009 according to A.D. Little.

The next section examines the factors that have the greatest influence on R&D expenses in the pharmaceutical industry compared to the other industries.

Data analysis

Univariate analysis

To highlight the difference between pharmaceutical firms and other firms with active R&D programmes, we begin by carrying out a simple univariate analysis. Table 1 presents the average value of several firm characteristics by quartile of R&D/sales for each of the two samples. The results for pharmaceutical firms are shown in Panel B while those for other R&D-active firms are shown in Panel A. Firm size is measured by three variables: LNTA is the log of total assets, LNMVE is the log of market value of equity, and LNSLS is the log of sales. Financial performance is gauged by operating cash flows over total assets (EBITDA) and the log of market-to-book value of assets (LNQ). Strength in the capital structure is measured by the ratio of total debt to total assets (DEBT) and the proportion of debt with a long-term maturity (MATU). The ratio cash and equivalent over total assets (LIQUID) provides a measure of the firm's liquidity position. Finally, DIVEQT is the dividend per share scaled by book value of equity and SLSG is sales growth over the next period.

Table 1.   Firm characteristics by R&D quartiles.

	R&D/sales quartiles				Difference		
	Q1 = low	Q2	Q3	Q4 = high	Q4 − Q1	t-stat	
Panel A: All firms excluding pharmaceuticals with positive R&D/sales							
R&D	0.250	0.959	2.323	5.463	5.21	47.21	***
LNTA	11.30	11.36	11.38	11.65	0.35	3.16	***
LNMVE	10.12	10.37	10.63	11.22	1.10	21.66	***
LNSLS	11.37	11.25	11.24	11.45	0.07	1.66	*
LNQ	0.034	0.067	0.129	0.237	0.20	8.44	***
EBITDA	2.96	3.74	4.35	4.72	1.75	7.17	***
DEBT	23.72	26.40	21.40	18.93	− 4.79	− 4.14	***
MATU	0.510	0.509	0.513	0.528	0.02	2.16	**
LIQUID	11.64	11.01	11.75	14.49	2.85	4.58	***
DIVEQT	1.44	1.46	1.45	1.53	0.09	2.31	**
SLSG	2.94	2.34	3.47	3.92	0.98	2.09	**
Panel B: Pharmaceutical companies only							
R&D	4.50	8.43	12.04	13.63	9.13	35.41	***
LNTA	11.21	11.44	12.48	11.71	0.50	2.68	***
LNMVE	10.90	11.37	12.68	11.90	1.00	4.63	***
LNSLS	10.89	11.15	11.97	10.94	0.05	0.22	
LNQ	0.27	0.34	0.52	0.49	0.22	2.42	**
EBITDA	4.10	4.74	6.78	4.55	0.45	0.55	
DEBT	22.72	14.41	8.09	7.01	− 15.71	− 6.94	***
MATU	0.54	0.59	0.64	0.80	0.26	5.69	***
LIQUID	11.53	13.88	16.61	20.56	9.03	4.25	***
DIVEQT	1.87	1.71	2.15	1.48	− 0.39	− 1.86	*
SLSG	3.33	1.98	2.73	3.41	0.07	0.04	

Table 2. Determinants of R&D expenditure.

	Pharmaceutical companies				Other R&D-active firms			
	(1)		(2)		(3)		(4)	
LNTA	0.0065	***	0.0069	***	0.0018	***	0.0018	***
	(4.53)		(4.11)		(7.05)		(7.26)	
LNQ	0.0022		0.0014		0.0034	***	0.0042	***
	(0.43)		(0.26)		(3.54)		(3.58)	
SLSG	−0.0143				−0.0045	***		
	(−0.73)				(−2.76)			
EBITDA			−0.0196				−0.0270	**
			(−0.41)				(−2.54)	
DEBT	−0.0553	***	−0.0552	***	−0.0089	***	−0.0098	***
	(−3.67)		(−3.59)		(−4.79)		(−5.25)	
MATU	0.0267	***	0.0270	***	0.0015		0.0016	
	(3.39)		(3.42)		(1.37)		(1.46)	
LIQUID	0.0573	**	0.0566	*	0.0180	***	0.0181	***
	(2.04)		(1.92)		(3.91)		(3.93)	
F value	10.28	***	9.92	***	48.95	***	47.96	***
R^2	0.2747		0.2735		0.4316		0.4329	
N observations	291		291		15,182		15,182	

The last column shows the difference between the high and low R&D quartiles (Q4 − Q1) to point out which variables may have an influence on a firm's R&D intensity.

The analysis regarding other R&D active firms presented in Panel A reveals significant differences for all the variables, except log of sales. Based on the other measures of firm size, R&D-intensive firms are noticeably larger. In fact, total assets and market value of equity are both monotonously increasing with R&D-intensity. However, the relation is U-shaped for log of sales, due to the presence of firms with a large turnover for a relatively small asset base (such as wholesalers) in the lower R&D quartile. R&D-intensive firms also tend to have higher cash flows (higher EBITDA), to be better valued (higher LNQ) and to hold more cash (higher LIQUID). They also appear to prefer equity financing (as indicated by their lower debt ratio) and to use a higher proportion of long term debt when they have to borrow. Finally, their dividend policy is characterized by a higher dividend to equity ratio (DIVEQT) and their current sales growth (SLSG) appears to be more favourable.

In Panel B where the focus is on pharmaceutical firms, inter-quartile differences are generally less significant. The positive relation between R&D-intensity and firm size observed in the other industries still exists, but is not as statistically significant. Similarly, cash flows to total assets which displayed a significant relation to R&D intensity with an inter-quartile difference of 1.75% are less significant with an inter-quartile difference of only 0.55% for pharmaceutical firms. This suggests that R&D expenses do not directly depend on the firm's internal cash flows because of the various environmental factors specific to the pharmaceutical industry.[7,8] Nonetheless, big R&D spenders exhibit a higher market-to-book value of assets, which indicates that investors anticipate a positive outcome from the firm's R&D investments. However, this favourable perspective may not lead to a higher risk-adjusted return (Nguyen et al., 2010).

R&D is scaled by sales. LNTA is the log of total assets. LNMVE is the log of market value of equity. LNSLS is the log of sales. LNQ is the log of market-to-book value of assets. EBITDA is earnings before interests, taxes and depreciation, over total assets. DEBT is total debt over total assets. MATU is the proportion of long term debt. LIQUID is cash and equivalent over total assets. SLSG is sales growth from the previous year. DIVEQT is dividend over book equity. T-statistics are adjusted for heteroskedasticity and clustering by firm. ***, ** and * denote significance at the 1%, 5% and 10% level.

Regarding the role of the financing variables, the negative relationship between leverage and R&D intensity observed for other industries is confirmed for pharmaceutical firms. In fact, the inter-quartile difference in debt is three times larger compared to the corresponding result in Panel A. The proportion of debt with a long term maturity is also much larger for high R&D pharmaceutical firms. Similarly, these firms tend to hold extremely large cash balances representing on average more than 20% of their total assets. Interestingly, low R&D spenders have comparable cash ratios of about 11.5% in both samples. These three variables (DEBT, MATU, and LIQUID) clearly distinguish pharmaceutical firms from other R&D active firms. Their strong relation with R&D expenses suggests a high degree of uncertainty as well as a wealth of opportunities. Pharmaceutical firms appear to respond to their underlying risks by avoiding debt, and if this is not possible by avoiding debt with a short maturity. They also tend to hold more cash to shield themselves against potentially negative outcomes (and obviously lower cash flows) but also to benefit from future investment opportunities that may unexpectedly arise. The negative relation between dividend payments (DIVEQT) and R&D reflects the same need to retain internal funds. Finally, there appears to be no difference in sales growth for pharmaceutical firms, at least in the immediate subsequent period, contrary to what firms in other sectors can expect. A possible explanation is the particularly extended horizon associated with pharmaceutical R&D investments.

Determinants of R&D intensity

Following this brief overview, we examine how R&D intensity is related to the above individual variables using multivariate regressions. The independent variables consist of firm size (LNTA), the market to book value of assets (LNQ), a cash flow indicator (EBITDA or SLSG), the financial leverage (DEBT) and the proportion of long-term debt (MATU), and the firm's cash position (LIQUID). All regressions include year dummies to control for economic fluctuations and industry dummies for R&D active firms. Standard errors are clustered at the firm level. The regression results are presented in Table 3.

For all industry sectors, R&D intensity increases with firm size, which supports the notion that the diversification of risk available to larger firms increases the incentives to engage in high risk R&D activities. Conversely, the lack of risk mitigation opportunities appears to increase the costs of undertaking R&D investments for smaller firms. This result is consistent with Hypothesis 1. Next, the market to book value of assets is associated with a significantly higher R&D intensity for all industries, but not so much for pharmaceutical firms. This suggests that market conditions play a lesser role in governing the investment policy of pharmaceutical firms, or equivalently, the latter have succeeded in insulating their R&D investments from market conditions. Similarly, revenues and operating cash flows have little impact on the R&D intensity of pharmaceutical firms consistent with what Mahlich and Roediger-Schluga (2006) obtained for an earlier period. Thus Hypotheses 2 and 3 appear to be empirically validated.

The dependent variable is R&D over sales. LNTA is the log of total assets. LNQ is the log of market to book value of assets. SLSG is sales growth from the previous year. EBITDA is earnings before interests, taxes and depreciation. DEBT is total debt over total assets. MATU is the proportion of long term debt. LIQUID is cash and equivalent over total assets. All regressions include year dummies (and industry dummies for non pharmaceutical firms). Robust t-statistics are indicated between brackets. ***, **, and * denote significance at the 1%, 5% and 10% level.

Regarding the role of financing variables, it is clear that debt has a strong negative impact on R&D investments, in and outside of the pharmaceutical industry. The magnitude of the effect is notable as it implies that a one standard deviation in the debt ratio (0.147 for pharmaceuticals) is associated with a $0.0553 \times 0.147 = 0.8\%$ change in the R&D/sales ratio. The maturity of debt also plays a significant role for pharmaceutical firms. The result indicates that high R&D firms borrow long term to avoid the challenge of renewing short term debt in adverse economic conditions or after mixed R&D outcomes. Again the magnitude is significant since a one standard deviation in the debt maturity (0.327 for pharmaceuticals) is associated with a $0.027 \times 0.327 = 0.9\%$ change in the R&D/sales ratio. Although the direction of the effect is similar for other R&D active firms, the effect is not particularly strong. Besides, the influence of cash reserves appears to be stronger among other R&D-active firms. But the effect is clearly positive for both groups of firms.

These results are totally consistent with Hypothesis 4 and show that risky investments such as R&D activities, which may induce a rapid cash burnout, should not be financed with debt which commits the firm to a strict schedule of cash outflows. Instead, they should be financed by equity which appears to promote R&D investments by providing assurance that they will not jeopardize the firm's survival. The recent work of Müller and Zimmermann (2009) confirms the importance of using equity to fund R&D activities. Likewise, Filatotchev and Piesse (2009) provide evidence that accumulated debt is a drag on R&D investments for newly-listed firms. In addition, if high R&D firms resort to debt financing they should preferably opt for long term debt for which the principal (or main cash outflow) is repaid only after several years. This also appears to take financial pressure off the firm, and thus supports greater R&D investments. Lastly, a bigger cushion of cash appears to have a positive effect, even after controlling for the firm's funding structure.

Effect on sales growth

Finally, we investigate whether R&D investments have any effect on future growth. Similar to the previous analysis, the independent variables consist of firm size (LNTA), an indicator of growth opportunities (LNQ), a measure of cash flows (EBITDA), the leverage ratio (DEBT), the composition of debt (MATU), and the cash position (LIQUID). In an alternate specification, current sales growth (SLSG) is included to control for potential unobserved factors. All regressions include year dummies to control for changes in the economic environment and industry dummies for the control sample of other R&D active firms. Standard errors are again clustered at the firm level. Table 3 presents the regression results.

Looking across the two samples, it appears that sales growth (SLSG) is persistent for other R&D active firms, but not for pharmaceutical companies. This means that for R&D-active firms sales increases (decreases) in a given year tend to be followed by sales increases (decreases) the next year. The coefficient on R&D investments (RND) indicates that they have a positive influence on future growth. However, the impact is statistically weak for pharmaceutical firms, possibly because the effect is measured immediately after the investments are made. As is well known, the payoff from pharmaceutical R&D is likely to occur after many years. Thus, the balance of evidence is weakly supportive of Hypothesis 5.

The dependent variable is sales growth over the following year. SLSG is sales growth from the previous year. RND is R&D expenses over sales. LNTA is the log of total assets.

Table 3.   R&D expenditure and subsequent sales growth.

	Pharmaceutical companies		Other R&D-active firms	
	(1)	(2)	(3)	(4)
RND	0.2246	0.2306	0.3665 ***	0.3834 ***
	(1.24)	(1.28)	(4.18)	(4.12)
SLSG		0.0487		0.0891 ***
		(0.46)		(5.65)
LNTA	− 0.0114 *	− 0.0104 *	− 0.0016 *	− 0.0017 **
	(− 1.87)	(− 1.71)	(− 1.87)	(− 1.97)
LNQ	0.0570 ***	0.0530 **	0.0784 ***	0.0715 ***
	(2.72)	(2.24)	(16.55)	(15.54)
EBITDA	0.7361 ***	0.7065 **	0.3637 ***	0.3252 ***
	(2.73)	(2.54)	(8.27)	(7.57)
DEBT	0.0471	0.0500	− 0.0230 ***	− 0.0199 **
	(0.63)	(0.69)	(− 3.19)	(− 2.45)
MATU	0.0047	0.0051	− 0.0006	− 0.0003
	(0.28)	(0.31)	(− 0.17)	(− 0.07)
LIQUID	− 0.0346	− 0.0340	− 0.0386 **	− 0.0380 **
	(− 0.47)	(− 0.45)	(− 2.33)	(− 2.35)
F value	3.47 ***	3.33 ***	66.72 ***	52.69 ***
R^2	0.1509	0.1528	0.2083	0.2149
N observations	288	288	14,827	14,827

LNQ is the log of market to book value of assets. EBITDA is earnings before interests, taxes and depreciation. DEBT is total debt over total assets. MATU is the proportion of long term debt. LIQUID is cash and equivalent over total assets. All regressions include year dummies (and industry dummies for non pharmaceutical firms). Robust t-statistics are indicated between brackets. ***, **, and * denote significance at the 1%, 5% and 10% level.

Firm size (LNTA), growth opportunities (LNQ) and cash flows (EBITDA) exhibit a similar effect in both samples. Unsurprisingly, larger firms are associated with lower sales growth. Firms with higher growth opportunities, as indicated by their higher market to book value (as a proxy for Tobin's Q) experience higher sales growth, especially among non pharmaceutical companies. Similarly, there is a strong relationship between sales growth and prior cash flows for both samples. Given the dispersion in cash flows (of about 4.3% for both samples, as measured by the standard deviation of EBITDA), the associated impact on sales growth appears to be quite significant (about 3.1% for pharmaceutical firms and 1.5% for other R&D active firms).

The remaining variables suggest that leverage (DEBT) does not affect the sales growth of pharmaceutical firms. This result may also come from the fact that these firms strive not to rely on debt to support their growth. Besides, high leverage can severely dent the growth of other R&D active firms. Finally, debt maturity presents an insignificant association with future sales growth, while the negative coefficient on cash reserves appears to reflect the fact that higher growth tends to deplete the firm's cash reserves.

Discussion

The analysis of R&D expenditures in the Japanese pharmaceutical industry provides several intriguing observations. First, we found a positive relation between R&D and firm size, which is totally opposite to the result obtained for the US and other countries, where a large share of R&D investment is carried out by small (often start-up) firms. Apart from suggesting the existence of economies of scale in the management of R&D projects, this relation highlights the role that size can play in mitigating the high level of risk affecting R&D active firms. This interpretation is consistent with the particularly low level of operational risk displayed by Japanese firms in cross-country comparisons of corporate risk taking. For instance, John *et al.* (2008) show that cash flow volatility in Japan is the lowest among all the countries included in their sample and several times lower relative to the cash flow volatility of US firms (2.1% against 9%). The fact that large firms have come to concentrate a disproportionate share of R&D investments in Japan may also be due to the relatively low return on R&D expenditures. This situation provides unsurprisingly little incentive for small firms to bear the considerable risk of undertaking projects that may never pay off and if so, only after a long and costly development cycle.

Consistent with earlier evidence presented by Mahlich and Roediger-Schluga (2006), we found that the financing of R&D investments in the pharmaceutical industry does not depend on the availability of internal funds, contrary to what Grabowski and Vernon (2000) have reported for US pharmaceutical companies. In Japan, R&D expenditures are much more determined by the firm's funding structure. More precisely, a solid balance sheet reflected in the prudent use of debt appears to stimulate R&D expenditures possibly because it helps instil greater confidence that the risk associated with these expenses can be absorbed if the R&D projects turn out to be unsuccessful. The importance of financing R&D activity with equity capital has recently been pointed out by Müller and Zimmermann (2009). Similarly, Filatotchev and Piesse (2009) indicate that debt financing is associated with a lower R&D intensity. The implication of inadequate funding is also illustrated by the sharp drop in R&D investments following leveraged buyouts (LBOs) in which target firms substitute a significant amount of debt to their existing equity (Long and Ravenscraft 1993). Furthermore, if pharmaceutical firms have to use debt, their preference is clearly in favour of long term loans which alleviate the financial pressure of renewing short term loans before the R&D projects start to generate positive cash flows. This financing behaviour seems to be specific to pharmaceutical firms probably because of the extended payback periods that characterize their R&D investments.

The positive correlation detected between a firm's R&D intensity and its liquidity position provides another piece of evidence in support of the notion that R&D activities need to be well funded and require appropriate financial resources to mitigate the high level of associated risk. This finding is consistent with the negative influence of debt for the reason that cash can be viewed as negative debt (since excess cash can be used to repay the firm's existing debt). We also observed that the market-to-book value of assets has little influence on the firm's R&D intensity, which suggests that pharmaceutical firms undertake their R&D projects regardless of the stock market's assessment of those investments. This result may have a lot to do with Japan's financial system which involves stable bank-firm relationships and gives less importance to investor sentiment (Hoshi and Kashyap 2001) . Accordingly, Japanese firms have a greater assurance of receiving funds even when stock market conditions are unfavourable. In contrast, investments in market-based economies depend to a larger extent on investor sentiment.

Another characteristic of the Japanese pharmaceutical industry is that sales growth appears to be weakly conditioned on past R&D investments. This finding is quite puzzling since there would be no reason to undertake high-risk investments without a clear benefit. However, this outcome could be due to the fact that we have measured the impact of R&D with a relatively short time lag. As it is well known, the benefits expected from R&D projects, whether they consist of higher sales or increased profits, are likely to take time to materialize. In addition, it is well known that R&D is a cumulative process. It follows that a measure of cumulated R&D expenditures might have been more suitable. Nevertheless, the analysis using a large control sample of firms with active R&D programmes reveals that R&D investments are generally associated with a significant increase in subsequent sales. Hence, the methodology used to assess the impact on future sales is not the likely cause of the insignificant results displayed by pharmaceutical firms. In this particular case, the competitive pressure induced by the saturation of the Japanese domestic market and the downward price spiral due to government attempts to contain mounting health expenditures (Oliver *et al.*, 1997, Ikegami and Campbell 2004) seem to be more credible explanations. The analysis also reveals that pharmaceutical firms exhibit a lower persistence in sales growth compared to other R&D active firms, which suggests that their commercial success is hard to sustain, consistent with highly competitive market conditions. Besides, strong internal cash flows contribute to improve the sales growth of firms in all industries.

Implication for theory and practice

Pharmaceutical firms have learned to operate in a high risk environment because they have been compelled to cope with an elevated rate of failure among their R&D projects. This experience is reflected in their financial policies. From a practical viewpoint, the main lesson for any high-risk firm is to secure a reliable source of funds in the form of equity capital. Debt financing is too hazardous given its relatively strict payment constraints. Short term debt is even worse because lenders may require the full amount to be repaid at short notice. The recent financial crisis is a timely reminder of the peril of over-leveraging and over-relying on short term debt. Surely, debt is cheaper than equity; and short-term debt most particularly. However, the precise reason why pharmaceutical firms avoid this type of financing is because they have learned that their cash flows, while potentially huge, are not dependable enough to commit to prompt capital outflows. Similarly, large cash reserves which have been repeatedly criticized for encouraging poor investments seem to be justified as an extra precaution against the risk of financial distress. It follows that when their risks are properly mitigated, R&D investments have the ability to spur sales which is eventually associated with higher profits. This virtuous circle can be noticed for all R&D intensive firms although the pricing pressure induced by current government policies appears to have clouded this effect in the case of pharmaceutical companies.

Conclusion

In this paper, we have analyzed the determinants and motives for undertaking R&D investments in a high risk industry. Unsurprisingly, the results underline the significant role played by risk considerations and thus, point to the importance of risk mitigation strategies. Consistent with the high degree of risk aversion generally displayed by Japanese companies, R&D investments are associated with strong balance sheets both on the right-hand side through solid equity funding, and on the left-hand side in the form of abundant cash reserves. Firms operating in a similar high-risk environment may be advised to follow this example and avoid compounding their operational risk with further financial risks.

Acknowledgements

We would like to thank the three anonymous referees for many helpful suggestions. Profesor Malcolm Warner, the APBR Co-editor, has also provided considerable advice that has greatly contributed to improve the paper.

Notes

1. Science, Technology and Competitiveness key figures report 2008/2009, European Commission. Available at http://ec.europa.eu/research/era/publication_en.cfm
2. Report on the survey of research and development, Statistics Bureau, MEXT, 2006. Available from http://www.mext.go.jp/english/news/2008/03/08021921/002/001.pdf
3. Ministry of Health, Labour and Welfare, and JETRO, *Japan Economic Monthly*, August 2005.
4. Trends in the pharmaceutical industry, *Japan Economic Monthly*, August 2005
5. In a similar vein, Hoshi *et al.* (1991) show that liquidity plays a lesser role in the financing of *keiretsu* affiliates.
6. Situation and perspectives of the pharmaceutical industry and biotechnologies, A.D. Little (Paris 2009)
7. These factors include the time lag between an investment and its final outcome, the duration of the investment cycle, and the profit margin strategy of the firm.
8. These factors include the time lag between an investment and its final outcome, the duration of the investment cycle, and the profit margin strategy of the firm.

References

Acemoglu, D. and Linn, J., 2004. Market size in innovation: theory and evidence from the pharmaceutical industry. *Quarterly journal of economics*, 119, 1049–1090.

Anderson, G. and Hussey, P., 2000. Population aging: a comparison among industrialized countries. *Health affairs*, 19, 191–203.

Bottazzi, G., Dosia, G., Lippi, M., Pammolli, F. and Riccaboni, M., 2001. Innovation and corporate growth in the evolution of the drug industry. *International journal of industrial organization*, 19, 1161–1187.

Filatotchev, I. and Piesse, J., 2009. R&D, internationalization and growth of newly listed firms: European evidence. *Journal of international business studies*, 40, 1260–1276.

Grabowski, H. and Vernon, J., 2000. The determinants in pharmaceutical research and development expenditures. *Journal of evolutionary economics*, 10, 201–215.

Griliches, Z., 1981. Market value, R&D, and patents. *Economic letters*, 7, 183–187.

Hall, B., 1980s. The stock market valuation of R&D investment during the 1980s. *American economic review*, 83, 259–264.

Hall, B., 2002. The financing of research and development. *Oxford review of economic policy*, 18, 35–51.

Hoshi, T., Kashyap, A. and Scharfstein, D., 1991. Corporate structure, liquidity and investment: evidence from Japanese panel data. *Quarterly journal of economics*, 100, 33–60.

Hoshi, T. and Kashyap, A., 2001. *Corporate financing and governance in Japan: the road to the future*. Cambridge, MA: MIT Press.

Hubbard, R., 1998. Capital market imperfections and investment. *Journal of economic literature*, 26, 193–225.

Ikegami, N. and Campbell, J., 2004. Japan's health care system: containing costs and attempting reform. *Health affairs*, 23, 26–36.

Jacobzone, S., 2000. Coping with ageing: international challenges. *Health affairs*, 19, 213–225.

John, K., Litov, L., and Yeung, B., 2008. Corporate governance and risk–taking. *Journal of finance*, 63, 1679–1728.

Lev, B., Radhakrishnan, S., and Ciftci, M., 2005. The stock market valuation of R&D leaders. Working paper, New York University.

Long, W. and Ravenscraft, D., 1993. LBOs, debt and R&D intensity. *Strategic management journal*, 14, 119–135.

Mahlich, J. and Roediger–Schluga, T., 2006. The determinants of pharmaceutical R&D expenditures: evidence from Japan. *Review of industrial organization*, 28, 145–164.

Megna, P. and Klock, M., 1993. The impact of intangible capital on Tobin's Q in the semiconductor industry. *American economic review*, 83, 265–269.

Müller, E. and Zimmermann, V., 2009. The importance of equity finance for R&D activity. *Small business economics*, 33, 303–318.

Myers, S., 1977. Determinants of corporate borrowing. *Journal of financial economics*, 5, 147–175.

Nguyen, P., Nivoix, S., and Noma, M., 2010. The valuation of R&D expenditures in Japan. *Accounting and finance*, 50 (4), 899–920.

Oliver, A., Ikegami, N., and Ikeda, S., 1997. Japan's ageing population: implications for healthcare. *Pharmaco economics*, 11, 306–318.

Sapienza, H., Autio, E., George, G., and Zahra, S., 2006. A capabilities perspective on the effects of early internationalization on firm survival and growth. *Academy of management review*, 31, 914–933.

Scherer, F., Harhoff, D., and Kukies, J., 2000. Uncertainty and the size distribution of rewards from innovation. *Journal of evolutionary economics*, 10, 175–200.

Schwartz, E., 2004. Patents and R&D as real options. *Economic notes*, 33, 23–54.

Leadership and performance in Japanese R&D teams

Jun Ishikawa

College of Business, Rikkyo University, Tokyo, Japan

This study examined the relative influence of transformational and gatekeeping leadership on team performance in a study of researchers working in industrial R&D teams in Japan. Potential effects of both internal and external communication and group norms for consensus were studied as possible mediating influences on the leadership-performance relationship. Results found that, while both forms of leadership enhanced communication processes within and between groups, only gatekeeping leadership served to reduce group norms for consensus. As a result, team cultures became somewhat more accepting of expressions of divergent opinions and new ideas from various team members, an important factor in R&D innovation and performance. By contrast, transformational leadership served to create team cultures in which divergence from group norms by various members was discouraged, leading to fewer innovative ideas and no performance increment. Results are discussed both in the context of the unique Japanese work environment and in the larger context of leadership processes across regions and cultures.

Introduction

Technological innovation has long been considered to be one of Japan's principal competitive assets in the highly volatile and high-stakes global economy. Developing new technologies, and new applications for existing technologies, are routinely cited as a principal reason for Japan's lead in markets such as consumer and industrial electronics, chemicals and pharmaceuticals and, increasingly, aerospace (Shibata 2006). At the centre of these efforts are the R&D research laboratories that churn out new products and applications at an unrelenting pace. At the heart of these labs is an approach to knowledge management that blends culture, technology, and process engineering (Nonaka 2005, Osono *et al.* 2008).

As a result of Japan's prominence on the world stage, numerous studies have been conducted over the years in an effort to explicate the principal factors that influence Japan's R&D laboratory performance (Clark and Fujimoto 1991, Nonaka and Takeuchi 1995, Kono and Clegg 2001, Lervek 2008, Ibata-Arens 2009, Motohashi 2009). Most of these studies have focused on the perceived uniqueness of Japan's culture, work ethic, engineering prowess, knowledge management systems, national innovation system, and industrial policies. A small subset of these studies focused specifically on leadership style as a potential influence. Given Japan's relatively strong cultural emphasis on collective behaviour, leadership style represents a potentially critical factor to consider in exploring how and why Japanese research teams perform at such high levels. However, even though leadership has long been identified as a key factor in team behaviour and effectiveness in other cultural settings, little is known about its relative impact on innovation and performance in the third largest economy of the world (Shibata 2006).

While the literature on leadership processes is rich in both theory and research, little has focused specifically on research and development teams, preferring other organizational settings such as manufacturing and marketing (Scott and Bruce 1998, Elkins and Keller 2003, Jackson and Tomioka 2004, Aycan 2008). Much of the research that exists tends to focus on the performance implications of *transformational leadership* (Bass and Roggio 2006). The principal finding here is that transformational, or charismatic, leaders can often create conditions in R&D teams that, not unlike other work environments, are conducive to exceptional effort and creativity. This, in turn, can lead to enhanced group performance (Elkins and Keller 2003).

The empirical question to be addressed here, however, is the extent to which transformational leadership (or any approach to leadership) can transcend cultural differences. Specifically, our question is whether transformational leadership, which some evidence suggests can lead to higher performance in Western research laboratories, can work equally effectively in non-Western settings. In point of fact, little evidence exists concerning the relative effectiveness of transformational leadership across cultures, particularly in East Asia (Avolio *et al.* 2005). Research by the GLOBE research project, for example, suggests that such leadership can be effective in some, but certainly not all, cultural environments (House *et al.* 2004, Dickson *et al.* 2009).

Because values and cognitive frameworks are different in collectivistic cultures compared to individualistic cultures, so too might we expect leadership styles to differ (Hooker 2003, Steers *et al.* 2010). For example, Abe (2010) suggested that leadership style, which promoted group oriented decision-making, was effective in Japan. Furthermore, in their systematic study, House *et al.* (2004) and Dickson *et al.* (2009) identified Japan as one environment where the effectiveness of Western-style leadership might be limited. In particular, strong consensus norms might negatively affect individual and organizational performance (particularly in teams) by curbing unique ideas that run counter to prevailing beliefs (Ishikawa 2008). If this is correct, the effects of transformational leadership on such norms should be examined in Japan. This study aims to investigate whether transformational leadership has a positive or negative impact on Japanese R&D team performance through norms for maintaining consensus. Previous studies have neglected this issue largely because it is not a concern in many Western settings. Nevertheless, it may be significant in a collectivistic culture like Japan.

Previous studies of transformational leadership across cultures are also limited in that they have routinely ignored the effects of communication patterns in team performance (Aycan 2008). It is argued here, that communication processes may be more important in R&D settings than other settings due to the creative and sometimes abstract interchanges that are required among team members. In this regard, several studies have found that variations in patterns of communication can significantly affect R&D team performance and knowledge creation (Katz and Tushman 1979, Kivimaki and Lansisalmi 2000, Hirst and Mann 2004, Halevy and Sagiv 2008). However, there have been few studies that examined the relationship between transformational leadership and team communication in R&D settings, and none focusing on Japan. In this study, it is proposed that transformational leadership will have a positive impact on R&D team performance through the team communication process in a Japanese sample. Thus, this study aims to examine the two kinds of influences of transformational leadership on R&D team performance: a positive influence through a norm for maintaining consensus and a negative influence through team communication.

Finally, this study compares *gatekeeping leadership* with transformational leadership to determine which leader behaviour is more effective in this environment. In contrast to transformational leadership, gatekeeping leadership emphasizes a supervisor's role in building bridges or making connections between employees and their need for information and resources to complete their assignments (Hirst and Mann 2004). Gatekeepers are facilitators, not cheerleaders; supporters, not commanders. Indeed, many effective gatekeepers may have little or no charismatic abilities. Still, they can play an important role in facilitating team effort and performance. In this study, it is proposed that gatekeeping leadership positively influences Japanese R&D team performance through a norm for maintaining consensus and through communication. In other words, it is proposed that gatekeeping leadership is more effective than transformational leadership in influencing independently measured performance in the Japanese context.

Transformational leadership and gatekeeping leadership

Transformational leadership

Transformational leadership has been defined as leader behaviour that influences followers to broaden and elevate their goals and provide them with the confidence to perform beyond the expectations specified in implicit or explicit exchange agreements (Dvir *et al.* 2002, Avolio *et al.* 2005, Dickson *et al.* 2009). Advocates of this model argue that most previous leadership models (generally referred to as transactional models) were premised on assumptions about followers' rational decision-making; that is, followers behaved in order to maximize their rewards in the organization, which required leaders to integrate followers' rewards with their goals. As such, a leader's principal responsibility is to set goals, clarify desired outcomes, provide feedback, and exchange rewards for accomplishments (Dvir *et al.* 2002). While advocates of transformational leadership do not disagree with the value of transactional exchanges, they argue that in reality followers do not necessarily always behave based solely on rational decision-making principles. Particularly in high performance work teams, they assert that followers will often emphasize their contribution to team performance over their rational exchange agreements with the organization.

According to Bass and Avolio (1990), Avolio *et al.* (2005), and Aycan (2008), transformational leadership consists of four factors: idealized influence, inspirational motivation, intellectual stimulation, and individualized consideration. The idealized influence is a behaviour that inspires followers and fosters identification with their leader. The inspirational motivation is a behaviour that encourages followers by expressing enthralling visions. The intellectual stimulation includes drawing followers' attention to problems and promoting novel perspectives and their intellectual curiosity. The individualized consideration involves realizing followers' needs and providing them with support and coaching. These behaviours encourage followers' ardent contribution to the achievement of team goals.

Transformational leadership has been studied extensively in recent years and has been found to be fairly consistently related to positive job attitudes (Podsakoff *et al.* 1990, Dumdum *et al.* 1991, Barling *et al.* 1996) and the job performance of followers (Dumdum *et al.* 1991, Howell and Avolio 1993, Yammarino and Dubinsky 1994, Barling *et al.* 1996, Lowe and Galen Kroeck 1996, Dvir *et al.* 2002). Only a small subset of these studies focused specifically on R&D teams, the principal focus of the present study. For example,

Keller (1992) found that transformational leadership was positively related to R&D team performance, which included project quality and budget/schedule rated by project members and managers, respectively. Transformational leadership significantly influenced project quality and budget/schedule in both research and development teams, although the significance of the correlation was more prominent in research projects than in development projects. Keller (2006) also noted that, based on a longitudinal study, that transformational leadership could predict five-year-later profitability and speed to market.

Berson and Linton (2005) compared the effects of transformational leadership in R&D settings with those in non-R&D settings and found that, although a significant correlation between transformational leadership and outcome variables including quality climate, job satisfaction, and overall satisfaction was observed in both R&D and non-R&D settings, it was stronger in R&D settings than in non-R&D settings. While job attitudes are important for management here, it is also possible that such leadership would also influence R&D performance, although the authors did not specifically study this relationship. Moreover, while Keller (1992, 2006) and Berson and Linton (2005) both found positive relationships between transformational leadership and R&D team performance, they did not search for possible factors that might mediate this relationship.

Finally, Shin and Zhou (2003) found that intrinsic motivation mediated the relationship between transformational leadership and the creativity of followers in Korean R&D settings, and that followers' collectivistic norms moderated the relationship between them. They indicated that these norms largely affected the efficiency of transformational leadership in the Korean work environment. However, since Shin and Zhou (2003) focused their study on an individual (as opposed to a group) level, it is difficult to generalize to groups. Moreover, some caution is in order here (and throughout this study) about over-generalizing about which style of leadership is most effective across cultures as significant differences can sometimes be found (Paik and Pak 2009).

The results of these studies indicate that transformational leadership was positively related to R&D team performance in the samples studied. Still, the question remains concerning both the external generalizability of these results (specifically, the potential applicability of these results to the Japanese work environment) and possible mediators of this relationship. Two mediators, a norm for maintaining consensus and communication patterns, are examined in this study.

Norm for group consensus

As mentioned above, some previous studies showed transformational leadership can positively influence R&D team performance in Western settings. Nevertheless it is possible that transformational leadership also has a negative impact on R&D team performance through the strong norm for maintaining consensus in Japanese settings. Japan is a collectivistic and high context culture in which group consensus is highly valued (Dulek and Fielden 1991, Kono and Clegg 2001, Abe 2010). Local management practices are designed to promote this, even in R&D divisions (Hara *et al.* 2008). Unlike in Britain, Germany, or the US, most Japanese R&D employees are recruited as new college graduates, and tend to devote themselves to a single company until retirement. Moreover, company-specific knowledge and skills are emphasized, and in-house training is regarded as important (McCormick 1995). Although Japanese companies nowadays are changing some of their traditional HRM practices to Western style practices, these shifts are occurring very slowly and cautiously. For example, performance-based compensation systems have been applied to limited hierarchies in the area of R&D (Benson and Debroux

2003, Hemmert 2009). Because of this, intellectual inbreeding often occurs and radical innovations may fail to emerge at a rate often found in the West.

It is possible that transformational leadership serves to reinforce these norms of group consensus that reinforce either the status quo or only marginal or evolutionary change or innovation. One reason is that transformational leadership has a strong impact on followers. Sometimes the impact is too strong for followers to confront their leaders' opinions. In particular, idealized influence, which is one dimension of transformational leadership, may have such an effect. This idealized influence promotes followers' identification with their leader. The result is very similar to that of charismatic leadership because the primary influence process of charismatic leadership is personal identification, which is the influence derived from followers' desire to please and imitate leaders (Conger 1989). Under such an influence, followers do not want to criticize their leaders and do not permit colleagues to criticize their leaders. From a review of previous studies, Yukl (2002) noted that being in awe of the leader can reduce good suggestions by followers and that a desire for leader acceptance can inhibit criticism by followers and be considered a possible dark side to charismatic leadership.

Other studies indicated that transformational leadership promotes cohesiveness of the team (Jung and Sosik 2002, Pillai and Williams 2004, Stanko and Gibson 2009). This is because transformational leadership fosters followers' commitment to the goal and influences followers to strive for the achievement of the goal in unison with other team members. In general, cohesiveness should have a positive impact on team performance, but excessive cohesiveness may also negatively impact performance by repressing opposing views or ideas. For example, Leana (1985) found that group cohesiveness was a major cause of groupthink. Therefore, transformational leadership may suppress some ideas and opinions expressed by team members.

In addition, transformational leadership often unites followers and creates a team climate, which is required for achievement of the goal (Liao and Chuang 2007). As a result, it may press followers not to behave contrary to the climate the leader aims to create. As a result, team members may be reluctant to diverge from prevailing norms; and indeed, they may even be punished for this. While similar norms are found in the West, the prevailing strength of consensus norms in Japan make it much more difficult for employees to take issue with prevailing ideas, oftentimes preventing them from opposing any consensus reached by the group or organization they belong to. As a result, many new ideas that do not quickly receive group approval can languish or die. For example, Postmes *et al.* (2001) found that strong norms for maintaining consensus adversely affected the quality of group decision making, and led to poor team performance. At the same time, such norms often reduce the diversity of information and opinions within a team, which is essential for team performance (Pelz and Andrews 1966, Halevy and Sagiv 2008).

Therefore, it can be posited that a strong norm for maintaining consensus, which undermines a diversity of new ideas, can eventually hinder team performance in the Japanese context.

Hypothesis 1: A norm for maintaining consensus mediates the relationship between transformational leadership and team performance in such a way that transformational leadership is positively related to a norm for maintaining consensus and this norm for consensus is negatively related to team performance.

Internal and external communication

For R&D teams to work together effectively, open, timely, and frank communication is essential (Menzel 1966, Halevy and Sagiv 2008, Stanko and Gibson 2009). While team members acquire technological information through books and papers, they also make extensive use of external communication with specialists outside of their organizations. Therefore, following the findings of Ancona and Caldwell (1992), we would expect external communication to affect team performance through promoting the acquisition of technological information.

However, information required for R&D performance is not only technological in nature. For example, it is also necessary for team members to acquire information about the manufacturing process and customer needs. In order to acquire this information, internal communication, or communication among members inside the organizations (e.g. members of manufacturing or marketing departments) is also useful. In particular, some studies indicate that high context communication inside organizations fosters knowledge creation in Japanese companies (Nonaka and Takeuchi 1995, Hentschel and Haghirian 2010). Therefore, following the consistent previous findings of the research, we would expect that ample availability of both external and internal communication to be positively related to R&D team performance (Kivimaki and Lansisalmi 2000, Hirst and Mann 2004).

In theory, at least, transformational leadership is, or ought to be, related to team communication. Transformational leadership clarifies the goal of followers (Nemanich and Keller 2007) and promotes goal commitment from them (Piccolo and Colquitt 2006). Such goals make followers clear about what information is necessary or important. New knowledge, which is the goal of R&D activities, is thus created by the composition and interpretation of available information. Furthermore, high commitment to these goals stimulates followers' information seeking activities because information is one of the most important resources for the achievement of team goals.

Individualized consideration, which is one of the four dimensions of transformational leadership, provides followers with support and coaching. Because of this, transformational leadership should have a positive impact on the development of followers (Dvir *et al.* 2002). This includes the advancement of communication skills and inducements for increased communication, since communication is a key factor in R&D performance. Under such influence from transformational leadership, the followers should – at least in theory – improve their communication patterns.

Intellectual stimulation, which is also one dimension of transformational leadership, encourages followers to promote novel perspectives and open their intellectual curiosity. Therefore, they should apply new ideas or try new methods in order to promote novel perspectives and stimulate their intellectual curiosity. Eventually, they should come to communicate more effectively because communication is an important tool for obtaining new ideas or methods.

Transformational leadership has also been found to positively influence leader-member exchange (Hui *et al.* 2005). Followers, who have good relationship with their leaders, desire to meet their demands. In this case, the demands from leaders typically involve goal achievement and the acquisition of information. Further, the ideal influence dimension contributes to followers' having more than just self-interest in mind, thus overcoming the fear of incurring personal costs in conducting various communication activities.

Hence, followers under transformational leadership should search for information that is required to achieve their goals. In this regard, Madzar (2001) found that transformational leadership was positively related to the information inquiry behaviours of followers, at least with respect to followers' behaviours that sought information from their leaders. However, as noted above, other types of information are also required to achieve team goals, including outside information. Accordingly, we posit that transformational leadership helps to promote both internal and external communications of followers:

Hypothesis 2a: Internal communication mediates the relationship between transformational leadership and team performance in such a way that transformational leadership is positively related to internal communication and internal communication is positively related to team performance.

Hypothesis 2b: External communication mediates the relationship between transformational leadership and team performance in such a way that transformational leadership is positively related to external communication and external communication is positively related to team performance.

Gatekeeping leadership

Gatekeeping leadership is a construct that has evolved from the more general construct of a gatekeeper. A number of empirical studies have focused on the role of gatekeepers in R&D team performance (Taylor and Utterback 1975, Hirst and Mann 2004). In particular, gatekeepers tend to be 'communication stars' that can perform both internal communication and external communication roles frequently and effectively. This is not necessarily easy to accomplish, since both contexts are different from each other. Nevertheless, gatekeepers can often perform both communication activities simultaneously and effectively. Indeed, they often perform important roles as a node in highly diverse information flows. Gatekeepers often have communication networks with specialists outside the organizations. In this sense, they bridge organizational boundaries. They not only acquire the technological information from the networks, which is required for R&D teams, but also translate such information into terms that are meaningful to other team members within an internal context. They also communicate with employees of other departments inside the organizations. Previous studies showed that in R&D teams gatekeepers positively influenced performance by encouraging communication with other team members.

Meanwhile, Allen (1977) suggested that gatekeepers were not always equivalent to team leaders. That is, leaders and gatekeepers may exist separately and play different roles in teams. However, if leaders and gatekeepers exist separately, the flow of directions and information may get confused. On the contrary, when leaders play the role of gatekeepers simultaneously, smoother communication within the team would be performed and team performance may increase.

In the present study, gatekeeping leadership is defined as leadership that plays the role of gatekeeper. In the teams where leaders display gatekeeping leadership, team members may actively perform communication and eventually have high performance. In this regard, Hirst and Mann (2004) show that leaders that performed the role of gatekeepers positively influenced R&D team performance. Furthermore, Kim and Min (1999) found that the gatekeeping role was one of the most important roles for R&D team leaders in a Korean sample. This suggests that gatekeeping leadership may be effective in collectivistic cultures.

Internal and external communication

Several early studies show that gatekeepers could influence the communication patterns and richness of other members in R&D teams (Allen 1977, Tushman 1977, Katz and Tushman 1979, Tushman and Katz 1980). For example, Tushman and Katz (1980) showed that gatekeepers influenced team performance through encouraging the external communication of other team members, while Tushman (1977) found that the gatekeeping role affected the internal communication of other members. Further, Harada (2003) noted that gatekeepers influenced the communication of other members in Japanese R&D settings. Finally, Tushman and Katz (1980) suggested that non-supervisor gatekeepers have a negative association between external communication and performance, although supervisor gatekeepers have a positive association. The results of these studies suggest that gatekeeping leadership positively influences the internal and external communication of team members.

Furthermore, gatekeeping leaders actively perform both external and internal communication because they understand that communication is critical for R&D performance. As a result, leader expectations have a significant impact on the learning behaviour of followers through goal setting, providing learning opportunities, and feedback (Bezuijen *et al.* 2009). Accordingly, if gatekeeping leaders offer goal setting for communication, communication opportunities, and feedback for team members' communication, team members come to perform communication more actively.

Because of these reasons, team members with gatekeeping leaders communicate more positively with internal or external individuals. Frequent communication promotes information sharing, such as technological information and internal information that includes the vision and strategy of the company, information about the manufacturing process, customer needs, and other information. Based on this, the following hypotheses are proposed:

Hypothesis 3a: Internal communication mediates the relationship between gatekeeping leadership and team performance in such a way that gatekeeping leadership is positively related to internal communication and internal communication is positively related to team performance.

Hypothesis 3b: External communication mediates the relationship between gatekeeping leadership and team performance in such a way that gatekeeping leadership is positively related to external communication and external communication is positively related team performance.

Norm for group consensus

Gatekeeping leaders bring various types of information to teams. Because of this, team members can share various types of information inside the teams. This means that they share various opinions, various values, and various points of view. Such sharing reduces the pressure that builds up consensus norm. Gatekeeping leaders understand that using various contexts is critical for R&D performance. Hence, they attach importance to the diversity of opinions, values, and points of views because such diversity is important in various contexts. Because of this, gatekeeping leaders would try to shape norms that regard diversity as important. Taggar and Ellis (2007) showed that leader expectations had a significant impact on norm creation. In this regard, Feldman (1984) found that norms are enforced when they facilitate team survival. Conversely, norms are weakened if team

114

members recognize that they do not contribute to team survival. Team members thus weaken norms for maintaining lock-step consensus because they regard diverse opinions to be important for team survival.

Moreover, it is possible that gatekeeping leadership facilitates communication among team members. It fosters team member behaviour that actively exchanges opinions inside the teams. As a result, team members share various opinions. The members in such teams do not shape consensus norms because they share and respect various kinds of opinions.

Because of these reasons, team members under gatekeeping leadership reduce norms for maintaining consensus. As mentioned above, norms for maintaining consensus would impede team performance. Hence, it is posited that:

Hypothesis 4: A norm for maintaining group consensus mediates the relationship between gate-keeping leadership and team performance in such a way that gate-keeping leadership is negatively related to norm for maintaining consensus and a norm for consensus is negatively related to team performance.

Method

Sample

The data for this study were obtained through a survey carried out during October 2007 and March 2008. The sample consisted of 122 R&D teams from seven industrial parts manufacturers in Japan. In addition to 122 team leaders (response rate: 100%), 683 R&D team members (response rate: 82.4%) and 25 managers (response rate: 100%) also participated in the study. Each team member belonged to a single team, and each team was managed by one of the 25 managers. Among the team leaders, 94.1% were men, 9.3% held a doctoral degree, and their average age was 36 years old. Among the team members, 89.1% were men, their average age was 30 years old, and their average tenure in the team was two years. The average team size was six persons.

Distribution and collection of the questionnaires was done on company premises and with the prior approval of the R&D department management of each firm. Because of this, response rate was high. The questionnaires were collected by the author in sealed envelopes, therefore confidentiality was maintained.

Measures

This study consisted of six questionnaire measures, plus control variables. Corresponding Japanese versions for all of the measures used in this study were constructed in accordance with the translation-back-translation procedure outlined by Brislin (1980).

Transformational leadership was measured by 20 items adapted from Bass's Multifactor Leadership Questionnaire (MLQ) Form 5X (Bass and Avolio 2004). Each team member was asked to rate his/her leader's behaviour on a five-point response scale. Four items were used to measure inspirational motivation, intellectual stimulation, and individualized consideration. Eight items were used to measure idealized influence. In order to verify that these four factors did contribute to an overall transformational leadership index, a confirmatory factor analysis was conducted. The result of the analysis suggested that a higher-order factor solution provided an adequate fit ($\chi^2 = 131.27$ ($p < 0.05$), AGFI $= 0.91$, CFI $= 0.94$, RMSEA $= 0.04$, NFI $= 0.93$).

Gatekeeping leadership was measured by five items adapted from Hirst and Mann (2004). An example of the items used in this scale is 'The leader coordinates the team's task efforts with outside stakeholders'. Each team member was asked to rate his/her leader's behaviour on a five-point scale, ranging from strongly agree to strongly disagree.

Internal and external communication were measured by three items each. Each team member was asked to rate the frequency of internal and external communication in his/her team on a five-point response scale, ranging from strongly agree to strongly disagree.

The norm for maintaining consensus was measured by three items adapted from Postmes *et al.* (2001). Each team member was asked to rate his/her group norm for maintaining consensus on a five-point response scale, ranging from very strong to very weak. For example, one of the three measuring items was 'People in this group generally adjust to one another with ease'.

A confirmatory factor analysis was conducted in order to see if transformational leadership, gate-keeping leadership, internal communication, external communication, and norm for maintaining consensus were the distinct construct in each category, respectively. The result of the analysis suggested that a five-factor solution had a better fit than other solutions.

Team performance was measured independently by four items adapted from Keller (2001); that is, technical quality, schedule performance, cost performance, and overall team performance. The managers, who are higher in rank than team leaders, were asked to rate each item on a five-point response scale.

Control variables include team size, which was provided by the leaders, and team members' average tenure provided by the team members.

Aggregation tests

Transformational leadership, gatekeeping leadership, internal communication, external communication, and norm for maintaining consensus were aggregated to mean values within each team, which was the unit of the analysis. To justify this aggregation, a within-group correlation (r_{wg}) was computed to assess the amount of agreement by the team members (James *et al.* 1984). The mean r_{wg} value was 0.87 for transformational leadership, 0.89 for gatekeeping leadership, 0.90 for internal communication, 0.89 for external communication, and 0.89 for norm for maintaining consensus. In addition, the ICC(1) values were as follows: transformational leadership, 0.22; gatekeeping leadership, 0.50; internal communication, 0.24; external communication, 0.36; and norm for maintaining consensus, 0.25. ICC(2) values were as follows: transformational leadership, 0.61; gatekeeping leadership, 0.85; internal communication, 0.64; external communication, 0.76; and norm for maintaining consensus, 0.65. The overall pattern of results across the r_{wg}, ICC(1), and ICC(2) analyses provided sufficient support for aggregating the data to team level of analysis.

Results

The mean values, standard deviations, and coefficient alphas, as well as a correlation matrix are shown in Table 1. As expected, transformational leadership had significant positive correlations with internal communication and a norm for maintaining consensus for this Japanese sample. However, it was not related to external communication or, perhaps most importantly, team performance. Contrarily, gatekeeping leadership showed positive correlations with internal communication, external communication and, again

Table 1. Descriptive statistics and correlations.

	Mean	s.d.	α	1	2	3	4	5	6	7
1. Team size	5.59	1.21								
2. Team tenure: Member	1.94	1.14		0.02						
3. Transformational leadership	3.15	0.59	0.93	0.01	0.04					
4. Gatekeeping leadership	3.36	0.75	0.81	−0.10	−0.02	0.23*				
5. Norm for maintaining consensus	2.38	0.72	0.81	0.16	0.19*	0.37**	−0.20*			
6. Internal communication	3.80	0.53	0.80	−0.04	0.18*	0.43**	0.54**	0.14		
7. External communication	2.50	0.84	0.85	−0.09	−0.21*	−0.04	0.39**	−0.41**	0.09	
8. Team performance	3.01	0.91	0.84	−0.12	0.12	0.17	0.32**	−0.24**	0.37**	0.17

Note: *$p < 0.05$, **$p < 0.01$.

importantly, team performance. Gatekeeping leadership was also negatively correlated with a norm for maintaining consensus.

To test the relationship between leadership and various potential mediators, structural equation modelling was conducted; the results are shown in Figure 1. As expected, this analysis found a significant positive correlation between transformational leadership consensus norms. Furthermore, transformational leadership was positively related to internal communication, but not to external communication. In contrast, gatekeeping leadership was negatively related to a norm for maintaining consensus and positively related to internal and external communication. In addition, there was a negative correlation between the norm for maintaining consensus and team performance and a positive correlation between internal communication and team performance. However, there was no significant correlation between external communication and team performance. These results suggest that external communication does not mediate between the two kinds of leadership and team performance. Moreover, this model did not show adequate fit ($\chi^2 = 38.09$ ($p < 0.05$), AGFI $= 0.82$, CFI $= 0.87$, RMSEA $= 0.11$, NFI $= 0.80$).

Hence, another model that excluded external communication was examined. Results are shown in Figure 2. This model shows an adequate fit ($\chi^2 = 20.25$ ($p > 0.05$),

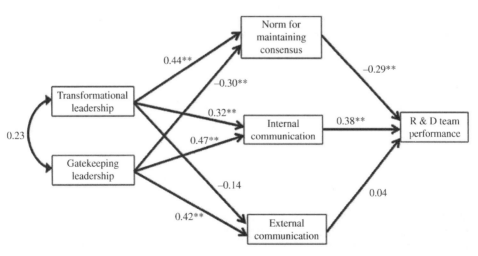

Figure 1. Result of SEM[a].
Note: **$p < 0.01$, [a]The effect of control variables are not shown.

AGFI = 0.89, CFI = 0.94, RMSEA = 0.08, NFI = 0.87), and all the paths shown in it were significant. A negative correlation was found only between a norm for maintaining consensus and team performance, while the other correlations were all positive. The result of this analysis suggests that the norm for maintaining consensus mediates the relationship between transformational leadership and team performance in such a way that transformational leadership was positively related to the norm for maintaining consensus, while the norm for maintaining consensus was negatively related to team performance. The result also indicates that the norm for maintaining consensus mediates the relationship between gatekeeping leadership and team performance in such a way that gatekeeping leadership was negatively related to the norm for maintaining consensus and the norm for maintaining consensus was negatively related to team performance. Meanwhile internal communication positively mediated the relationship between both leadership and team performance.

Although Figure 2 suggests an indirect relationship between leadership and team performance, it is possible that there is a direct relationship between them. Therefore, a partially mediated model, which was obtained by adding a direct path between both leadership and team performance, was conducted. The result of this analysis indicated an adequate fit ($\chi^2 = 17.16$ ($p > 0.05$), AGFI = 0.88, CFI = 0.95, RMSEA = 0.08, NFI = 0.89), but correlations between both leadership and team performance were not significant.

These results support Hypotheses 1, 2a, 3a, and 4, but not Hypotheses 2b and 3b.

Discussion

In this study, two different approaches to leadership (transformational and gatekeeping) were compared as they relate to independently measured job performance in Japanese R&D teams. The results indicate that gatekeeping leadership was directly related to team performance for this sample, while transformational leadership was not. As hypothesized, gatekeeping leadership enhanced internal communication among team members, while simultaneously tempering a norm for group consensus that could limit open discussions and disagreements – a typical success factor in research and development facilities. By contrast, transformational leadership served to increase both communication norms and norms for group consensus, and this combination led to less than optimal performance results. That is, a strong norm for maintaining group consensus restrained the critical analysis of various team members and reduced the overall quality of decision making as a team. Accordingly, transformational leadership affected team performance positively through internal communication, but negatively through the maintenance of a norm for

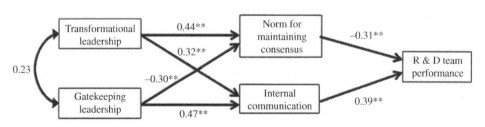

Figure 2. Result of SEM[b] excluded external communication.
Note: **$p < 0.07$, [b]The effect of control variables are not shown.

maintaining consensus, thereby yielding poor performance results. These findings are consistent with previous observations about knowledge management techniques in Japanese firms (Nonaka 2005, Osono *et al.* 2008).

According to theory, gatekeeping leaders encourage their followers to communicate frequently, even to the point of strong disagreements when it is in the interest of attaining project results (Hirst and Mann 2004). They understand that diverse information and opinions are necessary for research performance. Hence, it is likely that gatekeeping leaders understand not only various types of information processing, but also various cognitive frameworks and personal values that are necessary for R&D team performance and knowledge creation. Under such leadership, team members recognize that various contexts are required for team performance, and they feel it is acceptable to offer their own opinions and suggestions, even if these include criticism of the ideals of colleagues.

With these findings in mind, three study limitations must be identified. First, due to access limitations, this study was not designed as a comparative empirical study. Instead, the data collected here from Japanese employees were compared against reasonably consistent findings of similar employees from various Western studies (Avolio *et al.* 2005). Additional investigations would be helpful that incorporated samples from two or more cultures. This issue can be raised for studies of effective leader behaviour in general. That is, much of the existing research on leadership assumes that these theories are largely culture-free. The present findings call this generalization into question, inviting further studies along these lines.

A second potential limitation is that the present study focused on R&D teams. While a better understanding of leadership processes in such teams is clearly useful, it is not certain that employees and teams in other Japanese organizations or professions would respond in a similar manner. In view of the widespread collective nature of Japanese society, it is not unlikely that many other people in many different work environments would indeed respond in a similar way (Kono and Clegg 2001). This is an empirical question that the present study does not answer.

A third potential limitation of the present study is that the interrelated functions of research and development were not examined separately. A prior study by Keller (1992) suggested that the difference between research and development could be an important moderator in terms of the correlation between transformational leadership and R&D team performance. However, in the present study, companies did not differentiate between these two groups; indeed, the two groups worked as integrated team members, making differentiations impossible without losing the very concept of the teams that were under study.

Implications

It is believed that this study makes some contributions to the theory and practice. First, it raises questions concerning the universal applicability of transformational (or any other) leadership style. Most previous studies concluded, or simply argued without evidence, that transformational leadership had a positive effect on performance regardless of the situation or environment due largely to the uniform influence of charisma on subordinates (Bass and Roggio 2006). The results of the present study do not support this position. Moreover, previous studies have neglected to investigate why transformational leadership may not work equally across cultures. The present study found that transformational efforts adversely affected team performance through their reinforcement of norms for maintaining group consensus, at least in this Japanese setting. That is, transformational processes led employees to pull together in ways that inhibited the free or independent expression of ideas that may have been at odds with the group. This, in turn, led to fewer ideas or innovations being suggested, which resulted in poorer performance. Although this sequence of events may not have occurred in many Western work environments, its existence in a Japanese work environment is not surprising (Kono and Clegg 2001, Steers *et al.* 2010). This finding suggests that transformational leadership may have a negative impact on team performance in not only Japanese settings but also other collectivistic country settings.

Second, this study examined communication as the mediator between transformational leadership and team performance. Many prior studies indicated that communication had significant impact on R&D performance, and some studies showed that transformational leadership was effective in R&D settings. Nonetheless, there have been no previous studies that examined the relationship between transformational leadership, communication, and R&D team performance. The present study examined this relationship. Although transformational leadership had a negative impact on R&D team performance, it also had a positive impact on internal and external communication.

Third, the present study suggests that gatekeeping leadership is more effective than transformational leadership in collectivistic cultures such as that in Japan. In this sample, transformational leadership had a negative effect on R&D team performance, although it had a positive effect on consensus norms. In contrast, gatekeeping leadership influenced R&D team performance through a combination of a positive influence on group communication and a negative, or tempering, influence on rigid consensus norms. When leaders openly encouraged the frank expression and exchange of ideas that may have run counter to group norms, employees presumably felt more comfortable engaging in such behaviours, resulting in new ideas and subsequently improved performance.

The participants of this study were exclusively R&D employees. Hence, any generalizations of the effects of gatekeeping leadership are limited. However, communication may be a key factor for teams that need creativity beyond just R&D teams. Furthermore, norms for maintaining consensus may represent a major impediment to creativity in teams in general. Because gatekeeping leadership promoted the communication of team members and tempered the consensus norm in this study, it is likely that gatekeeping leadership has a positive impact on other types of teams in other collectivistic countries, compared to transformational leadership.

Conclusions

This study offers evidence concerning the lack of a one-size-fits-all theory of leadership around the globe. Instead, it suggests that future leadership research – as well as future managerial efforts to lead subordinates – must be tempered with a clear recognition of cultural and other local factors that can influence subordinate attitudes and behaviours. This study also suggests that leadership effectiveness in Japan, and possibly other Asian cultures, represents a fruitful area for future research. In point of fact, with few notable exceptions (e.g. Nonaka 2005, Osono *et al.* 2008), little theory-building research focusing on leadership in Asia can be found, despite the growing economic and political importance of this region. Because of this, rigorous research of a comparative nature, both within (e.g. Japan vs. Korea vs. China) and between Asia and other regions (e.g. Asia vs. North America vs. Europe), would prove useful for expanding our collective global understanding of influence processes around the world. In this endeavour, it is hoped that this study represents one useful step.

Acknowledgement

The author would like to thank Richard T. Mowday, Carlos Sanchez-Runde, and Richard M. Steers for their helpful comments on an earlier draft of this paper.

References

Abe, M., 2010. Introduction: Japanese management in the 21th century. *In*: P. Haghirian, ed. *Innovation and change in Japanese management*. Basingstoke: Palgrave Macmillan, 1–11.

Allen, T.J., 1977. *Managing the flow of technology*. Cambridge, MA: MIT Press.

Ancona, D.G. and Caldwell, D.F., 1992. Bridging the boundary: external activity and performance in organizational teams. *Administrative science quarterly*, 37, 634–665.

Avolio, B.J., Walumbwa, F.O., and Weber, T., 2005. Leadership: current theories, research, and future directions. *Annual review of psychology*, 60, 421–449.

Aycan, Z., 2008. Cross–cultural approaches to leadership. *In*: P. Smith, M. Peterson and D. Thomas eds. *Handbook of cross–cultural management research*. Los Angeles, CA: Sage, 219–232.

Barling, J., Weber, T., and Kelloway, E.K., 1996. Effects of transformational leadership training on attitudinal and financial outcomes: a field experiment. *Journal of applied psychology*, 81, 827–832.

Bass, B.M. and Avolio, B.J., 1990. Developing transformational leadership: 1992 and beyond. *Journal of European industrial training*, 14, 21–27.

Bass, B.M. and Avolio, B.J., 2004. *Multifactor leadership questionnaire (3rd. ed.) – form 5x – short*. Menlo Park, CA: Mind Garden.

Bass, B.M. and Roggio, R.E., 2006. *Transformational ledership*, (2nd ed.) Mahwah, NJ: Lawrence Erlbaum.

Benson, J. and Debroux, P., 2003. Flexible labour markets and individualized employment: the beginnings of a new Japanese HRM system. *Asia Pacific business review*, 9, 55–75.

Berson, Y. and Linton, J.D., 2005. An examination of the relationships between leadership style, quality, and employee satisfaction in R&D versus administrative environments. *R&D management*, 35, 51–60.

Bezuijen, X.M., Van Den Berg, P.T., Van Dam, K., and Thierry, H., 2009. Pygmalion and employee learning: the role of leader behaviors. *Journal of management*, 35, 1248–1267.

Brislin, R.W., 1980. Translation and content analysis of oral and written materials. *In*: H.C. Triandis and W.W. Lambert, eds. *Handbook of cross–cultural psychology*. Boston, MA: Allyn & Bacon, 349–444.

Clark, K.B. and Fujimoto, T., 1991. *Product development performance*. Boston, MA: Harvard Business School Press.

Conger, J.A., 1989. *The charismatic leader: behind the mystique of exceptional leadership*. San Francisco, CA: Jossey–Bass.

Dickson, M., Den Hartog, D., and Castano, N., 2009. Understanding leadership across cultures. *In*: R.S. Bhagat and R.M. Steers eds. *Handbook of culture, organizations, and work*. Cambridge, UK: Cambridge University Press, 219–243.

Dulek, R.E. and Fielden, J.S., 1991. International communication: an executive primer. *Business horizons*, 34, 20.

Dumdum, U.R., Fielden, J.S., and Hill, J.S., 1991. International communicating: an executive primer. *In*: B.J. Avolio and F.J. Yammarino, eds. *Transformational and charismatic leadership: the road ahead*. Oxford: Elsevier Science, 36–66.

Dvir, T., Eden, D., Avolio, B.J., and Shamir, B., 2002. Impact of transformational leadership on follower development and performance: a field experiment. *Academy of management journal*, 45, 735–744.

Elkins, T. and Keller, R.T., 2003. Leadership in research and development organizations: a literature review and conceptual framework. *Leadership quarterly*, 14, 587.

Feldman, D.C., 1984. The development and enforcement of group norms. *Academy of management review*, 9, 47–53.

Halevy, N. and Sagiv, L., 2008. Teams wihtin and across cultures. *In*: P. Smith, M. Peterson and D. Thomas eds. *The handbook of cross–cultural management research*. Los Angeles, CA: Sage, 253–268.

Hara, T., Kambayashi, N., and Matsushima, N., eds, 2008. *Industrial innovation*. London: Routledge.

Harada, T., 2003. Three steps in knowledge communication: the emergence of knowledge transformers. *Research policy*, 32, 1737.

Hemmert, M., 2009. Innovation management of Japanese and Korean firms: a comparative analysis. *In*: K. Jackson and P. Debroux eds. *Innovation in Japan: emerging patterns enduring myths*. London: Routledge, 8–29.

Hentschel, B. and Haghirian, P., 2010. Nonaka revisited: can Japanese companies sustain their knowledge management processes in the 21th century? *In*: P. Haghirian, ed. *Innovation and change in Japanese management*. Basingstoke: Palgrave Macmillan, 199–220.

Hirst, G. and Mann, L., 2004. A model of R&D leadership and team communication: the relationship with project performance. *R&D Management*, 34, 147–160.

Hooker, J., 2003. *Working across cultures*. Stanford: Stanford University Press.

House, R., Hanges, P., Javidan, M., Dorfman, P., and Gupta, V., 2004. *Culture, leadership, and organizations*. Los Angeles, CA: Sage.

Howell, J.M. and Avolio, B.J., 1993. Transformational leadership, transactional leadership, locus of control, and support for innovation: key predictors of consolidated–business–unit performance. *Journal of applied psychology*, 78, 891–902.

Hui, W., Law, K.S., Hackett, R.D., Duanxu, W., and Zhen Xiong, C., 2005. Leader–member exchange as a mediator of the relationship between transformational leadership and followers' performance and organizational citizenship behavior. *Academy of management journal*, 48, 420–432.

Ibata-Arens, M., 2009. Comparing national innovation systems in Japan and the United States: push, pull, drag, and jump factors in the development of new technology. *In*: K. Jackson and D. Philippe, eds. *Innovation in Japan*. London: Routledge, 30–53.

Ishikawa, J., 2008. Transformational leadership and R&D team performance in Japanese companies: focusing on negative effects of transformational leadership. *In: Asia academy of management annual conference proceedings*, 15–16 December 2008, Taipei, Taiwan.

Jackson, K. and Tomioka, M., 2004. *The changing face of Japanese management*. London: Routledge.

James, L.R., Demaree, R.G., and Wolf, G., 1984. Estimating within–group interrater reliability with and without response bias. *Journal of applied psychology*, 69, 85–98.

Jung, D.I. and Sosik, J.J., 2002. Transformational leadership in work groups: the role of empowerment, cohesiveness, and collective–efficacy on perceived group performance. *Small group research*, 33, 313.

Katz, R. and Tushman, M., 1979. Communication patterns, project performance, and task characteristics: an empirical evaluation and integration in an R&D setting. *Organizational behavior & human performance*, 23, 139–162.

Keller, R.T., 1992. Transformational leadership and the performance of research and development project groups. *Journal of management*, 18, 489.

Keller, R.T., 2001. Cross–functional project group in research and new product development: diversity, communications, job stress, and outcomes. *Academy of management journal*, 44, 547–555.

Keller, R.T., 2006. Transformational leadership, initiating structure, and substitutes for leadership: a longitudinal study of research and development project team performance. *Journal of applied psychology*, 91, 202–210.

Kim, Y. and Min, B., 1999. The roles of R&D team leaders in Korea: a contingent approach. *R&D management*, 29, 153.

Kivimaki, M. and Lansisalmi, H., 2000. Communication as a determinant of organizational innovation. *R&D management*, 30, 33.

Kono, T. and Clegg, S., 2001. *Trends in Japanese*. London: Palgrave.

Leana, C.R., 1985. A partial test of Janis' groupthink model: effects of group cohesiveness and leader behavior on defective decision making. *Journal of management*, 11, 5.

Lervek, J., 2008. Knowledge management and knowledge transfer in multinational enterprises. *In*: P. Smith, M. Peterson, and D. Thomas eds. *Handbook of cross–cultural management research*. Los Angeles, CA: Sage, 301–318.

Liao, H. and Chuang, A., 2007. Transforming service employees and climate: a multilevel, multisource examination of transformational leadership in building long–term service relationships. *Journal of applied psychology*, 92, 1006–1019.

Lowe, K.B. and Galen Kroeck, K., 1996. Effectiveness correlates of transformational and transactional leadership: a meta–analytic. *Leadership quarterly*, 7, 385.

Madzar, S., 2001. Subordinates' information inquiry: exploring the effect of perceived leadership style and individual differences. *Journal of occupational & organizational psychology*, 74, 221–232.

McCormick, K., 1995. Career paths, skill formation, and technological obsolescence. *In*: P. Shapira, ed. *The R&D workers: managing innovation in Britain, Germany, Japan, and the United States*. Westport: Quorum Books, 59–78.

Menzel, H., 1966. Information needs and uses in science and technology. *In*: C. Cuadra, ed. *Annual review of information science and technology*. New York: Wiley, 41–69.

Motohashi, K., 2009. Growing R&D collaboration of Japanese firms and policy implication for reforming the national innovation system. *In*: K. Jackson and D. Philippe eds. *Innovation in Japan*. London: Routledge, 54–76.

Nemanich, L.A. and Keller, R.T., 2007. Transformational leadership in an acquisition: a field study of employees. *Leadership quarterly*, 18, 49–68.

Nonaka, I., 2005. *Knowledge management: critical perspectives on business and management*. London: Routledge.

Nonaka, I. and Takeuchi, H., 1995. *The knowledge–creating company*. New York: Oxford University Press.

Osono, E., Shimizu, N. and Takeuchi, H., 2008. *Extreme Toyota: radical contradictions that drive sucess at the world's best manufacture*. Hoboken: Wiley.

Paik, Y. and Pak, Y., 2009. The changing face of Korean management of overseas affiliates. *In*: C. Rowley and Y. Paik, eds. *The changing face of Korean management*. London: Routledge, 165–188.

Pelz, D.C. and Andrews, F.M., 1966. *Scientists in organizations*. New York: John Wiley & Sons.

Piccolo, R.F. and Colquitt, J.A., 2006. Transformational leadership and job behaviors: the mediating role of core job characteristics. *Academy of management journal*, 49, 327–340.

Pillai, R. and Williams, E.A., 2004. Transformational leadership, self–efficacy, group cohesiveness, commitment, and performance. *Journal of organizational change management*, 17, 144–159.

Podsakoff, P.M., Mackenzie, S.B., Moorman, R.H., and Fetter, R., 1990. Transformational leader behaviors and their effects on followers' trust in leader, satisfaction, and organizational citizenship behaviors. *Leadership quarterly*, 1, 107–142.

Postmes, T., Spears, R., and Cihangir, S., 2001. Quality of decision making and group norms. *Journal of personality & social psychology*, 80, 918–930.

Scott, S.G. and Bruce, R.A., 1998. Following the leader in R&D: the joint effect of. *IEEE transactions on engineering management*, 45, 3.

Shibata, T., ed., 2006. *Japan: moving towards a more advanced knowledge economy*. Washington, DC: World Bank.

Shin, S.J. and Zhou, J., 2003. Transformational leadership, conservation, and creativity: evidence from Korea. *Academy of management journal*, 46, 703–714.

Stanko, T.L. and Gibson, C.B., 2009. The role of cultural elements in virtual teams. *In*: R.S. Bhagat and R.M. Steers eds. *Handbook of culture, organization, and work*. Cambridge, UK: Cambridge University Press, 272–303.

Steers, R.M., Sanchez–Runde, C., and Nardon, L., 2010. *Management across cultures: challenges and strategies*. Cambridge, UK: Cambridge University Press.

Taggar, S. and Ellis, R., 2007. The role of leaders in shaping formal team norms. *Leadership quarterly*, 18, 105–120.

Taylor, R.L. and Utterback, J.M., 1975. A longitudinal study of communication in research: technical and managerial influences. *IEEE transactions on engineering management*, 22, 80–87.

Tushman, M.L., 1977. Special boundary roles in the innovation process. *Administrative science quarterly*, 22, 587–605.

Tushman, M.L. and Katz, R., 1980. External communication and project performance: an investigation into the role of gatekeepers. *Management science*, 26, 1071–1085.

Yammarino, F.J. and Dubinsky, A.J., 1994. Transformational leadership theory: using levels of analysis to determine boundary conditions. *Personnel psychology*, 47, 787–811.

Yukl, G., 2002. *Leadership in organizations* (5th ed.). Upper Saddle River, NJ: Prentice–Hall.

The ownership structure of foreign subsidiaries and the effect of institutional distance: a case study of Japanese firms

Naoki Ando

Faculty of Business Administration, Hosei University, Tokyo, Japan

This study investigates how institutional distance between a home country and a host country affects the ownership structure of foreign subsidiaries. Using a sample consisting of foreign subsidiaries of Japanese firms, the effect of institutional distance on the ownership structure of foreign subsidiaries is tested. The results indicate that Japanese firms reduce equity shares in foreign subsidiaries as institutional distance increases. The study also finds that internationally experienced Japanese firms tend to have large equity ownership in institutionally distant countries. In addition, this study shows that complementing host country experience with international experience further mitigates uncertainty arising from institutional distance.

Introduction

The ownership structure of foreign subsidiaries is a critical strategic decision that multinational corporations (MNCs) encounter with foreign entry (Delios and Beamish 1999). Ownership structure reflects the level of control that a parent firm can exercise over foreign subsidiaries, the resource commitments of a parent firm, the level of exposure of a parent firm to investment risks and the need for host country resources (Anderson and Gatignon 1986, Gomes-Casseres 1990, Delios and Beamish 1999, Delios and Henisz 2000). Researchers have explored the pivotal question of what determines the level of equity ownership in foreign subsidiaries contingent on national difference (Kogut and Singh 1988, Xu and Shenkar 2002, Slangen and van Tulder 2009). National difference causes difficulty dealing with local idiosyncrasies and thus affects decision-making on strategic and managerial issues regarding the management of foreign subsidiaries (Dikova 2009, Dow and Larimo 2009). Among national differences, host country institutions have attracted the attention of researchers and are viewed as significantly influencing strategic decision-making (Delios and Beamish 1999, Slangen and van Tulder 2009).

This study emphasizes institutional dissimilarity between a host country and a home country to understand how cross-country differences affect decisions regarding the ownership structure of foreign subsidiaries. For this purpose, we focus on the impact of institutional distance on the ownership structure. Most previous studies on international management have addressed institutional advancement and its impact on the strategic decision-making of MNCs (Delios and Beamish 1999, Yiu and Makino 2002, Slangen and van Tulder 2009). Several studies, however, suggest that not only the level of institutional advancement of a host country but also the level of institutional dissimilarity between a host country and a home country can cause external uncertainty (Gaur and Lu 2007, Dow and Larimo 2009). Compared with the effect of institutional advancement, not much is known about the effect of institutional dissimilarity on the choice of ownership structure of foreign subsidiaries. This study aims to fill this research gap. In addition to the main effect of institutional distance on the ownership structure, this study incorporates two moderators: international experience and host country experience. Based on an organizational learning perspective, this study examines how experience in foreign operations moderates the effect of institutional distance on ownership strategy.

This paper is organized as follows. The next section briefly reviews the literature on institution theory and its application to foreign entry strategy. Then, hypotheses are presented regarding the relationship between institutional distance and the ownership structure of foreign subsidiaries. We next report on the results of the empirical analysis that uses a sample comprised of foreign subsidiaries of Japanese firms. Finally, we discuss the implications of the study as well as its limitations and directions for future research.

Literature search/review and theory

Transaction cost theory contends that foreign firms choose an ownership structure to minimize transaction costs arising from asset specificity, uncertainty and transaction frequency (Williamson 1985, Anderson and Gatignon 1986, Hennart 1991). They argue that when foreign firms need access to complementary assets owned by local firms, but full or partial acquisition of those assets through market transaction is difficult or costly due to market imperfections, foreign firms are inclined to form partnerships with local firms (Williamson 1985, Hennart 1991,Yiu and Makino 2002). In comparison, when the assets involved are highly specific to the transaction, and the exposure to behavioural and contextual uncertainty is possible, firms prefer forming wholly owned subsidiaries (Williamson 1985, Hennart 1991, Yiu and Makino 2002). Applying transaction cost theory, Hennart (1991) conducted an empirical study and found that Japanese firms choose joint ventures when they need to combine with other firms' intermediate inputs that are subject to high market transaction costs. Similarly, Delios and Henisz (2000) conducted an empirical study by using a sample of Japanese firms and found that they minimize expropriation hazards by increasing their ownership position in foreign subsidiaries as asset specificity increases.

Institutional theory is gaining visibility in the international management literature that explores the effects of cross-country differences in institutions on MNCs' behaviour and performance (North 1990, Delios and Beamish 1999, Delios and Henisz 2000, Brouthers 2002). Institutions are defined as the rules of the game in a society, or the humanly devised constraints that shape human interaction (North 1990). By establishing stable structures that facilitate economic transactions, institutions can reduce transaction costs in uncertain and complex environments (North 1990, Hoskisson *et al.* 2000). Institutional variation across countries, however, can alter the costs of conducting business in one host country compared to another (Henisz 2004, Chan *et al.* 2008). Foreign firms may encounter unfamiliar institutional settings in a host country, which may raise transaction costs and impede their business activities (Delios and Beamish 1999, Brouthers 2002). Because institutions can cause transaction costs to either increase or decrease, a better understanding of international management may be achieved if transaction cost theory is complemented with institution theory (Brouthers 2002, Yiu and Makino 2002, Meyer and Nguyen 2005).

Most previous studies applying institution theory to international management have focused on institutional voids in emerging and transition economies (Khanna and Palepu 2000, Chan *et al.* 2008). In general, these economies lack reliable market information, efficient intermediary institutions, predictable government actions and efficient bureaucracies (Khanna and Palepu 2000, Chan *et al.* 2008). These voids make market-based transactions costly and perceived uncertainty greater (Anderson and Gatignon 1986, Delios and Henisz 2000, Peng 2003, Chan *et al.* 2008). To mitigate external uncertainty arising from institutional voids, MNCs may tap into knowledge held by local firms (Hennart 1991, Delios and Henisz 2000, Meyer *et al.* 2009). Because local knowledge is generally tacit and uncodified, however, foreign firms have difficulty acquiring it through market transactions. Due to market imperfection, acquisition of local knowledge would impose high transaction costs (Hennart 1991, Lu 2002). Partnering with local firms may allow foreign firms to tap into local knowledge with reduced transaction costs (Hennart 1988, Lu 2002). Previous studies also argue that as uncertainty increases, foreign firms prefer lower control modes to retain and increase flexibility in case of environmental changes if transaction-specific assets are absent (Anderson and Gatignon 1986, Yiu and Makino 2002). Similarly, prior studies contend that MNCs decrease commitment to operations in institutionally underdeveloped countries as a result of minimizing risk exposure (Feinberg and Gupta 2009). These studies suggest that foreign firms tend to have lower ownership stakes in foreign subsidiaries in institutionally less-developed countries. Empirical evidence supports this negative relationship between institutional advancement and equity ownership (Uhlenbruck *et al.* 2006, Demirbag *et al.* 2007, Meyer *et al.* 2009, Slangen and van Tulder 2009). For example, using Japanese FDI into East and South-East Asia as a sample, Delios and Beamish (1999) found that legal restrictions on foreign ownership reduce equity ownership in foreign subsidiaries. Delios and Henisz (2000) also used a sample of Japanese firms and found that the political hazards of host countries are negatively associated with equity ownership. Similarly, Chan and Makino (2007) found that Japanese firms take a lower ownership stake in foreign subsidiaries when they face political instability in host countries. Mani *et al.* (2007) used a dataset of 4,459 subsidiaries established by 858 Japanese firms across 38 countries and found that higher country risk is negatively associated with wholly owned entry mode. Taylor *et al.* (2000) also found that Japanese firms tend to choose a low control entry mode when host government restrictions on operations of foreign firms are present.

Although previous studies have extensively examined the effect of the degree of institutional advancement on ownership structure of foreign subsidiaries, the degree of dissimilarity in institutions may also affect decisions on the ownership structure (Gaur and Lu 2007, Dow and Larimo 2009). MNCs from developed countries will have difficulty operating in host countries with underdeveloped institutions, while MNCs from emerging and transition economies may encounter unfamiliar institutional environments in developed countries. For example, MNCs from emerging and transition economies need to learn how to compete in market-based economies where they cannot exploit capabilities developed in network-based economies (Peng 2003). Thus, there is a rationale for addressing a degree of institutional dissimilarity. To address dissimilarity between institutional environments of two countries, this study defines institutional distance as the extent of dissimilarity in the formal and informal aspects of institutions in two countries (Kostova and Zaheer 1999, Xu and Shenkar 2002, Gaur and Lu 2007). Institutional distance will increase external uncertainty as perceived by foreign firms (Anderson and Gatignon 1986, Gaur and Lu 2007). In addition, they may have difficulty applying their organizational practices to foreign subsidiaries in dissimilar institutional environments because the practices have been developed in the context of their home country (Kostova 1999, Xu and Shenkar 2002, Brouthers *et al.* 2008). Large institutional distances may require organizational practices developed in the home country to be supplemented with local knowledge (Brouthers *et al.* 2008). These arguments suggest that dissimilarity in institutions between a host country and a home country significantly affects MNCs' strategic decision-making. However, few studies have addressed the effect of institutional distance on MNCs' behaviour (Gaur and Lu 2007, Brouthers *et al.* 2008). This paucity of studies needs to be fulfilled.

Hypotheses

Dissimilarity in institutions will be a critical source of uncertainty as perceived by foreign firms (Chan *et al.* 2008). A lack of familiarity with host country institutions and the resulting perception of uncertainty will discourage foreign firms from engaging in complex operations (Anderson and Gatignon 1986, Meyer 2001). Facing perceived uncertainty, foreign firms need local knowledge to cope with idiosyncrasies in legal, political, economic and social environments. Local knowledge is also necessary when transferring intangible assets to foreign subsidiaries. To gain a competitive advantage, foreign firms may transfer their intangible assets to foreign subsidiaries operating in institutionally distant countries; however, intangible assets developed in the home country need to be complemented with local knowledge or other local resources (Brouthers *et al.* 2008). However, the acquisition of local knowledge or other complementary assets would impose high transaction costs on foreign firms due to market imperfections resulting from the tacit and uncodifiable nature of the resources (Hennart 1991, Meyer 2001, Lu 2002). Partnering with local firms that are intimate with the host country's institutional environments would allow foreign firms to tap into local resources while keeping transaction costs manageable, which would help overcome perceived uncertainty arising from institutional distance (Hennart 1988, Yan and Luo 2001, Lu 2002). Foreign firms may gain the commitment of local partners by conceding larger equity stakes to them (Nakamura and Yeung 1994). Highly committed local partners will be willing to transfer their knowledge to foreign subsidiaries. Thus, faced with substantial dissimilarity in institutions, foreign firms will attempt to overcome external uncertainty by lowering the control level over foreign subsidiaries and extracting commitment from local partners to access their local knowledge. These arguments lead to the following hypothesis:

> Hypothesis 1: The greater the institutional distance between a home country and a host country, the greater the preference by the parent firm for lower equity shares in a foreign subsidiary.

Uncertainty as perceived by foreign firms is not static over time because, through their experience in international operations, they learn how to manage business activities in unfamiliar environments (Slangen and Hennart 2008, Dow and Larimo 2009). International experience is defined as a firm's experience with managing operations outside its home country, without reference to specific host countries (Slangen and Hennart 2008). At the outset, foreign firms are at a disadvantage compared to local firms in dealing with institutions in the host country (Delios and Beamish 2001). After experiential learning in various countries, foreign firms will incrementally improve their capability to manage operations in unfamiliar locations and deal with dissimilarity in external environments (Chang 1995, Delios and Beamish 2001, Cho and Padmanabhan

2005, Dow and Larimo 2009). The capabilities acquired through experiential learning can be applied to new locations to cope with local idiosyncrasies and overcome the liabilities of foreignness (Johanson and Vahlne 1977). Thus, foreign firms with international experience will perceive less uncertainty when facing greater institutional distance. They can increase their commitment to foreign operations and reduce their need for complementary resources held by local firms as a result of a reduced perception of uncertainty (Johanson and Vahlne 1977). Internationally experienced firms will have the capability to adjust their organizational practices to the form that best matches local institutions without gaining substantial support from local firms (Delios and Henisz 2000, Brouthers *et al.* 2008). These arguments lead to the following hypothesis:

Hypothesis 2: The negative impact of institutional distance on the level of equity shares in a foreign subsidiary is weaker for the parent firm with more international experience.

As foreign firms accumulate operational experience in a host country and grow to understand local idiosyncrasies, they will perceive less uncertainty in the host country. Host country experience is defined as a firm's experience with a particular host country (Slangen and Hennart 2008). Through operations in a host country, foreign firms can acquire knowledge and capabilities that help them manage foreign subsidiaries effectively, accommodate local business practices and build relations with local suppliers and governments (Zaheer 1995, Barkema and Vermeulen 1998, Chang and Rosenzweig 2001, Wilkinson *et al.* 2008). By using local knowledge acquired through experiential learning in a host country, firms can mitigate uncertainty arising from institutional distance (Gaur and Lu 2007).

Foreign firms, however, may confront difficulty in effective exploitation of local knowledge because the capability to process and exploit knowledge obtained through experience in a host country varies across firms (Jensen and Szulanski 2004, Gaur and Lu 2007). Less-capable firms cannot exploit local knowledge enough to overcome institutional dissimilarity, which may depend on a parent firm's capability to absorb and exploit local knowledge (Cohen and Levinthal 1990). International experience may enable firms to substantially and successfully absorb and exploit knowledge learned from their host country experience. Firms with international experience would be better able to detect potential problems in distant markets and better understand the subtleties of a host country (Evans *et al.* 2008, Dow and Larimo 2009). They can effectively process information about the unique qualities of a host country in order to deal with idiosyncratic institutional environments. Thus, internationally experienced firms can successfully reduce external uncertainty because they are better able to understand, absorb and exploit local knowledge (Cohen and Levinthal 1990, Dikova 2009). Accordingly, firms with more international experience and more host country experience can substantially overcome institutional dissimilarity and effectively manage foreign subsidiaries in institutionally distant countries. These arguments lead to the following hypothesis:

Hypothesis 3: The negative impact of institutional distance on the level of equity shares in a foreign subsidiary is weaker for the parent firm with both more international experience and more host country experience.

Methodology

Sample and data collection

The hypotheses are examined using a sample comprised of foreign subsidiaries of Japanese firms, which are derived from a CD-ROM version of the 2008 *Kaigai Shinshutsu Kigyo Soran* (Overseas Japanese Companies Data) compiled by *Toyo Keizai Shimposha*. The 2008 *Kaigai Shinshutsu Kigyo Soran* includes data on 21,317 foreign subsidiaries of Japanese manufacturers and non-manufacturers in which a Japanese firm has at least 10% equity ownership. The initial sample included foreign subsidiaries of Japanese manufacturers. To eliminate the influence of non-primary Japanese parent firms, 2,338 foreign subsidiaries established by more than one Japanese parent firm were dropped from the sample. The data on foreign subsidiaries were collected from *Kaigai Shinshutsu Kigyo Soran*, while the data on parent firms were collected from the *Nikkei NEEDS* database compiled by *Nihon Keizai Shimbun*. The host country data were primarily collected from *World Competitiveness Yearbook* compiled by IMD and *Global Competitiveness Report* compiled by the World Economic Forum. Due to missing data, the final sample contained 5,081 foreign subsidiaries of Japanese manufacturers in 38 countries.

Measures

The dependent variable is the ownership structure of foreign subsidiaries. The ownership structure is measured by equity shares in a foreign subsidiary that a Japanese parent firm owns. Data on equity shares in foreign subsidiaries were provided by *Kaigai Shinshutsu Kigyo Soran*. This dependent variable is a ratio, ranging from 0.1 to 1.0.

Institutional distance is the extent of dissimilarity in institutions between two countries (Kostova 1999, Gaur and Lu 2007). To operationalize institutional dissimilarity, this study uses data from the World Bank Governance Indicators (Kaufmann *et al.* 2005), primarily because the Governance Indicators encompass a broad range of institutional issues and are based on several hundred individual variables drawn from 37 separate data sources constructed by 31 organizations (Kaufmann *et al.* 2005, Dikova 2009). Kaufmann *et al.* (2005) have identified six institutional dimensions: *voice and accountability* (political, civil, and human rights); *political instability and violence* (the likelihood of violent threats to or changes in government, including terrorism); *government effectiveness* (the competence of bureaucracies and the quality of public service delivery); *regulatory burden* (the incidence of market-unfriendly policies); *rule of law* (the quality of contract enforcement, the police, and the courts, as well as the likelihood of crime and violence); and *control and corruption* (the exercise of public power for private gain, including both petty and grand corruption and state capture). Scores for each dimension range from -2.5 to 2.5, with higher values indicating advanced institutions. To obtain the proxy for institutional distance, this study adopts Kogut and Singh's (1988) approach for cultural distance scores, using the following formula:

$$\text{Institutional Distance}_j = \frac{1}{6}\sum\nolimits_{i=1}^{6}\left\{\frac{(I_{ij} - I_{ih})^2}{\sigma_i^2}\right\} \tag{1}$$

where Institutional Distance$_j$ is the institutional distance between host country j and Japan, I_{ij} is country j's score of the ith institutional dimension, I_{ih} is Japan's score of the ith institutional dimension, and σ_i^2 is the variance of the ith institutional dimension.

This study includes two moderators: international experience and host country experience, both at the parent firm level. Host country experience is measured by adding the number of operation years of all subsidiaries in the host country. To measure international experience, operation years for all foreign subsidiaries under an MNC are added. Both scores are log-transformed. When the international experience score is matched with each foreign subsidiary, the host country experience score of the MNC is subtracted.

To control for the effect of factors that cause uncertainty other than institutional distance, cultural distance is incorporated. Cultural distance between host countries and Japan is measured by using scores of four cultural dimensions developed by Hofstede (2001). This study follows Kogut and Singh's (1988) approach to measure cultural distance:

$$\text{Cultural Distance}_j = \frac{1}{4} \sum_{i=1}^{4} \left\{ \frac{(C_{ij} - C_{ih})^2}{\sigma_i^2} \right\} \tag{2}$$

where Cultural Distance$_j$ is the cultural distance between host country j and Japan, C_{ij} is country j's score of the ith cultural dimension, C_{ih} is Japan's score of the ith cultural dimension, and σ_i^2 is the variance of the ith cultural dimension. To control for the country risk of host countries, foreign ownership restrictions, exchange rate stability and inflation rates are incorporated. Data on foreign ownership restrictions and inflation rates were collected from the *2006–2007 Global Competitiveness Report*. For foreign ownership restrictions, scores were used of a survey item that asks 'Foreign ownership of companies in your country is (1 = rare, limited to minority stakes, and often prohibited in key sectors; 7 = prevalent and encouraged).' The data on exchange rate stability were collected from the *2006 World Competitiveness Yearbook*.

To control for firm-level effects, the R&D intensity of a parent firm, foreign entry through diversification, the foreign sales ratio of a parent firm and the size of a parent firm are incorporated. The R&D intensity of a parent firm is measured by a ratio of R&D expenditure to total sales. Foreign entry through diversification is a dummy variable, taking a value of one when a foreign subsidiary engages in an industry different from its parent firm and taking a value of zero otherwise. For the foreign sales ratio of a parent firm, the ratio of foreign sales to total sales is used. For the size of a parent firm, the number of employees is used, which is log-transformed. Data on the R&D intensity, the foreign sales ratio, and the size of a parent firm were collected from the *Nikkei NEEDS* database. The diversification dummy was based on information from *Kaigai Shinshutsu Kigyo Soran*. In addition, to control for industry-specific effects, this study incorporates five dummy variables indicating the industry in which a parent firm engages: electric and electronic products; machinery; chemical; automobile; and precision equipment.

Data analysis

Table 1 shows descriptive statistics and correlation coefficients of the variables. In foreign subsidiaries in the sample, Japanese parent firms have an average of 89% equity ownership. Seventy-four per cent of foreign subsidiaries in the sample are wholly owned. The mean value of the subsidiary age is 15.4, which indicates that the sample includes relatively mature foreign subsidiaries. Parent firms engage in the following industries: electric and electronic products (31.5%); machinery (17.2%); chemical (14.4%); automobile (8.3%); precision equipment (4.9%); and others. Correlation coefficients in Table 1 are low overall, with the highest being the correlation between host country experience and the size of a parent firm ($r = .51, p < .05$). From the correlation matrix, it

Table 1. Descriptive statistics and correlation matrix.

	Mean	S.D.	1	2	3	4	5	6	7	8	9	10	11
1 Ownership	0.89	0.22											
2 Insitutional distance	1.20	1.17	−0.21*										
3 International experience	2.16	0.99	0.03*	0.00									
4 Host country experience	3.29	0.95	−0.06*	−0.03	−0.33*								
5 Cultural distance	2.89	0.98	0.01	0.07*	0.01	0.00							
6 Ownership restriction	5.28	0.68	0.25*	−0.46*	0.07*	−0.01	0.18*						
7 Inflation	2.80	1.93	−0.08*	0.24*	0.08*	−0.02	−0.22*	−0.22*					
8 Exchange rate stability	0.06	0.05	−0.09*	0.18*	0.13*	−0.09*	−0.09*	−0.25*	0.25*				
9 R&D intensity	4.00	11.04	0.03*	−0.04*	0.01	−0.01	−0.01	0.03*	−0.01	−0.01			
10 Diversification	0.63	0.48	0.20*	−0.29*	0.10*	−0.04*	−0.02	0.23*	−0.14*	−0.08*	0.00		
11 Foreign sales ratio	40.13	19.94	0.10*	−0.09*	0.30*	0.16*	−0.03*	0.10*	−0.02	0.01	0.02	0.08*	
12 Parent size	8.80	1.68	0.00	0.03	0.47*	0.51*	0.00	0.02	0.06*	0.03*	−0.01	0.02	0.31*

Note: $*p < .05$.

appears that any severe problem of multicollinearity is not present. To further detect potential multicollinearity problems, variance inflation factors (VIF) were calculated. All VIF scores were much lower than 10 (the highest was 3.17).

A Tobit model is used to test the hypotheses because the dependent variable is a proportion. A Tobit model is preferred to ordinary least squares (OLS) regression analysis when a dependent variable is truncated because OLS can lead to biased coefficient estimates (Delios and Henisz 2000). A double-censored Tobit model is employed for this study, as the dependent variable is truncated at the values of 0.1 and 1.0.

Table 2 reports the result of Tobit regressions. Model 1 contains control variables and moderators, while Model 2 adds institutional distance to Model 1. The interaction term of institutional distance with international experience is added in Model 3, and the three-way interaction of institutional distance, international experience and host country experience is added in Model 4. To reduce the problem of multicollinearity, a mean-centring technique was used to form interaction terms. The explanatory power of all models is good, as Chi-square values are all significant ($p < .001$). H1 predicts that the institutional distance is negatively related to the ownership level in foreign subsidiaries. The result of Model 2 shows that institutional distance has a negative and significant impact on the level of equity ownership in foreign subsidiaries ($p < .001$). A log-likelihood ratio test achieved significance, indicating that adding institutional distance to Model 1 significantly increases the explanatory power of Model 1. Thus, H1 was supported.

Model 3 examines H2, which predicts that international experience positively moderates the relationship between institutional distance and equity ownership. Model 3 shows that the interaction term of institutional distance with international experience is positive and significant ($p < .01$). A log-likelihood ratio test is also significant, showing that adding the interaction term results in a significant increase in model fit over Model 2. These results lend support to H2, implying that, compared to less-experienced counterparts, internationally experienced firms tend to have more equity ownership in foreign subsidiaries when encountering large institutional distance.

Model 4 examines H3, which expects that firms with both international and host country experience hold larger equity shares in foreign subsidiaries when facing greater institutional distance. Model 4 shows that the three-way interaction term among institutional distance, international experience and host country experience is significant and positive ($p < .05$). In addition, a log-likelihood test indicates a significant increase in model fit over Model 3. These findings support H3, implying that firms with more international and host country experience tend to hold a greater level of ownership in foreign subsidiaries compared with less experienced firms at the same level of institutional distance. To check the robustness of the results in Models 2 to 4, a sequence of Tobit regressions was run by incorporating different sets of control variables. Except for a slight decrease in the significance level in some regressions, the coefficients for the main and interaction effects remained significant for different sets of control variables.

Model 1 shows that the main effects of international and host country experience are negative and significant. In addition, cultural distance is significant and negative. The negative effect of cultural distance, however, turns out to be insignificant after incorporating institutional distance. This finding is comparable to Zhao *et al.*'s (2004) results, which show that among the six transaction cost-related factors they examined, cultural distance is the least influential as a determinant of ownership structure. Other host country variables, such as foreign ownership restrictions, exchange rate stability and inflation, are all significant. The results of these three variables suggest that greater country risk leads to a lower level of equity ownership in foreign subsidiaries. Among firm-level

Table 2. Results of Tobit regression.

	Model 1 b	Model 1 S.E.	Model 2 b	Model 2 S.E.	Model 3 b	Model 3 S.E.	Model 4 b	Model 4 S.E.
Institutional distance			−0.06 ***	0.01	−0.06 ***	0.01	−0.05 ***	0.01
Institution * International experience					0.03 **	0.01	0.02 *	0.01
Institution * Host country experience							−0.04 ***	0.01
International experience * Host country experience							−0.01	0.01
Institution * International experience * Host country experience							0.02 *	0.01
International experience	−0.12 ***	0.02	−0.12 ***	0.02	−0.13 ***	0.02	−0.12 ***	0.02
Host country experience	−0.13 ***	0.02	−0.14 ***	0.02	−0.14 ***	0.02	−0.12 ***	0.02
Cultural distance	−0.03 *	0.01	−0.01	0.01	−0.01	0.01	−0.01	0.01
Ownership restriction	0.24 ***	0.02	0.20 ***	0.02	0.20 ***	0.02	0.20 ***	0.02
Inflation	−0.02 ***	0.00	−0.01 *	0.00	−0.02 ***	0.01	−0.02 ***	0.01
Exchange rate stability	−0.51 **	0.20	−0.48 *	0.20	−0.45 *	0.20	−0.41 *	0.20
R&D intensity	0.01 †	0.00	0.01 †	0.00	0.01 †	0.00	0.01 †	0.00
Diversification	0.21 ***	0.02	0.19 ***	0.02	0.19 ***	0.02	0.18 ***	0.02
Forign sales ratio	0.00 ***	0.00	0.00 ***	0.00	0.00 ***	0.00	0.00 ***	0.00
Parent size	0.05 ***	0.01	0.05 ***	0.01	0.06 ***	0.01	0.05 ***	0.01
Industry 1	0.05	0.03	0.05	0.03	0.05	0.03	0.04	0.03
Industry 2	0.02	0.03	0.02	0.03	0.02	0.03	0.02	0.03
Industry 3	0.05 †	0.03	0.05 †	0.03	0.05 †	0.03	0.06 *	0.03
Industry 4	−0.12 **	0.04	−0.12 **	0.04	−0.12 ***	0.04	−0.12 ***	0.04
Industry 5	0.19 ***	0.05	0.19 ***	0.05	0.18 ***	0.05	0.18 ***	0.05
Constant	0.11	0.10	0.34 **	0.11	0.37 ***	0.11	0.32 **	0.11
Log Likelihood	−2666.78		−2645.00		−2640.53		−2629.26	
Chi-square	709.30 ***		752.85 ***		761.79 ***		784.33 ***	
n	5081		5081		5081		5081	

Note: ***$p < .001$; **$p < .01$; *$p < .05$; †$p < .10$.

variables, foreign entry through diversification, the foreign sales ratio of a parent firm and the size of a parent firm are positive and significant.

Discussion

This study explored how institutions in host countries affect ownership structure of foreign subsidiaries. The empirical results indicated that when a host country is perceived as institutionally dissimilar, Japanese firms are more likely to choose a lower level of ownership in foreign subsidiaries. The results also revealed that the negative impact of institutional distance on the ownership level weakens with international experience. In addition, the study found that firms with more international experience and host country experience tend to own larger equity shares in foreign subsidiaries under the given level of institutional distance.

The first contribution of this study is an emphasis on institutional distance. Whereas most previous studies have extensively focused on institutional voids in emerging and transition economies, this study focused on dissimilarity in institutions between two countries. Shifting the focus from institutional underdevelopment to institutional distance enables us to recognize institutional dissimilarity between developed countries, which research emphasizing institutional advancement has not noticed. The second contribution of this study is its simultaneous examination of international experience and host country experience as moderators, whereas previous studies have examined how uncertainty arising from host country environments is mitigated by either international experience or host country experience. This study incorporated the two experience variables into the regression model as a three-way interaction term. In the following section, we discuss theoretical and practical implications of this study.

Implications

For theory/theory development and readers

This study showed that institutional distance affects behaviour of foreign firms regarding decisions on the ownership structure of foreign subsidiaries. Previous studies have extensively emphasized the level of institutional voids and examined its effect on the behaviour of MNCs (e.g. Chan *et al.* 2008). In comparison, this study focused on how institutional dissimilarity between a host country and a home country affects MNCs' behaviour. Our results imply that it is possible that MNCs perceive uncertainty even when entering institutionally advanced countries if institutions are dissimilar to those in the home country. This suggests that foreign firms may incur large transaction costs in developed countries. There has been a paucity of research on how MNCs from developed countries behave when facing institutional dissimilarity in institutionally advanced countries. By examining the effect of institutional distance on ownership strategy, this study took a small step towards advancing our understanding of this issue. Future research should explore how MNCs from a developed country cope with institutional dissimilarity that confronts them in other developed countries. It may also investigate whether MNCs react the same or differently to institutional distance in institutionally advanced countries and institutionally underdeveloped countries.

Local knowledge is essential to reduce environmental uncertainty arising from institutional dissimilarity. It is likely that partnering with local firms is a vital source of local knowledge and a valuable option for coping with institutional dissimilarity. This study also implies that experiential learning through foreign operations helps overcome institutional distance. It has been argued that foreign firms can acquire capabilities to cope with environmental uncertainty through international and host country experience (Johanson and Vahlne 1977). A decrease in external uncertainty through foreign operations is likely to drive foreign firms to choose greater control over foreign subsidiaries, along with more commitment of resources. In this sense, experiential learning through foreign operations can reduce the relative importance of local partners as a source of local knowledge. In comparison, inexperienced firms have to trade their ownership for a local partner's commitment and local knowledge, which compensates for its lack of international experience (Nakamura and Yeung 1994). Even if they have a preference for a higher level of ownership in foreign subsidiaries, inexperienced firms cannot adopt the preferred level of ownership due to a necessity for local knowledge. It seems that experience in foreign operations enables firms to retain flexibility in managing foreign subsidiaries. Because experienced firms do not need to rely on external resources possessed by local firms, they can adopt preferred ownership structures of foreign subsidiaries. Firms may prefer practices or policies that have been formed through their past experience. Future research may explore how institutional distance and the resulting necessity for local resources discourage firms from adopting their preferred practices.

While this study considered local partners and experiential learning to reduce uncertainty arising from institutional distance, a possible alternative to local partners and experiential learning may be the utilization of host country nationals (HCNs). HCNs are assumed to possess better local knowledge; they are more capable of addressing local idiosyncrasies associated with institutional settings of the host country (Harzing 2001). Given their familiarity with local environments, HCNs can work as an uncertainty-reducing mechanism for foreign firms. An effective deployment of human resources has been considered one of the critical factors in successfully managing foreign subsidiaries (Gong 2003, Belderbos and Heijltjes 2005). Future research should examine the effectiveness of HCNs in dealing with institutional distance compared with local partners and experiential learning. Future studies can also identify other mechanisms to overcome institutional distance.

From the results of the three-way interaction term, it appears that learning through international experience complements learning through host country experience in mitigating institutional distance, suggesting that international experience and host country experience work as complementary assets. Host country experience will provide foreign firms with local knowledge specific to a host country, while international experience will help foreign firms understand and exploit idiosyncratic local knowledge. The simultaneous use of international and host country experience appears to further mitigate external uncertainty caused by institutional dissimilarity. Although we found that the two experiences are complementary assets, the process through which international experience interacts with host country experience to reduce external uncertainty has remained underexplored. Future research may theoretically explore how international experience is combined with host country experience to mitigate institutional distance. A possible perspective to explore the interaction of international and host country experience may be to view the relationship between headquarters and a foreign subsidiary as a principal–agent relationship (O'Donnell 2000). A favourable relationship between headquarters and foreign subsidiaries may facilitate the effective combination of international and host country experience. To exploit local knowledge accumulated in a foreign subsidiary, headquarters will encourage the subsidiary to act in a way that contributes to benefits of the whole MNC. However, it is plausible that foreign subsidiaries do not always act in accordance with the benefits of the whole MNC. Due to the potential asymmetry between the goals of headquarters and those of foreign subsidiaries, the problem of economic incentive misalignment may occur (Björkman *et al.* 2004). Foreign subsidiaries may give priority to the achievement of their economic interests over the headquarters' interests. Future research may explore how a headquarter–subsidiary relationship affects the effectiveness of a combination of international and host country experience in overcoming institutional distance.

For business and management practice

Managers may benefit if they consider institutional dissimilarity between a host country and a home country when making decisions regarding foreign subsidiary management. Previous studies have extensively emphasized institutional voids in emerging and transition economies and have thus provided suggestions about how to cope with underdeveloped institutions. This study suggests that MNCs need to take institutional dissimilarity into consideration when entering developed as well as developing countries. It is plausible that they encounter difficulties in managing foreign operations in developed countries if the countries are institutionally distant. MNCs from developed countries should adopt ownership strategies that accommodate the degree of institutional dissimilarity even when they manage foreign operations in developed countries. MNCs from developing countries should also understand that institutions in developed countries are different from those in their home country or other developing countries. They need capabilities to manage foreign operations in well-developed institutions, which are different from the capabilities that are required to implement relationship-based and personalized transactions (Peng 2003). Firms managing foreign operations also should recognize the value of host country and international experience. The former gives managers valuable information about a host country's environment, while the latter allows them to better understand and exploit local knowledge. Both kinds of experience will reduce environmental uncertainty arising from institutional distance. To make the best use of international and host country experience, managers should develop organizational practices through which the two experiences complement each other.

Conclusions

Although the results presented herein are believed to contribute to the literature on foreign ownership strategy, this study has several limitations. First, the sample of this study consists solely of foreign subsidiaries of Japanese manufacturers, which limits the generalizability of the findings. MNCs from the US and Europe may act differently from Japanese MNCs when facing greater institutional distance. Future research needs to examine the effect of institutional distance by using datasets consisting of MNCs from other countries than Japan. Another limitation concerns operationalization of the variables. This study addressed complex concepts, such as distance, experience, knowledge and ownership. Our approach to operationalization may capture only limited aspects of these complex concepts. Limitations regarding operationalization may be overcome by using other research methods, such as an in-depth case study. In addition, several perspectives, such as strategic alliance, experiential learning, knowledge, perceived distance and ownership, are related to ownership strategy. These perspectives should be considered to advance and deepen our understanding of ownership strategy. Further, the results are based on cross-sectional data, so that the dependent variable is not equal to the ownership position at the time of entry. Future research may use panel data to uncover the evolutionary process of ownership strategy. Finally, this study did not incorporate variables related to the performance of foreign subsidiaries and did not offer performance implications to researchers and managers. Future research should examine the relationship among institutional distance, ownership level and foreign subsidiary performance.

References

Anderson, E. and Gatignon, H., 1986. Modes of foreign entry: a transaction cost analysis and propositions. *Journal of international business studies*, 17 (3), 1–26.

Barkema, H.G. and Vermeulen, F., 1998. International expansion through start-up or acquisition: a learning perspective. *Academy of Management journal*, 41 (1), 7–26.

Belderbos, R.A. and Heijltjes, M.G., 2005. The determinants of expatriate staffing by Japanese multinationals in Asia: control, learning and vertical business groups. *Journal of international business studies*, 36 (3), 341–354.

Björkman, I., Barner-Rasmussen, W., and Li, L., 2004. Managing knowledge transfer in MNCs: the impact of headquarters control mechanisms. *Journal of international business studies*, 35 (5), 443–455.

Brouthers, K.D., 2002. Institutional, cultural and transaction cost influences on entry mode choice and performance. *Journal of international business studies*, 33 (2), 203–221.

Brouthers, K.D., Brouthers, L.E., and Werner, S., 2008. Resource-based advantages in an international context. *Journal of management*, 34 (2), 189–217.

Chan, C.M., Isobe, T., and Makino, S., 2008. Which country matters? Institutional development and foreign affiliate performance. *Strategic management journal*, 29 (11), 1179–1205.

Chan, C.M. and Makino, S., 2007. Legitimacy and multi-level institutional environments: implications for foreign subsidiary ownership structure. *Journal of international business studies*, 38 (4), 621–638.

Chang, S.J., 1995. International expansion strategy of Japanese firms: capability building through sequential entry. *Academy of Management journal*, 38 (2), 383–407.

Chang, S.J. and Rosenzweig, P.M., 2001. The choice of entry mode in sequential foreign direct investment. *Strategic management journal*, 22 (8), 747–776.

Cho, K.R. and Padmanabhan, P., 2005. Revisiting the role of cultural distance in MNC's foreign ownership mode choice: the moderating effect of experience attributes. *International business review*, 14 (3), 307–324.

Cohen, W.M. and Levinthal, D.A., 1990. Absorptive capacity: a new perspective on learning and innovation. *Administrative science quarterly*, 35 (1), 128–152.

Delios, A. and Beamish, P.W., 1999. Ownership strategy of Japanese firms: transactional, institutional, and experience influences. *Strategic management journal*, 20 (10), 915–933.

Delios, A. and Beamish, P.W., 2001. Survival and profitability: the roles of experience and intangible assets in foreign subsidiary performance. *Academy of Management journal*, 44 (5), 1028–1038.

Delios, A. and Henisz, W.J., 2000. Japanese firms' investment strategies in emerging economies. *Academy of Management journal*, 43 (3), 305–323.

Demirbag, M., Glaister, K.W., and Tatoglu, E., 2007. Institutional and transaction cost influences on MNEs' ownership strategies of their affiliates: evidence from an emerging market. *Journal of world business*, 42 (4), 418–434.

Dikova, D., 2009. Performance of foreign subsidiaries: does psychic distance matter? *International business review*, 18 (1), 38–49.

Dow, D. and Larimo, J., 2009. Challenging the conceptualization and measurement of distance and international experience in entry mode choice research. *Journal of international marketing*, 17 (2), 74–98.

Evans, J., Mavondo, F.T., and Bridson, K., 2008. Psychic distance: antecedents, retail strategy implications, and performance outcomes. *Journal of international marketing*, 16 (2), 32–63.

Feinberg, S.E. and Gupta, A.K., 2009. MNC subsidiaries and country risk: internalization as a safeguard against weak external institutions. *Academy of Management journal*, 52 (2), 381–399.

Gaur, A.S. and Lu, J.W., 2007. Ownership strategies and survival of foreign subsidiaries: impacts of institutional distance and experience. *Journal of management*, 33 (1), 84–110.

Gomes-Casseres, B., 1990. Firm ownership preferences and host government restrictions: an integrated approach. *Journal of international business studies*, 21 (1), 1–22.

Gong, Y., 2003. Subsidiary staffing in multinational enterprises: agency, resources, and performance. *Academy of Management journal*, 46 (6), 728–739.

Harzing, A.W., 2001. Who's in charge? An empirical study of executive staffing practices in foreign subsidiaries. *Human resource management*, 40 (2), 139–158.

Henisz, W.J., 2004. The institutional environment for international business. *In*: P.J. Buckley, ed. *What is international business?* New York: Palgrave Macmillan, 85–109.

Hennart, J.F., 1988. A transaction costs theory of equity joint ventures. *Strategic management journal*, 9 (4), 361–374.

Hennart, J.F., 1991. The transaction costs theory of joint ventures: an empirical study of Japanese subsidiaries in the United States. *Management science*, 37 (4), 483–497.

Hofstede, G., 2001. *Culture's consequences: comparing values, behaviors, institutions, and organizations across nations*. 2nd ed. Thousand Oaks, CA: Sage.

Hoskisson, R.E., *et al.*, 2000. Strategy in emerging economies. *Academy of Management journal*, 43 (3), 249–267.

IMD, 2006. *IMD world competitiveness yearbook 2006*. Lausanne, Switzerland: International Institute for Management Development.

Jensen, R. and Szulanski, G., 2004. Stickiness and the adaptation of organizational practices in cross-border knowledge transfers. *Journal of international business studies*, 35 (6), 508–523.

Johanson, J. and Vahlne, J.E., 1977. The internationalization process of the firm – a model of knowledge development and increasing foreign market commitments. *Journal of international business studies*, 8 (1), 25–34.

Kaufmann, D., Kraay, A., and Mastruzzi, M., 2005. *Governance matters IV: governance indicators for 1996–2004*. World Bank policy research paper 3630.

Khanna, T. and Palepu, K., 2000. The future of business groups in emerging markets: long-run evidence from Chile. *Academy of Management journal*, 43 (3), 268–285.

Kogut, B. and Singh, H., 1988. The effect of national culture on the choice of entry mode. *Journal of international business studies*, 19 (3), 411–432.

Kostova, T., 1999. Transnational transfer of strategic organizational practices: a contextual perspective. *Academy of Management review*, 24 (2), 308–324.

Kostova, T. and Zaheer, S., 1999. Organizational legitimacy under conditions of complexity: the case of the multinational enterprise. *Academy of Management review*, 24 (1), 64–81.

Lu, J.W., 2002. Intra- and inter-organizational imitative behavior: institutional influences on Japanese firms' entry mode choice. *Journal of international business studies*, 33 (1), 19–37.

Mani, S., Antia, K.D., and Rindfleisch, A., 2007. Entry mode and equity level: a multilevel examination of foreign direct investment ownership structure. *Strategic management journal*, 28 (8), 857–866.

Meyer, K.E., 2001. Institutions, transaction costs, and entry mode choice in Eastern Europe. *Journal of international business studies*, 32 (2), 357–367.

Meyer, K.E., *et al.*, 2009. Institutions, resources, and entry strategies in emerging economies. *Strategic management journal*, 30 (1), 61–80.

Meyer, K.E. and Nguyen, H.V., 2005. Foreign investment strategies and sub-national institutions in emerging markets: evidence from Vietnam. *Journal of management studies*, 42 (1), 63–93.

Nakamura, M. and Yeung, B., 1994. On the determinants of foreign ownership shares: evidence from US firms' joint ventures in Japan. *Managerial and decision economics*, 15 (2), 95–106.

Nihon Keizai Shimbun. *Nikkei NEEDS database*. Tokyo: Nihon Keizai Shimbun.

North, D.C., 1990. *Institutions, institutional change and economic performance*. New York: Cambridge University Press.

O'Donnell, S.W., 2000. Managing foreign subsidiaries: agents of headquarters, or an interdependent network? *Strategic management journal*, 21 (5), 525–548.

Peng, M.W., 2003. Institutional transitions and strategic choices. *Academy of Management review*, 28 (2), 275–296.

Slangen, A.H.L. and Hennart, J.F., 2008. Do multinationals really prefer to enter culturally distant countries through greenfields rather than through acquisitions? The role of parent experience and subsidiary autonomy. *Journal of international business studies*, 39 (3), 472–490.

Slangen, A.H.L. and van Tulder, R.J.M., 2009. Cultural distance, political risk, or governance quality? Towards a more accurate conceptualization and measurement of external uncertainty in foreign entry mode research. *International business review*, 18 (3), 276–291.

Taylor, C.R., Zou, S., and Osland, G.E., 2000. Foreign market entry strategies of Japanese MNCs. *International marketing review*, 17 (2), 146–163.

Toyo Keizai Shimposha, 2008. *Kaigai shinshutsu kigyo soran* [CD-ROM]. Tokyo: Toyo Keizai Shimposha.

Uhlenbruck, K., *et al.*, 2006. The impact of corruption on entry strategy: evidence from telecommunication projects in emerging economies. *Organization science*, 17 (3), 402–414.

Wilkinson, T.J. *et al.*, 2008. The diminishing effect of cultural distance on subsidiary control. *Journal of international management*, 14 (2), 93–107.

Williamson, O.E., 1985. *The economic institutions of capitalism: firms, markets, relational contracting*. New York: Free Press.

World Economic Forum, 2006. *The global competitiveness report 2006–2007*. New York: Palgrave Macmillan.

Xu, D. and Shenkar, O., 2002. Institutional distance and the multinational enterprise. *Academy of Management review*, 27 (4), 608–618.

Yan, A. and Luo, Y., 2001. *International joint ventures: theory and practice*. New York: M.E. Sharpe.

Yiu, D. and Makino, S., 2002. The choice between joint venture and wholly owned subsidiary: an institutional perspective. *Organization science*, 13 (6), 667–683.

Zaheer, S., 1995. Overcoming the liability of foreignness. *Academy of Management journal*, 38 (2), 341–363.

Zhao, H., Luo, Y., and Suh, T., 2004. Transaction cost determinants and ownership-based entry mode choice: a meta-analytical review. *Journal of international business studies*, 35 (6), 524–544.

Epilogue: retrospect and prospects: the significance of the 'lost decades' in Japan

W. Miles Fletcher III and Peter W. von Staden

The contributions to this Symposium on Japan present varied analytical perspectives that capture different economic realities during the past two decades and thus point to different prognoses for the economy. Implicit to each perspective is that the actors in question, whether government, business elites, or company managers, to some degree are part of the reason for the onset of the economic downturn, and each can play a role in helping the economy recover its vigor. In this sense, then, the key to understanding the significance of the lost decade is the appreciation of not only the constituent parts of the whole but what these parts mean when considered together.

Government is responsible at the macro-level for helping Japan through its transition from a high growth economy to its next stage. Firms affect the policy making process through their representative organizations, such as Keidanren (now, Nippon Keidanren) as W. Miles Fletcher points out (Fletcher 2012). Of course, firms, both large and small, make the economy work. If government can reconfigure the structure of incentives and provide crucial infrastructure, private companies must respond. Officials cannot alone create economic growth. Executives in the private sector must take advantage of new opportunities. Therefore, one must consider what the preceding essays convey about the significance of the lost decade for government, business elites and company management.

The extent of change

On the surface, the experience of the lost decade has been traumatic for Japan. Indeed one may say that when the bursting of the speculative bubble in the late 1980s ushered in more than 10 years of sluggish growth from 1990–2003, the heady confidence of the 1980s vanished. Observers no longer claimed that Japan was 'number one.' Foreign 'Japan bashers,' who used to lambast 'Japan, Inc.' as an unfair trader, fell silent. Yet, a suspicion lurks that not much in Japanese business has changed at all. A commentary by Malcolm Warner (2011) in a recent issue of the *Asia Pacific Business Review* notes that the effects of the economic stagnation linger as the nation has not found a way out of its economic purgatory of slow growth over the past two decades.

The contributions in this Symposium present a complicated landscape of change and continuity in Japan. For example, W. Miles Fletcher (2012) shows how Keidanren remained a formidable representative 'lobby' in the complex web of government-business relations. Ulrike Schaede (2012) argues most forcefully for change by pointing out the many legal changes enacted by the government that could have a great impact on the managerial practices of companies. She contends that the government has, in effect, abandoned attempts at the 'administrative guidance' that marked the glory days of the postwar economy. The liberalization of 'cross-border financial transactions' in a new Foreign Exchange Law has removed the main levers that civil servants could use to control foreign participation in the economy. In 2003, a revision of the 1948 Labor Standards Act has made layoffs easier for companies to carry out. In response, many Japanese firms are following a strategy of 'choose and focus' by shedding unprofitable units and emphasizing core businesses.

In many ways, these developments have fulfilled the deep wishes of big business, as effectively represented, according to W. Miles Fletcher's account, by Keidanren (Fletcher 2012). If its proposals helped to inhibit a vigorous government fiscal response in the early 1990s, the group became a staunch advocate of broad long-term changes in terms of fiscal probity, smaller government, and the deregulation of the economy. Yet, one must remember that the leaders of Keidanren forged these goals in 1985, several years before the bursting of the bubble. They were reacting, instead, to the challenges at that time posed by the rapid rise in the value of the yen, pressure to limit Japanese exports from their largest market, the United States, the predicted ageing of the society, and increased competition from rivals in a globalized economy. Moreover, the neo-liberal policies enacted by the administration of Ronald Reagan in the United States served as a model. The economic crisis that unfolded after 1990 did not affect these goals; instead, they determined the response of Keidanren to that crisis.

Peter von Staden's analysis of the fascinating debates in government sponsored councils (shingikai) in 1999 casts doubt on the degree to which the governing elites have wanted change (von Staden 2012). The politicians whom he quotes clearly express reservations about permitting the introduction of unfettered competition within Japan. If one tries to read between the lines of the leaders' laments about the loss of 'virtue' within Japanese society, they seem to blame the nation's economic downfall not on an overly protective or over-bearing government but on an outbreak of extreme capitalistic selfishness and greed. To them, a reassertion of traditional values of duty may be more important than revamping policies or institutions. As von Staden (2012) contends, changes in law may not mean much if Japanese firms do not take advantage of them. Although Schaede argues that Japanese firms have made significant changes in strategy, she suggests that firms may well require another decade to fully implement those changes (Schaede 2012).

Research presented here and elsewhere argues that the managers of Japanese companies continue to struggle with the challenges of adapting to Japan's post-high growth economy. While pointing out that most studies of the lost decade stress the impact of 'macro-economic conditions' and look to governmental policies for solutions, Tsuyoshi Numagami, Masaru Karube and Toshihiko Kato (2010) emphasize problems in firms' management. Numagami et al. argue that firms themselves have contributed to the prolongation of the economic downturn, because they have not adapted effectively to new conditions. They argue that the consensus-based managerial structure that worked so well through the 1980s is ill-suited to the current business environment. As Shige Makino and Tom Roehl explain, the efficient use of and improvement of existing technologies and the creation of economies of scale and scope propelled firms' growth. Within this context consensus management worked well to 'move quickly to get to the easily visible targets....[and middle management fulfilled a] key role in finding ways to achieve these corporate goals' (Makino and Roehl 2010, p. 390). The problem is that the high costs of middle management coordination are affordable during rapid growth periods but not so during lean times as experienced during the lost decade. Japanese firms have become burdened with 'organizational deadweight' because of the over-emphasis on consensus decision-making and the resulting inability to make timely strategic decisions – what Numagami *et al.* (2010) call a dearth of 'strategic connoisseurship.' They suggest the need for greater organizational discipline.

The four case studies that follow in this Symposium pertaining to specific practices of Japanese firms, suggest that some have been successful but that they have not changed their practices in major ways. Bruno Amman and Jacques Jassaud (2012) convincingly show that large family businesses have drawn on innate strengths to survive the economic downturn comparatively well. Their financial prudence in avoiding debt plus a willingness to invest during difficult times has proved effective, but they evidently have not changed their basic management practices. Similarly, according to Sophie Nivoix and Pascal Nguyen (2012), large pharmaceutical companies have benefitted from similar policies, as they have been able to continue funding research and development (R&D) without taking on large amounts of debt. As Mark Metzler observes, these companies may provide useful lessons in effectively handling an extended economic crisis (Metzler 2012). Further studies to examine whether or not such firms are inherently less prone toward problems of 'organizational deadweight' would be helpful. Ishikawa Jun's study of leadership styles in R&D teams indicates that changing the emphasis on consensus in Japanese management may be difficult (Ishikawa 2012). While charismatic 'transformational' leadership by a single individual can work well in Western companies, the ineffectiveness of this approach in Japanese pharmaceutical firms suggests that 'collectivist' values in Japanese organizations remain strong. Naoki Ando's analysis of decisions by Japanese companies regarding direct investment in overseas subsidiaries hints at managers' inflexibility in arguing that their main concern is the degree of familiarity with the specific institutional circumstances of a subsidiary overseas (Ando 2012).

To be sure, there are other areas of the Japanese economy that merit examination to determine the extent of change. For example, what might be specific examples of 'organizational deadweight' hindering strategic decisions by companies? Has the modification of the Large Store Law led to a significant reduction in small retail shops and a more efficient retail sector? If the deregulation of foreign exchange has induced a large rise in foreign investment in Japan, what impact has it had on Japanese firms? Have the rate of investment by Japanese firms overseas or the pattern of that investment changed?

Prognosis

Of rising urgency is the question of what Japan should do next to break out of its economic slump. The standard levers of economic policy of maintaining low interest rates and injecting a fiscal stimulus have helped avoid a deep depression but evidently can do little more to boost the economy, no matter how persistently some economists argue for robust government spending (Krugman and Wells 2010). The Bank of Japan has held the discount rate near zero since 1995; the national debt since then has soared to double the annual throughput of the national economy. *The Economist* (2010) has argued that Japan needs a variety of radical reforms, a 'grand plan' to deal with the burdens of a rapidly ageing society with an economy replete with inefficiencies as detailed in a special 14 page report. The suggestions include infusing vitality into the economy to diversify companies' work force by recruiting more women, foreigners, and Japanese with international experience; to promote immigration; to provide more venture capital to encourage new businesses; to entice the elderly to invest their large savings more aggressively and/or to consume more. Warner (2011) agrees that Japan needs 'economic, political, and social reform in spades.' In this issue, Schaede (2012) advocates a much more liberalized and competitive economy. In fact, she views the past two decades not as a 'lost' era but as one that has presented exciting possibilities for economic renewal. von Staden seems sympathetic toward the prospect of basic reforms in arguing that the Japanese have resisted changes in economic practices and that they need to decide what kind of 'new political-economic system' they want (von Staden 2012). Metzler, however, doubts the utility of seeking a restoration of a unified vision of a high growth economy. He posits that just as Japan in the 1950s and 1960s was in the vanguard in pioneering high speed economic growth based on bank credit and then in experiencing a major deflation in the 1990s, the nation is now entering a second industrial era in which quantitative growth may be unsustainable and the 'grow-or-die' strategy may be obsolete (Metzler 2012). Indeed, the combination of a stubbornly persistent deflation and a projected shrinking of the nation's population presents Japan with a unique circumstance in its modern history and powerful obstacles to robust economic growth in the conventional sense. Hence, trying to conceptualize a new vision of political economy to achieve these goals may be unrealistic.

Whether or not Japan is on the front lines of coping with a new historical epoch, the Japanese in the private and public sectors may have no choice but to grope incrementally toward a new type of solution to their current predicament. There is probably not a magic potion, a coherent strategic vision that will quickly restore the economy to strong and steady growth. If the belated injection of a massive public stimulus has not yielded great success, the effects of more neo-liberal policies are uncertain. Japan has at least been successful in keeping the official unemployment rate comparatively low at a little over 5%, even if the price has been the survival of too many firms with low productivity and profits (*The Economist* 2010, 9–11) or of what some call 'zombie firms' (Warner 2011). Adopting policies and strategies to promote more internal economic competition would undoubtedly raise that rate in return for possible gains in productivity that might or might not be large enough to help the overall economy. Accepting a context of a relatively low demand as a 'new normal' so to speak, firms and government agencies may have to experiment with various types of initiatives to find out what policies, strategies, and tactics work. Some of these may entail government support, while others may take advantage of deregulation. As Schaede (2012) notes, even if a number of firms have embarked on substantively new strategies, significant results may not appear for a decade. In addition, however strong sentiment in the business community might be for a smaller government, the tragic earthquake, and tsunami that devasted northeastern Japan on 11 March 2011 will most like require a sharp increase public expenditures to support recovery. The Japanese political and corporate elites will have to decide what kind of political economy they want. They most probably will do so in stages. This new system may well take a shape that is difficult to envision now, and building it will require persistence and patience.

References

Amman, B. and Jassand, J. 2012. Family and non-family business resilience in an economic downturn in Japan. *Asia Pacific business review*, 18 (2), 201–221.

Ando, N., 2012. The ownership structure of foreign subsidiaries and the effect of institutional distance: a case study of Japanese firms. *Asia Pacific business review*, 18 (2), 257–272.

Fletcher, W.M., 2012. 'Dreams of economic transformation and the reality of economic crisis: Keidanran in the era of the 'bubble' and the 'lost decade' from the mid-1980s to the mid-1990s. *Asia Pacific business review*, 18 (2), 149–165.

Ishikawa, J., 2012. Leadership and performance in Japanese R&D teams. *Asia Pacific business review*, 18 (2), 239–256.

Krugman, P. and Wells, R., 2010. The slump goes on: why? *The New York Review of Books*, 30 September. Available from: http://www.nybooks.com/articles/archives/2010/sep/30/slump-goes-why [Accessed 22 December 2010].

Makino, S. and Roehl, T., 2010. Learning from Japan; a commentary. *Academy of management perspectives*, 24 (4), 38–45.

Metzler, M., 2012. Introduction: Japan at an inflection point. *Asia Pacific business review*, 18 (2), 135–147.

Nivoix, S. and Nguyen, P., 2012. Characteristics of R&D expenditures in Japan's pharmaceutical industry. *Asia Pacific business review*, 18 (2), 223–238.

Numagami, T., Karube, M. and Kato, T., 2010. Organizational deadweight: learning from Japan. *Academy of management perspectives*, 24 (4), 25–37.

Schaede, U., 2012. From developmental state to the 'New Japan': strategic inflection point in Japanese business. *Asia Pacific business review*, 18 (2), 167–184.

The Economist, 2010. Into the unknown: a special report on Japan, 20 November, 1–16.

von Staden, P., 2012. Fettered by the past in the march forward: ideology as an explanation for the malaise in today's Japan. *Asia Pacific business review*, 18 (2), 185–200.

Warner, M., 2011. Commentary: whither Japan? Economy, management, and society. *Asia Pacific business review*, 17 (1), 1–5.

Index

Abdellatif, M. 72, 76, 85
Abe, M. 108, 110
Abegglen, J.C. 34
accounting: consolidated 40–1, 44; financial industry reform (1998) 40–1; mark-to-market valuations 44
Acemoglu, D. 93
aerospace industry 107
ageing population *see* demography
agency theory 71
agricultural/food imports 20, 21
Allen, T.J. 113, 114
Allouche, J. 69, 70, 71, 76
Amann, B. 8, 9, 10, 143
Amyx, J.A. 15, 17, 40, 53, 58, 59
Ancona, D.G. 112
Anderson, E. 125, 126, 127, 128
Anderson, G. 92
Ando, N. 7, 143
antitrust law 40, 46; United States 36
Archer, M. 55
Arrègle, J.-L. 71, 72
Asaba, S. 47
asset prices 2, 16, 21–2, 23, 25, 27; mark-to-market valuations 44
Astellas Pharma 93
auditing 46
automobile industry 93
Avolio, B.J. 108, 109, 119
Aycan, Z. 108, 109

Bank of Japan: discount rate 16, 17, 22, 23, 143; money supply 16; public funds to replenish capital of banks 24
banking sector 3, 6, 11, 22–3, 46, 75; bank inspections 41; banking crisis (mid-1990s) 37, 39–41; consolidation 3, 40, 75; mismanagement 17; non-performing loans 3, 16, 17, 24, 25, 27, 39, 40, 41, 44; pharmaceutical R&D 95, 103; post-war period 36, 144
bankruptcies 6, 36, 41, 42, 44
Barclay, M. 71

Barkema, H.G. 129
Barling, J. 109
Bass, B.M. 109, 115, 119
Beason, D. 15, 16
Belderbos, R.A. 136
Benson, J. 110–11
Berle, A.A. 71
Berson, Y. 110
Bezuijen, X.M. 114
Bhaskar, R. 55
Björkman, I. 137
Blyth, M. 65
board of directors 45, 46
Bottazzi, G. 93, 94
Boyd, J.P. 64
Brazil 20, 98
Brislin, R.W. 115
Brouthers, K.D. 126, 128, 129
Burgelman, R.A. 35
Burkart, M. 71
business community 3–4, 5, 141; deliberation councils (*shingikai*) 4, 42, 53–4, 59–63, 64, 65, 142; Japan Chamber of Commerce 23, 24, 25; Keidanren *see separate entry*; *see also* companies/groups/firms
business groups, horizontal (*keiretsu*) 3, 5, 45, 70, 95
business law 34–5, 42–6; bankruptcy 44; financial industry reform (1998) 40–1

Carney, M. 71
carry trade 6
Chami, R. 72
Chan, C.M. 126, 127, 128, 135
Chang, S.J. 128, 129
Charreaux, G. 71
chemical industry 107
China 4, 6, 26, 34, 36, 47, 48, 98
Cho, K.R. 128
choose and focus strategy 4–5, 34–5, 43, 46–7, 48, 142; deflationary times 10; hostile takeover, possibility of 46
Chrisman, J.J. 71, 72

Printed in Great Britain
by Amazon